DRUG CONTROL AND HUMAN RIGHTS IN INTERNATIONAL LAW

Human rights violations occurring as a consequence of drug control and enforcement are a growing concern, and raise questions of treaty interpretation and of the appropriate balancing of concomitant obligations within the drug control and human rights treaty regimes. Tracing the evolution of international drug control law since 1909, this book explores the tensions between the regime's self-described humanitarian aspirations and its suppression of a common human behaviour as a form of 'evil'. Drawing on domestic, regional and international examples and case law, it posits the development of a dynamic, human rights-based interpretative approach to resolve tensions and conflicts between the regimes in manner that safeguards human rights. Highlighting an important and emerging area of human rights inquiry from an international legal perspective, this book is a key resource for those working and studying in this field.

DR RICHARD (RICK) LINES is a key figure in the emerging field of human rights and drug policy. His work explores areas including international drug control law, prisoners' rights, harm reduction and the death penalty for drug offences. He is Chair of the International Centre on Human Rights and Drug Policy at the Human Rights Centre, University of Essex, where he is a Visiting Fellow. He holds a PhD in Law from the University of Middlesex.

DRUG CONTROL AND HUMAN RIGHTS IN INTERNATIONAL LAW

RICHARD LINES

Foreword by WILLIAM A. SCHABAS

Middlesex University, London, and Universiteit Leiden

CAMBRIDGE
UNIVERSITY PRESS

CAMBRIDGE
UNIVERSITY PRESS

University Printing House, Cambridge CB2 8BS, United Kingdom

One Liberty Plaza, 20th Floor, New York, NY 10006, USA

477 Williamstown Road, Port Melbourne, VIC 3207, Australia

4843/24, 2nd Floor, Ansari Road, Daryaganj, Delhi – 110002, India

79 Anson Road, #06-04/06, Singapore 079906

Cambridge University Press is part of the University of Cambridge.

It furthers the University's mission by disseminating knowledge in the pursuit of education, learning, and research at the highest international levels of excellence.

www.cambridge.org
Information on this title: www.cambridge.org/9781107171176
DOI: 10.1017/9781316759707

First published 2017

A catalogue record for this publication is available from the British Library.

Library of Congress Cataloging-in-Publication Data
Names: Lines, Richard, 1965– author.
Title: Drug control and human rights in international law / Dr. Richard Lines, University of Essex; foreword by Professor William Schabas.
Description: Cambridge [UK] ; New York : Cambridge University Press, [2017] | Includes bibliographical references.
Identifiers: LCCN 2016044388 | ISBN 9781107171176
Subjects: LCSH: Drugs – Law and legislation. | Drug control – International cooperation. | Human rights. | Narcotic laws.
Classification: LCC K3641.L56 2017 | DDC 341.4/8–dc23
LC record available at https://lccn.loc.gov/2016044388

ISBN 978-1-107-17117-6 Hardback

For my parents, Kathy and Malcolm, who taught me to recognise right from wrong, to have a healthy scepticism of authority and to always root for the underdog.

CONTENTS

FOREWORD

The control of narcotic drugs has been a concern of the international community from long before the creation of the United Nations and, with it, the modern legal system for the protection of human rights. The International Opium Convention of 1912 was the first international drug treaty. It was followed by the International Convention relating to Dangerous Drugs in 1925 and the International Convention for Limiting the Manufacture and Regulating the Distribution of Narcotic Drugs in 1931. The Covenant of the League of Nations had given the organisation explicit responsibility for 'the general supervision over the execution of agreements with regard to the traffic in women and children, and the traffic in opium and other dangerous drugs'. No similar formulation appears in the Charter of the United Nations, to whom the responsibilities of the League in the area of narcotic drugs were nevertheless transferred.

When the United Nations was established, human rights was given great prominence in its activities. There were several important references to the protection of human rights in the Charter of the United Nations. Its entry into force was followed by the negotiation of the International Bill of Rights. The crowning achievement was adoption of the Universal Declaration of Human Rights, on 10 December 1948 in Paris. Perusal of the *travaux préparatoires* of the Declaration does not suggest any interest at all in the subject of drugs. More generally, within the framework of United Nations activities, drug control was then only one issue among many international concerns.

But over the years, the focus on drugs within the activities of the United Nations appears to have gathered some steam. Today, one of the main institutions within the United Nations is called the Office on Drugs and Crime. There is a kind of equivalence within the United Nations, with its Office on Drugs and Crime based in Vienna and its Office of the High Commissioner for Human Rights based in Geneva. Some have called them 'parallel universes', although it would not be fair to suggest that the Vienna-based drugs and crime officials are indifferent to human rights any more than one can say the Geneva-based human rights officials neglect issues relating to drugs and crime. But like crime, the relationship between human rights and drugs remains enigmatic. This important study by Richard Lines provides much needed clarity in this respect. It also maps out a way forward.

Drug use and drug-related harms are of course a serious concern that impact on the right to health, enshrined in Article 25 of the Universal Declaration of Human Rights as well as in subsequent treaties such as the International Covenant on Economic, Social and Cultural Rights. From a human rights perspective, the so-called drug addict must be viewed not as a problem but as a person. Not only does this compel an approach based upon protection and the reduction of harm, it also shifts the emphasis to the abuses of human rights associated with campaigns to deal with drug use as well as the manufacture and traffic of illicit substances.

Although millions are affected by violations of human rights associated with drug suppression, the most acute form this takes is in the use of capital punishment. The sometimes hysterical obsession with criminalisation of drugs at the international level has provided a pretext for several States to impose capital punishment for drug-related offences. They frame the justification for the death penalty with language about protecting society. Obviously, the international drug treaties say nothing about the death penalty. The UN Office on Drugs and Crime speaks clearly about the inadmissibility of capital punishment, be it for drug crimes in particular or more generally.

It is difficult to provide any precise figure about the number of executions carried out worldwide, essentially because of the refusal of the People's Republic of China to provide any data. What we can say is that China is responsible for thousands of executions each year of which a significant portion is for crimes related to drug traffic. In Iran, which has the highest rate of execution per capita, the death penalty is on the increase, contrary to general trends. There the vast majority of executions are for drug crimes. Some countries in Southeast Asia continue to execute drug traffickers although the numbers are relatively small. There the rhetoric used to justify maintaining capital punishment, in a region where the death penalty seems to be losing momentum, is its alleged value in combating the drug trade.

The executioners face a major international legal obstacle. Not only the applicable human rights treaties but also customary international law require that any States that continue to carry out capital punishment confine its use to the 'most serious crimes'. Drug crimes cannot, according to contemporary legal authority, be included in this category.

Detention has always been at the forefront of human rights concerns. The earliest human rights treaty of general application, the European Convention of Human Rights, allows for detention 'of persons for the prevention of the spreading of infectious diseases, of persons of unsound mind, alcoholics or drug addicts or vagrants'. But the provision does not seem ever to have been applied in the context of drugs, suggesting that European practice does not in fact countenance this. Very recently, the United Nations Commission on Crime Prevention and Criminal Justice adopted the Mandela Rules, a much-updated version of the Standard Minimum Rules that have been in force since the 1950s. The Mandela Rules reflect progressive attitudes to the detention of offenders and others deprived of their liberty.

Yet alongside these very positive developments sits the terrible reality that many hundreds of thousands of people are deprived of their liberty for drug-related reasons, many of them individuals who are dependent upon drugs and those whose only crime is possession. Then are the multitudes of petty traffickers, 'mules' and other poor players in the global drug trade. In addition to the human rights violations associated with the detention itself, which may often be characterised as arbitrary, are the appalling prison conditions that must be endured.

Francis Bacon once said 'the remedy is worse than the disease'. That seems an apt portrayal of the relationship between drug control and human rights. It may be impossible to forsake the remedy at the present time. But it can be greatly attenuated by a much-heightened role for human rights norms and principles. Both prevention and repression of drug use need more human rights than they get today.

Richard Lines initially wrote this book as a doctoral thesis that I had the honour to supervise. The word 'supervise' is a bit of a grandiose term because with the best students, and Rick was one of them, the academic director plays a very minor role. It was clear from the outset that this would be the work of a scholar *éngage*, who would aspire to the highest standards of scholarly achievement yet always with an eye to the practical. I think this has been accomplished. This study is a precious contribution on a long-neglected issue. Campaigning to change the approach of international law to drug control so that it is more in line with human rights standards needs more than an authoritative monograph, but at the same time the campaign cannot fulfil its objectives without one.

Prof William A. Schabas OC MRIA

PREFACE

On 28 September 2015 I found myself sitting in the United Nations headquarters in Geneva, observing the first-ever panel at the UN Human Rights Council on 'the impact of the world drug problem on the enjoyment of human rights'. What the session lacked in content, it more than made up for in significance.

Ten years earlier, when I and a tiny handful of colleagues around the world began the work of developing the subject of human rights and drug control into a serious issue of international legal scholarship, research and advocacy, the idea of the Human Rights Council convening such a session was only a fantasy. At that time, there was little serious discourse on the human rights impacts of drug control, either within the scholarly literature or the work of UN bodies. At the time we started this work, gaining even a cursory mention of 'human rights' in the context of drug control within the statements of the UN Commission on Narcotic Drugs, UN Office on Drugs and Crime, the Office of the High Commissioner for Human Rights or the many UN human rights treaty bodies or Special Procedures was a hard-won achievement. Few of us would have imagined in those early days that the Human Rights Council would stage a thematic session specifically on the topic, into which over twenty Member States and over forty non-governmental organisations would make formal written submissions.

Even fewer of us would have imagined that human rights would be selected as one of the cross-cutting themes to be formally examined during the UN General Assembly Special Session on the World Drug Problem in April 2016. The inclusion of human rights within the Special Session on drugs is even more surprising given the experience the previous time human rights was seriously debated within a UN drug control forum. That debate took place in March 2008, during the annual meeting of the UN Commission on Narcotic Drugs in Vienna, when the first human rights resolution ever to come before that body was proposed. I was also present at that session, and along with a handful of colleagues assisted supportive Member States in efforts to have it adopted.

During those debates, many States argued that having the Commission even consider a resolution on human rights was absurd, a feeling summed up neatly by the Chinese delegation, which stated that it was 'not appropriate to address human rights within the mission of CND' and that it was 'ridiculous to require us to work in accordance with human rights law'.[1] In this hostile environment, even agreeing on a simple preambular statement recognising the sixtieth anniversary of the 1948 Universal Declaration of Human Rights was the subject of heated debate, and this during the year that the UN had proclaimed the celebration of that anniversary its key overarching theme.

Looking back, we can see that progress has clearly been made in bringing about a more robust consideration of the human rights impacts of drug control. The story of that ten-year journey, conceptualised and driven by a small group non-governmental organisations working alongside an even smaller number of UN human rights monitors and scholars, is one that has yet to be written. Just as the full impact of that work, which has now been embraced and advanced by many others in government, the UN and civil society, has yet to be felt. While the human rights impacts of drug control are now increasingly becoming a mainstreamed part of the debate, moving from rhetoric to policy and programmatic change remains a significant challenge.

The barriers to achieving real human rights progress in this area are many and complex, and are exacerbated by the corrosive influence of decades of the 'war on drugs' mentality on the design, construction, implementation and measurement of 'success' of drug control efforts. In this legal and policy environment, drugs are seen as 'a grave threat to the health and well-being of all mankind, the independence of States, democracy, the stability of nations, the structure of all societies, and the dignity and hope of millions of people and their families',[2] to cite the 1998 UN Political Declaration on Drugs; people who grow, manufacture, transport or sell drugs are seen as existential enemies of the global community; and people who use drugs are at best seen as weak-willed victims of 'chemical slavery', and at worst as a 'contagion' threatening to spread throughout the 'normal' populace.

1 Author's notes from the meeting.

2 UN General Assembly, 'Political Declaration' (21 October 1998) UN Doc No A/RES/S-20/2, 1.

In such a climate, where millions of people are fundamentally and systematically dehumanised, it is hardly surprising that drug control and enforcement efforts have routinely resulted in mass violations of human rights. The real surprise is that it is only during the most recent part of the one hundred year history of international drug control law that such abuses have started to be recognised as a problem.

This book is an effort to contribute to the growing discourse and scholarship on the issue of human rights and drug control. In particular, it seeks to move beyond the identification of abuses and provide a legal framework for preventing those abuses. It offers guidance on the often contentious and misunderstood question of treaty interpretation in this context, and how concomitant obligations within international drug control law and international human rights law should be considered and balanced. Most importantly, it offers a framework to ensure human rights violations occurring in the name of drug control can never be justified by States or their defenders as a necessary and unavoidable part of fulfilling international drug control obligations.

ACKNOWLEDGEMENTS

There are many people who have assisted and supported me in the preparation of this book that I would like to thank.

First, I would like to thank Professor William A. Schabas and Dr Nadia Bernaz of the School of Law, Middlesex University, for their encouragement, advice and patience over the course of this project. I would particularly like to recognise Professor Schabas, who over nearly ten years as my postgraduate academic supervisor never ceased to be enthusiastic and encouraging of my research into what was, at the time I began, a non-existent area of international human rights scholarship. I am also grateful for his contribution of the Foreword to this book.

I would like to thank Professor Neil Boister of the University of Waikato, New Zealand, and Dr David Keane of Middlesex University for their review of an earlier draft of this manuscript and their encouragement to publish.

I would like to thank Professor Noam Lubell, Head of Law at the University of Essex, for his ongoing advice and support. I would also like to thank the faculty and students at the Human Rights Centre at the University of Essex, where as a Visiting Fellow I have been able to develop some of these ideas. In particular, I would like to recognise Professor Paul Hunt, whose work on the right to health in the context of drug policy during his time as UN Special Rapporteur was an early inspiration, and who has been a friend and mentor to me in this area.

I would like to thank my colleagues and the students at the International Centre on Human Rights and Drug Policy at the Human Rights Centre, University of Essex, where I have had the opportunity to explore many of the ideas that appear in this book. In particular, I want to thank my colleague, friend and co-founder of the Centre, Damon Barrett, whose ideas and research have been inspirational to my own thinking on these topics. Damon is one of those rare people with whom I have worked so closely over such a long period of time that it is often impossible to know where his ideas end and mine begin, and vice versa. Suffice it to say this book would not exist without him. I also want to give a special thanks to Munira Ali for her help preparing the Table of Cases for the book.

I would like to thank Professor Joshua Castellino, Dean of Law at Middlesex University, for his constant enthusiasm for my work and Dr Helena Wray, who provided a review of two early chapters. I would also like to thank the graduate students and faculty at the Irish Centre for Human Rights, National University of Ireland Galway, where I developed the early stages of this research.

I would like to thank the many colleagues who have helped shape and influence my thinking on this topic over the course of many years and many conversations: Dave Bewley-Taylor, Julia Buxton, John Collins, Joanne Csete, Niamh Eastwood, Richard Elliott, Patrick Gallahue, Julie Hannah, Robert Husbands, Ralf Jürgens, Kasia Malinowska, Richard Pearshouse, Gen Sander, Rebecca Schleifer, Daniel Wolfe and Bi Yingxi.

I would like to thank Luciana Pols and Mariano Fusero for pointing me in the direction of important Latin American case law on this topic, and in helping me understand the relevant domestic legal systems.

I would like to thank Jim Barnes, who taught me while I was still a teenager that the law could be used as a tool for achieving social change, and that doing that work was a lifetime's calling.

I would like to thank my colleagues at Harm Reduction International. I would especially like to thank our former Executive Director, Professor Gerry Stimson, who encouraged me to pursue doctoral studies in this area.

I would like to thank the team at Cambridge University Press for their help and support in bringing this book to publication.

I would like to thank Shannonbrooke Murphy for all her help and support. Finally, I would especially like to thank my partner, Halle, for giving me the support and encouragement to see the book through to completion.

TABLE OF INTERNATIONAL INSTRUMENTS

Drug Control Instruments

Pre-League of Nations

League of Nations

United Nations

Human Rights Instruments

Other International Instruments

TABLE OF INTERNATIONAL DOCUMENTS

Council of Europe

Economic and Social Council of the United Nations

International Law Commission

International Narcotics Control Board

Raymond Yans, President, International Narcotics Control Board', Prevention Strategy and Policy Makers: A 'Solidarity Consortium' (10 October 2010). 149n6

'Report of the International Narcotics Control Board for 2010' (2011) UN Doc No E/INCB/2010/1. 155n34

'Report of the International Narcotics Control Board on the Availability of Internationally Controlled Drugs: Ensuring Adequate Access for Medical and Scientific Purposes' (2011) UN Doc No E/INCB/2010/1/Supp.1. 85n53

'International Narcotics Control Board Regrets Bolivia's Denunciation of the Single Convention on Narcotic Drugs' (5 July 2011) UN Doc No UNIS/NAR/1114. 104, 169n87

'Report of the International Narcotics Control Board for 2011' (2012) UN Doc No E/INCB/2011/1. 92n94

'Improving the implementation of the international drug control conventions through enhanced capacity of national drug control administrations: Statement by Raymond Yans, President, International Narcotics Control Board' (Rome, 10 October 2012). 129–130n22

'Report of the International Narcotics Control Board for 2013' (2014) UN Doc No E/INCB/2013/1. 149n5

'Contribution of the INCB to the high-level review of the implementation by Member States of the Political Declaration and Plan of Action on International Cooperation towards an Integrated and Balanced Strategy to Counter the World Drug Problem' (2014). 100n140

'Report of the International Narcotics Control Board for 2014' (2015) UN Doc No E/INCB/2014/1. 85n58

'Statement by Dr. Lochlan Naidoo, President, International Narcotics Control Board', Fifty-eighth session of the Commission on Narcotic Drugs Special segment on preparations for the special session of the General Assembly on the world drug problem (UNGASS) to be held in 2016 Vienna, 9–17 March 2015. 178n23

'Statement by Mr. Werner Sipp, President, International Narcotics Control Board (INCB), Fifty-ninth session of the Commission on Narcotic Drugs, Preparations for the special session of the General Assembly on the world drug problem to be held in 2016' (14 March 2016). 178n25

International Opium Commission

'Report of the International Opium Commission: Vol. I – Report of the Proceedings' (North-China Daily News & Herald Ltd 1909). 20n23

League of Nations

'Conference on the Limitation of the Manufacture of Narcotic Drugs', Information Secretariat, League of Nations, 1932. 120

Office of the United Nations High Commissioner for Human Rights

United Nations Commission on Human Rights

United Nations Commission on Crime Prevention and Criminal Justice

United Nations Commission on Narcotic Drugs

United Nations Committee of Economic, Social and Cultural Rights

United Nations Committee on the Elimination of Racial Discrimination

United Nations Committee on the Rights of the Child

United Nations Conference on International Organization

United Nations Conference for the Adoption of a Single Convention on Narcotic Drugs

'Official Records Volume II' (24 January–25 March 1961) UN Doc No E/CONF.34/24/Add. 1. 56n40, 119n53&55, 136n57, 163n61

United Nations Conference for the Adoption of a Convention Against Illicit Traffic in Narcotic Drugs and Psychotropic Substances

'Official Records Volume I' (25 November–20 December 1988) UN Doc No E/CONF.82/16/Add.1. 119n56

United Nations Depository Notifications

Permanent Mission of Bolivia to the United Nations, 'Single Convention on Narcotic Drugs, 1961, as amended by the Protocol amending the Single Convention on Narcotic Drugs, 1961: Proposal of Amendments by Bolivia to Article 49 paragraphs 1(c) and 2(e)' (12 March 2009) UN Doc No C.N.194.2009.TREATIES-2 (Depositary Notification). 103n161

Permanent Mission of Bolivia to the United Nations, 'Single Convention on Narcotic Drugs, 1961, as amended by the Protocol amending the Single Convention on Narcotic Drugs, 1961: Denunciation' (30 June 2011) UN Doc No C.N.421.2011.TREATIES-26 (Depositary Notification). 103–104n162

Permanent Mission of the United States to the United Nations, 'United States: Objection to the Reservation contained in the communication by the Plurinational State of Bolivia' (3 July 2012), UN Doc. No. C.N.101.2012.TREATIES-VI.18 (Depository Notifications). 169n85

Permanent Mission of the United Kingdom to the United Nations, 'United Kingdom: Objection to the Reservation contained in the communication by the Plurinational State of Bolivia' (14 December 2012), UN Doc No C.N.719.2012.TREATIES-VI.18 (Depository Notifications). 169n86

Permanent Mission of Italy to the United Nations, 'Italy: Objection to the Reservation contained in the communication by the Plurinational State of Bolivia' (28 December 2012) UN Doc No C.N.101.2013.TREATIES-VI.18 (Depository Notifications). 121n65

Permanent Mission of Bolivia to the United Nations, 'Single Convention on Narcotic Drugs, 1961, as amended by the Protocol amending the Single Convention on Narcotic Drugs, 1961: Accession' (22 January 2013) UN Doc No C.N.94.2013.TREATIES-VI.18 (Depositary Notification). 104n163

Permanent Mission of Ireland to the United Nations, 'Ireland: Objection to the Reservation contained in the communication by the Plurinational State of Bolivia' (9 January 2013) UN Doc No C.N.101.2013.TREATIES-VI.18 (Depository Notifications). 121n67

Permanent Mission of Japan to the United Nations, 'Japan: Objection to the Reservation contained in the communication by the Plurinational State of Bolivia' (15 January 2013). 111n17

United Nations General Assembly

United Nations Human Rights Committee

United Nations Human Rights Council

United Nations Official Commentaries

United Nations Office on Drugs and Crime

United Nations Permanent Forum on Indigenous Issues

'Report of the Eighth Session of the UN Permanent Forum on Indigenous Issues' (18–19 May 2009) UN Doc No E/2009/42-EC/C.19/2009/14. 103n159

United Nations Security Council

Res 1377 (12 November 2001) UN Doc No S/RES/1377. 71n115

United Nations Working Group on Arbitrary Detention

'Report of the Working Group on Arbitrary Detention' (15 December 2003) UN Doc No E/CN.4/2004/3. 95

'Report of the Working Group on Arbitrary Detention' (10 July 2015) UN Doc No A/HRC/30/3. 91n86

World Health Organization

'Effectiveness of Sterile Needle and Syringe Programming in reducing HIV/AIDS among Injecting Drug Users' (World Health Organization 2004). 96n117

World Health Organization, UN Office on Drugs and Crime and UNAIDS, 'Position Paper: Substitution maintenance therapy in the management of opioid dependence and HIV/AIDS prevention' (World Health Organization 2004). 96n118

World Health Organization, UN Office on Drugs and Crime and UNAIDS, 'Technical Guide for Countries to set targets for Universal Access to HIV Prevention, Treatment and Care for Injecting Drug Users' (World Health Organization 2009). 155n35

World Health Organization Western Pacific Region, 'Assessment of Compulsory Treatment of People Who Use Drugs in Cambodia, China, Malaysia and Viet Nam: An Application of Selected Human Rights Principles' (2009). 91n85

Other Sources

'Washington Conversations on International Peace and Security Organization. October 7, 1944', chap IX, para 1 in Pamphlet No. 4, Pillars of Peace: Documents Pertaining To American Interest In Establishing A Lasting World Peace: January 1941–February 1946 (Book Department, Army Information School 1946). 30

Government of Singapore, 'Letter dated 27 June 1997 from the Permanent Mission of Singapore to the United Nations Office at Geneva addressed to the Special Rapporteur on Extrajudicial, Summary or Arbitrary Executions' (5 December 1997) UN Doc No E/CN.4/1998/113. 87n64

TABLE OF CASES AND NATIONAL LEGISLATION

European Court of Justice

India

Indonesia

Inter-American Court of Human Rights

International Court of Justice

Israel

Singapore

South Africa

United Nations Human Rights Committee

United Kingdom

R v Lambert (Steven) [2001] UKHL 37; [2001] 3 WLR 206; [2001] 3 All ER 577. 66n90

Director of Public Prosecutions v Farrell [2009] IEHC 368 (High Court) 66n91

World Trade Organization (Appellate Body)

Standards for Reformulated and Conventional Gasoline (29 April 1996) WT/DS2/AB/R. 140n76

United States – Import Prohibition of Certain Shrimp and Shrimp Products – Report of the Appellate Body (22 October 2001) WT/DS58/AB/R. 130–131

EC – Measures Affecting the Approval and Marketing of Biotech Products (7 February 2006)WT/DS291–293/INTERIM. 131–132

1

Drug Control, Human Rights and 'Parallel Universes'

1.1 Background and Context

1.1.1 Quincy Wright and the 'Three Stages' of Drug Control

Writing in the American Journal of International Law in 1924 on 'the opium question', Professor Quincy Wright described what he termed the 'three stages' of international drug control contemporary to that era. The 'first stage' Wright described as beginning in 1729, continuing up until the early 1900s. This period might today be characterised as the pre-multilateral era of drug control, during which time a handful of States adopted what were essentially national or bilateral measures on drugs. In 1729, Chinese Emperor Yongzheng issued the first edict prohibiting the smoking of opium.[1] It is also from this year that the earliest records exist of a European opium trade, in this case conducted by the Portuguese.[2] The first stage of drug control was characterised by the monopoly trade in opium by the British East India Company from 1773,[3] which led to the important role of opium within international affairs in the eighteenth century.[4] Opium smoking was a tolerated activity in many British colonies and territories in Asia at that time, despite the 'official' disapproval of the British government, and the sale of opium via these State monopolies was an important source of government revenue.[5] This period saw the increase in domestic opium production in China, and

[1] Quincy Wright, 'The Opium Question' (1924) 18/2 American Journal of International Law 281. See also James Windle, 'How the East Influenced Drug Prohibition' (2013) 35/5 The International History Review 1185.

[2] Kenneth W. Makowski, 'Narcotics Regulation: A Study in Irresolution' (1960–1961) 34 Temple Law Quarterly 310, 311.

[3] Alfred McCoy, *The Politics of Heroin: CIA Complicity in the Global Drug Trade, Afghanistan, Southeast Asia, Central America, Colombia* (3rd ed, Lawrence Hill Books 2003) 5.

[4] William M. Hepburn, 'International Legislation on Social Questions' (1931–1932) 9 New York University Law Review 310, 321.

[5] John Collins, 'Regulations and Prohibitions: Anglo-American Relations and International Drug Control, 1939–1964' (PhD thesis, London School of Economics London, 2015) 32.

attempts by China to stop British opium imports into the country, leading to the first and second Opium Wars fought between the countries in the mid-1800s, as the British attempted to maintain their markets.[6] The first of these wars led to the cession of Hong Kong to England in 1842,[7] an early illustration of how drug control was to shape global politics in the years to come. This 'first stage' also included the negotiation of numerous treaties and trade agreements intended to suppress or restrict the opium trade, particularly among and between China, Great Britain, France and the United States.[8]

Wright's 'second stage' covers what was essentially the first phase of multilateral efforts in drug control, when control measures 'became a matter of international law, but without a specific international supervisory machinery'.[9] Beginning with the International Opium Commission in Shanghai in 1909, and the subsequent resolutions emerging from that meeting, and continuing into 1912, with the convening of the second International Opium Conference at The Hague. The International Opium Convention that emerged from the Hague conference codified the resolutions adopted in 1909 into the first truly international treaty on drug control. Over the ensuing years, efforts were made to encourage other States to ratify the treaty and to participate in the newly created international regime it defined.[10]

A significant boost to those efforts came via the Treaty of Versailles that ended the first World War. The British Government realised well before the war ended that 'the peace treaties . . . might furnish a convenient vehicle by which most of the nations of the world could be brought into the antiopium movement'.[11] It was seen as a particular opportunity to bring the defeated States of Germany, Austria, Hungary and Turkey into the regime, important producing and manufacturing countries which had not ratified the Opium Convention, and whose reluctance was seen to be providing a rationale for other States to similarly refuse. According to Taylor, 'It was felt that if all the belligerents were brought within the purview of the Convention, the neutral states would eventually be forced

[6] Frank Dakota, Lars Laamann and Zhou Xun, *Narcotic Culture: A History of Drugs in China* (University of Chicago Press 2004) Chapter 3.

[7] Makowski (n 2) 311. [8] Wright, 'The Opium Question' (n 1) 281–285.

[9] Herbert L. May, 'Narcotic Drug Control' (1951–1952) 29 International Conciliation 491, 497.

[10] Wright, 'The Opium Question' (n 1) 281–285.

[11] Arnold H. Taylor, *American Diplomacy and the Narcotics Traffic, 1900–1939: A Study in International Humanitarian Reform* (Duke University Press 1969) 141.

to follow suit.'[12] As a result, based upon the British and US proposals, Article 295 was inserted into the Treaty of Versailles during the Paris Peace Conference.[13] It committed the High Contracting Parties who were not already Parties to the 1912 Convention to ratify the treaty within a year. Furthermore, Article 295 specified that in the case of those Powers that were not yet State Parties to the Opium Convention, the ratification of the Treaty would itself 'be deemed in all respects equivalent to the ratification of the Convention and to the signature of the Special Protocol . . . for bringing the said Convention into force'.[14] Similar clauses were also inserted into other peace treaties at the conclusion of the war.[15]

Wright's 'third stage' begins with the foundation of the League of Nations in 1920, and is characterised by an increased commitment to international cooperation in drug control, and the creation of a 'permanent international control machinery'.[16] This is reflected in the adoption of Article 23(c) of the Covenant of the League of Nations, which 'intrust[s] the League with general supervision over the execution of agreements with regard to traffic in . . . opium and other dangerous drugs'.[17] This third stage sees increased and expanded multilateral efforts to control opium and other drugs, including the creation of new supervisory bodies under the auspices of the League, the adoption of new resolutions, a growing number of States agreeing to come into the regime and, in the decade after Wright's article was published, the adoption of new treaties under the supervision of the League that expanded the scope of international legal obligations in this area.[18]

Using the evolutionary stages posited by Wright in 1924, this book examines what it calls the 'fourth stage' of international drug control, namely the system established by the international community after 1945 under the United Nations. At the level of international law, the UN period is marked by the drafting and ratification of three new conventions that incorporate and expand upon the previous League of Nations instruments.[19] It includes the creation of new and invigorated supervisory

12 Ibid 142. 13 Ibid 142–143. 14 Peace Treaty of Versailles 1918, art 295.

15 Adolf Lande, 'The Adjustment of the International Opium Administration to an Eventual Dissolution of the League of Nations' (1945) 45 Columbia Law Review 392, 396, Taylor (n 11) 144.

16 May (n 9) 497.

17 Covenant of the League of Nations (adopted 28 April 1919) (Covenant) art 23(c).

18 Wright, 'The Opium Question' (n 1) 285.

19 International Opium Convention (adopted 19 February 1925) 81 LNTS 319 (1925 Convention); Convention for Limiting the Manufacture and Regulating the Distribution of

bodies, and increased State participation in the regime to the point where the treaties today enjoy near universal ratification. However, this fourth stage of drug control differs in several ways from the League of Nations era that preceded it. In addition to the developments described above, the fourth stage of international drug control is marked by the increased use of penal laws to suppress drugs,[20] resulting in what the United Nations Office on Drugs and Crime describes as the negative 'unintended consequences' of the regime.[21]

Despite the robust nature of the modern international drug control system, and the near universal ratification of the core instruments, the demand for and consumption of the drugs prohibited under the treaties remains high.[22] According to the UN Office on Drugs and Crime, the negative unintended consequences of this fourth stage regime are many and include the creation of huge criminal markets for drugs, controlled by cartels that often use violence and the corruption of State officials to maintain their vast profits, destabilising weak States; untold billions of dollars spent each year in largely ineffective drug interdiction efforts, at the expense of public investment in health, education and social services; exploding prison populations in many parts of the world, often driven by the prosecution of drug-related offences; and millions dead from, and many millions more infected with, HIV as a result of sharing of syringes for injecting drug use.[23] Another of the unintended consequences of the fourth stage of drug control is the negative impact of the regime on human rights. Addressing this 'unintended consequence' forms the basis of this book.

1.1.2 Human Rights in Drug Control's 'Fourth Stage'

One need only scratch the surface of domestic and international efforts to control illicit drugs during the United Nations era to see the potential for

Narcotic Drugs (adopted 13 July 1931) 139 LNTS 303 (1931 Convention); Convention of 1936 for the Suppression of the Illicit Traffic in Dangerous Drugs (adopted 26 June 1936) 198 LNTS 301 (1936 Convention).

20 Neil Boister, 'The Interrelationship between the Development of Domestic and International Drug Control Law' (1995) 7 African Journal of International and Comparative Law 906, 913 (Interrelationship).

21 UN Commission on Narcotic Drugs, 'Making Drug Control "Fit for Purpose": Building on the UNGASS Decade: Report by the Executive Director of the United Nations Office on Drugs and Crime as a contribution to the review of the twentieth special session of the General Assembly' (7 March 2008) UN Doc No E/CN.7/2008/CRP.17 (Fit for Purpose).

22 See, for example, UN Office on Drugs and Crime, 'World Drug Report 2015' (2015) United Nations, New York.

23 UN Commission on Narcotic Drugs, 'Fit for Purpose' (n 21) 10–12.

human rights concern. Indeed, drug control and enforcement activities are prime areas for the abuse of human rights, not least because, as noted by Barrett and Nowak, the very indicators of success of drug control efforts – number of criminal offences prescribed; number of people arrested and successfully prosecuted; number of people in detention; number of traffickers punished (in some countries by execution); number of people in drug treatment (whether voluntarily or involuntarily); number of hectares of crops destroyed; number of successful military operations against insurgents or criminal gangs – are also indicators of human rights risk, if not actual evidence of human rights violations.[24] As a result, the negative human rights consequences occurring during the fourth stage of drug control are mammoth, spanning all regions of the world, and include the execution of up to 1,000 people annually for drug offences;[25] the arbitrary detention of up to half a million people worldwide under the guise of 'drug treatment';[26] the denial of due process rights and rights to consent to treatment in the context of drug cases;[27] and the denial of the right to health to millions of people who inject drugs by legally prohibiting access to effective HIV prevention measures.[28]

The negative unintended consequences on human rights also highlight another unique aspect of this fourth stage that the international law on drug control during the United Nations era has developed alongside of, and in parallel with, the modern system of international human rights law, beginning with the Universal Declaration of Human Rights in 1948. Despite the contemporaneous development of these two international

[24] Damon Barrett and Manfred Nowak, 'The United Nations and Drug Policy: Towards a Human Rights-Based Approach' in A Constantinides and N. Zaikai (eds), *The Diversity of International Law: Essays in Honour of Professor Calliope K. Kpufa* (Martinus Nijhoff 2009) 468.

[25] See Patrick Gallahue and Rick Lines, 'The Death Penalty for Drug Offences: Global Overview' (International Harm Reduction Association 2010), Patrick Gallahue, 'The Death Penalty for Drug Offences: Global Overview 2011' (International Harm Reduction Association 2011).

[26] See, for example, Richard Elliott, Rick Lines and Roxanne Schleifer, 'Treatment or torture? Applying international human rights standards to drug detention centers' (Open Society Foundations 2011) 3.

[27] See, for example, Juhi Gupta, 'Interpretation of Reverse Onus Clauses' (2012) 5/1 NUJS Law Review 49, Drug Policy Alliance, 'Drug Courts are Not the Answer: Towards a Health Centered Approach to Drug Use' (Drug Policy Alliance 2011), Joanne Csete, 'Costs and Benefits of Drug-Related Health Services' in J. Collins (ed) *Ending the Drug Wars: Report of the LSE Expert Group on the Economics of Drug Policy* (LSE Ideas 2014) 75–76.

[28] See, for example, UN General Assembly, 'Report of the Special Rapporteur on the right of everyone to the enjoyment of the highest attainable standard of physical and mental health' (6 August 2010) UN Doc No A/65/255, paras 50–58 (Special Rapporteur Health 2010).

legal regimes, in practice there has been little cross fertilisation between the two. The United Nations drug control system has rarely considered the human rights impacts of the regime, and the human rights system has rarely considered drug control efforts within its mandate. In practice, this gap means that human rights violations in the name of drug control largely occur in the absence of human rights scrutiny, and in some cases are even justified by States on the basis that the abusive policies or practices are supported under the UN drug control treaties. The current status quo prompted the former Special Rapporteur on the right to the highest attainable standard of health, Paul Hunt, to conclude that '[i]t is imperative that the international drug control system . . . and the complex international human rights system that has evolved since 1948, cease to behave as though they exist in parallel universes'.[29]

Within the United Nations system, nowhere is the disconnect between the 'parallel universes' of drug control and human rights more apparent than on the 26th of June each year. On 7 December 1987, the UN General Assembly declared June 26th as the International Day Against Drug Abuse and Illicit Trafficking.[30] This date was chosen as it coincided with the closing of the International Conference on Drug Abuse and Illicit Trafficking, which met earlier that year to agree on the final text of the United Nations Convention against Illicit Traffic in Narcotic Drugs and Psychotropic Substances.[31] This third UN drug treaty, which was adopted in 1988, obligates States Parties to implement strict penal sanctions within their domestic law to punish drug offences. However, 26 June 1987 was also the date that the UN Convention Against Torture and Other Cruel, Inhuman or Degrading Treatment or Punishment entered into force.[32] Ten years later, in December 1997, the General Assembly commemorated this achievement by designating the 26th of June as the International Day in Support of Victims of Torture, 'with a view to the total eradication of torture and the effective functioning of the Convention'.[33]

[29] Paul Hunt, 'Human Rights, Health and Harm Reduction: States' Amnesia and Parallel Universes' (International Harm Reduction Association 2008) 9.

[30] UN General Assembly, 'International Conference on Drug Abuse and Illicit Trafficking' (7 December 1987) UN Doc No A/RES/42/112, para 5.

[31] UN Convention against the Illicit Traffic in Narcotic Drugs and Psychotropic Substances (20 December 1988) 1582 UNTS 95 (1988 Convention).

[32] Convention Against Torture and Other Cruel, Inhuman or Degrading Treatment or Punishment (10 December 1984) 1465 UNTS 85 (Torture Convention).

[33] UN General Assembly, 'UN International Day in Support of Victims of Torture' (18 February 1998) UN Doc No A/RES/52/149.

The ensuing years have illustrated how uncomfortably these two United Nations commemorative dates sit together, as some States choose to 'celebrate' the International Day Against Drug Abuse and Illicit Trafficking by staging the execution of drug traffickers, most visibly in China where the executions are often public and *en masse.*[34] In fact, in the decade following the entry into force of the 1988 drug convention, the number of States legislating to impose capital punishment for drug offences increased significantly,[35] this during a period when scholars were documenting an overall downward trend in the use of the death penalty worldwide.[36] There is a case to be made that the increase in States prescribing capital punishment for drug offences came as the direct result of the ratification of the 1988 Convention, which created international obligations for States to impose punitive domestic laws and penalties for drug offences. That the above executions are explicitly carried out to mark the International Day Against Drug Abuse and Illicit Trafficking, despite the fact that the UN human rights system has concluded that the death penalty for drug offences constitutes a violation of international human rights law,[37] illustrates 'the contradictions faced by the United Nations as it seeks to protect and expand human rights while also acting as the international community's guarantor of conventions to control licit and illicit drugs'.[38]

Given that June 26th marks the International Day in Support of Victims of Torture, this disconnect between human rights and drug control is also illustrated by the increasing international documentation of the infliction of torture, or other forms of cruel, inhuman or degrading treatment, in the name of 'drug treatment'.[39] In March 2012, a group of twelve United Nations agencies – including the Office of the High Commissioner for Human Rights, the World Health Organization, the UN Office on

[34] Rick Lines, 'A "Most Serious Crime"? The Death Penalty for Drug Offences and International Human Rights Law' (2010) 21 *Amicus Journal* 21.

[35] See, Rick Lines, 'The Death Penalty for Drug Offences: A Violation of International Human Rights Law' (International Harm Reduction Association 2007) 7, Rick Lines, 'A "most serious crime"? International Human Rights Law and the Death Penalty for Drug Offences' (18th International Conference on the Reduction of Drug-Related Harm, Warsaw, 15 May 2007).

[36] William A. Schabas, *The Abolition of the Death Penalty in International Law* (3rd ed, Cambridge University Press 2002) 19, Roger Hood and Carolyn Hoyle, *The Death Penalty: A Worldwide Perspective* (4th ed, Oxford University Press 2008) 13–18.

[37] See generally, Lines, 'A "Most Serious Crime"?' (n 34).

[38] Emma Bonino, 'Crimes without Victims: Appropriate Policy Responses to Drug Use' in *Protecting the Human Rights of Injection Drug Users: The Impact of HIV and AIDS* (Open Society Institute 2005) 17.

[39] See generally, Elliott, Lines and Schleifer (n 26).

Drugs and Crime and UNICEF – released a joint statement calling for the closure of all compulsory drug detention and rehabilitation centres, where many such abuses have been documented.[40] The UN Special Rapporteur on torture has also raised specific concern about 'a number of areas where torture and ill-treatment occur as a direct or indirect result of current approaches to drug control',[41] including the use of the death penalty. In his 2009 report, Special Rapporteur Manfred Nowak noted with concern that 'the international drug control system has evolved practically detached from the United Nations human rights machinery'.[42] In his 2013 report, the subsequent Special Rapporteur, Juan Mendez, again highlighted violations linked to drug control law and policy.[43] Clearly the gap in law and practice that currently exists between drug control and human rights is one that needs to be bridged.

The disengagement evident at the UN level between human rights and drug control is also reflected in the literature. Writing in 1996, Professor Norbert Gilmore of McGill University noted that 'little has been written about drug use *and* human rights. Human rights are rarely mentioned expressly in drug literature and drug use is rarely mentioned in human rights literature'.[44] Twenty years later, the literature examining drug control issues through the lens of international human rights law has grown, but the total body of peer-reviewed commentary and analysis in the area would barely rank the issue as a footnote in the broader human rights lexicon. The relative dearth of legal scholarship in the area of human rights and drugs stands in sharp contrast to the many human rights issues

[40] International Labour Organization; Office of the High Commissioner for Human Rights; United Nations Development Programme; United Nations Educational, Scientific and Cultural Organisation; United Nations Population Fund; United Nations High Commissioner for Refugees; United Nations Children's Fund; United Nations Office on Drugs and Crime; United Nations Entity for Gender Equality and the Empowerment of Women; World Food Programme; World Health Organization; and Joint United Nations Programme on HIV/AIDS, 'Joint Statement: Compulsory drug detention and rehabilitation centres' (March 2012).

[41] UN Human Rights Council, 'Report of the Special Rapporteur on torture and other cruel, inhuman or degrading treatment or punishment, Manfred Nowak' (14 January 2009) UN Doc No A/HRC/10/44, para 17 (Nowak Report).

[42] Ibid para 51.

[43] UN Human Rights Council, 'Report of the Special Rapporteur on torture and other cruel, inhuman or degrading treatment or punishment, Juan E. Mendez' (1 February 2013) UN Doc No A/HRC/22/53. (Mendez Report).

[44] Norbert Gilmore, 'Drug Use and Human Rights: Privacy, Vulnerability, Disability, and Human Rights Infringements' (1996) 12 Journal of Contemporary Health Law and Policy 355, 356.

engaged by drug control, and the litany of documented human rights abuses resulting from drug enforcement practices.

While some of the more recent literature seeks to close this gap, other literature seeks to reinforce it. Takahashi argues there is no link between the international drug control regime and capital punishment because most countries do not execute people for drug offences,[45] and makes the case that the death penalty for drug offences is in fact not a drug control issue at all, but one related to broader rule of law concerns. In an interesting example of the Hunt's concept of 'parallel universes' in action, Takahashi states 'the death penalty [for drugs] issue is not so much of a drug control issue as much as it is an issue of human rights',[46] and that while accepting that executions for drug offences are clearly violations of international human rights law, 'it is not relevant whether [these executions] were done enforcing drug control laws or during a campaign to cut down on traffic violations'.[47] The suggestion that the legal context underpinning and justifying executions is not relevant to, or should be shielded from, human rights scrutiny is unusual. In fact, a 2001 report by the UN Secretary-General recorded a 50 per cent increase in the number of countries prescribing the death penalty for drugs into domestic law between 1985 and 2000,[48] the exact period during which 1988 drug treaty was being drafted, adopted and ratified at State level. This suggests that, at minimum, the link between the international drug control regime and the use of the death penalty is a reasonable area of human rights inquiry to explore. However, Takahashi argues that human rights leaders who have spoken out on drug control issues, such as several UN High Commissioners for Human Rights, have been 'fooled' or 'tricked' into doing so.[49] In effect, attempting to dismiss or ridicule the very notion

45 Saul Takahashi, 'Drug Control and Human Rights: Frequently Asked Questions' (World Federation Against Drugs 2013) 8.

46 Saul Takahashi, 'Drug Control, Human Rights, and the Right to the Highest Attainable Standard of Health: By No Means Straightforward Issues' (2009) 31 Human Rights Quarterly 748, 761.

47 Saul Takahashi, 'Introduction: The Perils of Sectionalism' in S. Takahashi (ed) *Human Rights, Human Security, and State Security: The Intersection*, vol. 1 (Praeger, 2014) xx.

48 UN Commission on Crime Prevention and Criminal Justice, 'Capital punishment and implementation of the safeguards guaranteeing protection of the rights of those facing the death penalty: Report of the Secretary-General' (29 March 2001) UN Doc No E/CN.15/2001/10, para. 90.

49 Ibid xx-xxi. Although Takahashi mentions only Louise Arbour in his critique, both former High Commissioner, Navanethem Pillay, and current High Commissioner, Zeid Ra'ad Al Hussein, have also spoken out on human rights abuses driven by drug control.

of a broader systemic impact of the international drug control on human rights, and the work of those scholars and bodies that highlight these concerns.

However, this perspective is not reflective of the broader literature, nor the evolving practice of UN mechanisms, on the question of the human rights impacts of drug control. For example, in April 2016 more than sixty Member States used the occasion of the UN General Assembly Special Session on the world drug problem to specifically voice their opposition to the death penalty for drug offences.[50] This would suggest these States considered a discussion of human rights issues such as capital punishment completely appropriate for highest level United Nations meeting on drug control.

1.2 Scope and Objectives

1.2.1 Bridging the 'Parallel Universes' of Drug Control and Human Rights

International legal instruments on drug control date back more than one hundred years.[51] Since the adoption of the International Opium Convention in 1912, eight other treaties on drugs have been agreed under the auspices of the League of Nations and later the United Nations, and drug control has been the subject of more than one hundred resolutions of the UN General Assembly.[52] The international law of drug control therefore predates by several decades the modern system of international human rights law that has emerged since 1948, and the numerous United Nations and regional human rights treaties that have been ratified subsequently. The lessons of the fourth stage of drug control, and the impacts of these 'parallel universes' on human rights as described above, demand a new paradigm, one that closes the gaps in law and practice, and prevents human rights violations occurring due to drug control and enforcement activities.

Despite their differing histories, drug control and human rights treaties today exist as part of a larger common body of public international law. As

50 The author is grateful to the International Drug Policy Consortium for sharing its contemporaneous notes from the General Assembly Special Session, 19–21 April 2016.

51 International Opium Convention (signed 23 January 1912) 1922 LNTS 189 (1912 Convention).

52 UN General Assembly, 'Resolutions' www.un.org/documents/resga.htm accessed 15 May 2014.

described by McLachlan, 'treaties are themselves creatures of international law. However wide their subject matter, they are all nevertheless limited in scope and are predicated for their existence and operation on being part of the international law system'.[53] Within this larger body of international law, obligations between the drug control and human rights regimes interact with one another at various times and in various ways. In many cases, the human rights violations linked to drug control activities are driven by domestic and/or international efforts to meet the obligations enshrined within the three United Nations drug control conventions, creating a situation where seeking to fulfil the requirements of the drug treaties encourages or justifies policies and practices that violate international human rights law. The question, then, is how are States (or international organisations) to resolve situations in which efforts to control drugs come into conflict with obligations to protect and promote human rights? How are these conflicts, whether potential or actual, to be resolved in a manner that is consistent with the obligations of States Parties under both treaty regimes, yet at the same time ensure human rights are protected? Addressing these questions raises issues of treaty interpretation, and the appropriate balancing of obligations within the two legal regimes.

Questions of treaty interpretation, conflict of laws, and of what has come to be known as the 'fragmentation' of international law[54] are of increasing interest among international legal scholars and practitioners. The appropriate application of Articles 31–33 of the Vienna Convention of the Law of Treaties on interpretation, and the specific application of rules of treaty interpretation within world trade law in order to balance trade obligations with human rights and/or environmental concerns, are but two of the areas that have seen increased academic attention in recent years.[55] In particular, the work of the Study Group on the Fragmentation of International Law of the International Law Commission has highlighted

[53] Campbell McLachlan, 'The Principle of Systemic Integration and Article 31(3)(c) of the Vienna Convention' (2005) 54 International and Comparative Law Quarterly 279, 280.

[54] International Law Commission, 'Fragmentation of International Law: Difficulties Arising from the Diversification and Expansion of International Law - Report of the Study Group of the International Law Commission' (13 April 2006) UN Doc No A/CN.4/L.682, 208, para 414 (Fragmentation Report).

[55] See, for example, Joost Pauwelyn, *Conflict of Norms in Public International Law: How WTO Law Relates to Other Rules of International Law* (Cambridge University Press 2003), Rudiger Wolfrum and Nele Matz, *Conflicts in International Environmental Law* (Springer Verlag 2003), Seyed-Ali Sadat-Akhavi, *Methods of Resolving Conflicts between Treaties* (Brill Academic Publishers 2003), Richard K. Gardiner, *Treaty Interpretation* (Oxford University Press 2008).

the complications arising from the 'manifold' growth in specialised multilateral treaties over the past fifty years,[56] and the increasing likelihood that two or more rules or principles of international law will be applicable in respect to specific situations, necessitating a process to determine the relationship between them. However, despite the multiple areas in which drug control laws and activities engage human rights, and the slow yet growing attention among human rights monitors to these concerns, the question of treaty interpretation in this context is largely unaddressed. The primary scholarly works written in the area of international drug control law do not address the question of interpretation in any detail, if at all.[57] Some attempts have been made in the health and human rights literature to bridge these 'parallel universes', either through recourse to Article 103 of the Charter of the United Nations,[58] or through conceptualising human rights law as a '"normative counterweight" to those harmful aspects of the international legal regime of drug control'.[59] However, despite their value in advancing the discourse on this question, these proposals remain either unsatisfactory or incomplete attempts to address the complexities of treaty interpretation in this context. Other attempts have been made in the public international law literature to grapple with these questions in the context of a single case.[60] However, such case studies are, by definition, narrow in focus, making them of little general use in assessing broader interpretive questions between the two regimes. A 2015 report from a UK Parliamentary group on drug policy issues took the position that drug control obligations are 'subordinate' to human rights obligations in 'every aspect of drug policy', a conclusion for which the report argues '[t]here is no ambiguity'.[61] However, this position is too sweeping in scope, and

[56] Fragmentation Report (n 54) 10, para 7.

[57] Neil Boister, *Penal Aspects of the UN Drug Conventions* (Kluwer 2001), Syamal Kumar Chatterjee, *Legal Aspects of International Drug Control* (Martinus Nijhoff 1981).

[58] See, for example, Damon Barrett, Rick Lines, Rebecca Schleifer, Richard Elliott and Dave Bewley-Taylor, 'Recalibrating the Regime: The Need for a Human Rights-Based Approach to International Drug Policy' (Beckley Foundation Drug Policy Programme 2008) 1, Rick Lines and Richard Elliott, 'Injecting Drugs into Human Rights Advocacy' (2007) 18 International Journal of Drug Policy 453, 455.

[59] Richard Elliott, Joanne Csete, Evan Wood and Thomas Kerr, 'Harm Reduction, HIV/AIDS, and the Human Rights Challenge to Global Drug Control Policy' (2005) 8/2 Health and Human Rights 104, 121.

[60] Sven Pfeiffer, 'Rights of Indigenous Peoples and the International Drug Control Regime: The Case of Traditional Coca Leaf Chewing' (2013) 5/1 Goettingen Journal of International Law 287.

[61] All Party Parliamentary Group on Drug Policy Reform, 'Guidance on Drug Policy: Interpreting the UN Drug Conventions' (August 2015) 4.

lacks the legal specificity necessary to offer serious interpretive guidance to States or jurists in resolving conflicts. As a consequence, the issue of treaty interpretation in the context of human rights and drug control constitutes a significant gap in the literature, one which impedes the development of human rights-based approaches to drug law and policy.

1.2.2 Towards a 'Fifth Stage' of Drug Control

This book poses the question of how the international law of drug control should be interpreted within the context of international human rights law. It examines the interplay between the fourth stage of international drug control law and the concomitant development of international human rights law during the same period. Tracing the evolution of international drug control law since 1909, it explores the historic tensions within the regime between its often stated humanitarian aspirations on the one hand, and its drive to suppress a common human behaviour as a form of 'evil' on the other. Drawing from this history, it explores the object and purpose of the United Nations drug treaties, and adopts a teleological approach to the question of treaty interpretation. Building upon this approach, as well as those of the International Court of Justice and of international human rights courts and treaty bodies, it makes the case that international drug control law must be interpreted in an evolutive or dynamic fashion that considers treaty obligations in light of present-day conditions and developments in international law. In doing so, the book posits the development of what it calls a 'fifth stage' of drug control, a dynamic, human rights-based interpretative approach emerging from the engagement between the two regimes. Drawing upon illustrative examples from the jurisprudence or proceedings of domestic, regional and international legal bodies, it concludes by exploring basic principles for resolving tensions and conflicts between the two regimes in a manner that safeguards human rights.

Chapter 2 reviews the evolution of the international law of drug control through the 'three stages' described by Wright, with a particular focus on the treaties and supervisory organs that define the fourth stage United Nations regime. Beginning with the findings of the Shanghai Opium Commission of 1909 and the subsequent adoption of the International Opium Convention in 1912, it traces the normative development of the drug control regime through the League of Nations period and into the United Nations era. Not intended as a detailed historical or legal analysis, it instead reviews the normative evolution of the regime in broad terms, focussing on key developments in structure and law, and providing a context to the challenges of defining a 'fifth stage' of international drug control that will be explored later.

Following from the legal development of the modern drug treaties, Chapter 3 explores the two related yet ultimately contradictory paradigms that have historically defined the evolution of the international drug control regime. The first is that 'addiction' to drugs is a form of 'evil' constituting a threat not only to individuals but to the fabric of society as a whole, creating a moral obligation on States to suppress drug cultivation, manufacturing, trafficking and use. The second is that coordinated international drug control activities, which by definition are morally demanded to fight this 'evil', represent a collective humanitarian mission by the international community. The interplay between these paradigms creates and perpetuates an atmosphere of human rights risk, in which the global cause of drug control is framed in a manner in which abusive practices and policies are not only considered necessary but are morally justified by the righteousness of the humanitarian end goal itself.

Chapter 4 begins an exploration of consequences of these conflicting paradigms, namely the human rights violations related to drug control and enforcement emerging during the United Nations era. Drug control's fourth stage has three main elements distinguishing it from its predecessors. The first two are the increased international obligations to use penal sanctions as tools of drug suppression, and near universal ratification of the regime itself, resulting in this penal approach becoming domestic law in almost every country of the world. However, this increasingly punitive and universal approach to drug enforcement sits uncomfortably alongside the third unique element of this fourth stage: the fact that the United Nations drug control regime has developed in parallel to an increasingly robust system of international human rights treaty law. Using several case studies, the chapter illustrates the often strained nature of the relationship between these two legal regimes, highlighting examples of tensions and conflicts between the obligations within the two systems.

Building from the examples of regime tensions and conflicts examined in Chapter 4, Chapter 5 begins an exploration of the challenges of treaty interpretation within the context of international drug control law. Using guidance provided within the Vienna Convention on the Law of Treaties, as well as other legal and historical sources, the chapter examines the object and purpose of the international law of drug control, which will be critical to later questions of treaty interpretation and adjudication of regime conflicts. It adopts an approach that considers the object and purpose as a single term, yet one embodying two separate concepts. The first of these concepts is the immediate or utilitarian object and purpose of the treaty, which Chapter 5 concludes is to limit controlled drugs to medical and scientific purposes. The second concept is the ultimate goal or *telos* of the treaty, the state of affairs the treaty hopes to achieve. Chapter 5 concludes that this *telos* is to promote the health and welfare of humankind.

Chapter 6 examines the question of treaty interpretation. Exploring various interpretive approaches, and drawing on both the object and purpose identified in Chapter 5 as well as the jurisprudence of the International Court of Justice, it makes the case that a teleological approach, often described as 'dynamic' or 'evolutive' interpretation, is the most appropriate to apply in this context, particularly in instances where drug control activities engage human rights obligations. Furthermore, it makes the case that this evolutive interpretation must be driven by human rights considerations, and at minimum be consistent with, and at best advance, core human rights principles and obligations.

Having proposed the development of a dynamic, human rights-based approach to treaty interpretation, Chapter 7 considers where such a process should take place, and how it might be applied. In short, what might a 'fifth stage' of international drug control law look like in practice. It reviews the key international and domestic fora through which a dynamic interpretation of drug control law might take place. It also considers how a dynamic human rights-based interpretation of international drug control law might proceed, using the examples of regime tensions and conflicts identified in Chapter 4, and offering guidance on resolving them in a manner that promotes human rights.

Finally, Chapter 8 explores the potential future of a 'fifth stage' of drug control. Using illustrative examples from domestic, regional and United Nations case law, it reviews cases where a dynamic, human rights-based approach has been used by courts and international bodies to examine drug control questions. In doing so, it highlights the potential for such an approach to be put into practice, and mitigate the negative human rights impacts of drug control efforts.

2

The 'Fourth Stage' of Drug Control

Development, Structure and Law

2.1 Introduction

This chapter reviews the evolution of international drug control law through the 'three stages' described by Wright, with a particular focus on the treaties and supervisory organs that define the 'fourth stage' United Nations regime. It is not intended as a comprehensive historical or legal analysis of the development of drug control under the League of Nations and the UN, as this work has been done by others.[1] Nor is it intended to review past or current developments in international drug policy or politics, what is sometimes termed 'drug diplomacy', as again this ground is already well represented in the literature.[2] Rather, this chapter reviews the historical and normative evolution of the regime in broad terms, focussing on key developments in structure and law, and provides a context to the challenges in defining a 'fifth stage' of international drug control that will be explored later.

As described in 1957 by the former Chief of the League of Nations Drug Control Service, the international drug control regime 'represent[s] the first concerted attempt by governments to regulate a single industry throughout the world, from the point at which the raw materials enter the international trade to the point at which they finally reach the legitimate consumer . . . Nothing similar or as far-reaching in international cooperation has ever been attempted'.[3] To pursue this goal, international drug control law establishes a system of indirect control, under which

[1] See Bertil A Renborg, *International Drug Control: A Study of International Administration by and Through the League of Nations* (Carnegie Endowment for Peace 1947), Chatterjee (see chapter 1 n 57), Boister, *Penal Aspects* (see chapter 1 n 57).

[2] See David R Bewley-Taylor, *International Drug Control: Consensus Fractured* (Cambridge University Press 2012) (International Drug Control), William B. McAllister, *Drug Diplomacy in the Twentieth Century: An International History* (Routledge 2000), Collins (see chapter 1 n 5), Taylor (see chapter 1 n 11).

[3] Bertil A. Renborg, 'International Control of Narcotics' (1957) 22 Law and Contemporary Problems 86, 110.

multilateral treaties define the laws and administrative practices that States are required to implement within their own territories, as well as creating supervisory organs to monitor and assist State progress in fulfilling these obligations. This system of indirect control, common among so-called suppression regimes,[4] is one that heightens the risk of human rights violations linked to drug control at national level.

Although the modern regime of international drug control law has evolved over the course of one hundred years, the functional aspects of the commodity control elements of the system were established at an early stage. These primarily include internal domestic controls limiting distribution and consumption to medical and scientific needs, controls on international trade and international limitations on domestic manufacturing. However, as the regime developed in the United Nations era, an important second element emerged alongside the commodity control function of the regime: the use of strict domestic penal sanctions to suppress illicit production, manufacturing, trafficking and possession. Indeed, as drug control's fourth stage progressed, the system of law enforcement and penal sanctions, rather than that of commodity control, increasingly came to define the regime. Although both elements of the system have potential human rights implications, it has been the emergence and expansion of the penalisation regime, implemented in the context of the system of indirect control allowing States wide latitude to pursue the general aim of drug suppression, that has fueled most of the human rights abuses related to drug control documented around the world in the modern era.

2.2 Early Development of the Multilateral Regime

Prior to the twentieth century, drug control was seen as primarily a domestic concern, and the earliest attempts at regulating opium during the first stage of drug control in the eighteenth and nineteenth centuries were primarily national or bilateral in scope. However, at the dawn of the new century, it 'became apparent that the problem would have to be treated on a universal basis'.[5] Popular agitation for international action

[4] See Neil Boister, 'Human Rights Protections in the Suppression Conventions' (2002) 2 Human Rights Law Review 199, 210. (Suppression Conventions). Nadelmann uses the term 'prohibition regimes'. See Ethan Nadelmann, 'Global Prohibition Regimes: The Evolution of Norms in International Society' (1990) 44 International Organization, 479–526.

[5] Robert W. Gregg, 'The Single Convention for Narcotic Drugs' (1961) 16/4 Food, Drugs and Cosmetic Law Journal 187, 189.

on 'the opium question' had been growing in the United States,[6] and Chatterjee notes that '[b]y coincidence, the anti-opium movement started at a time when the idea of internationalism itself was gaining momentum'.[7] The existence of large and well-financed domestic opposition movements to other 'moral vices', such as alcohol consumption and 'white slavery', also meant that the anti-opium cause found itself in a receptive political environment and attracted the attention of both the US President and Secretary of State.[8] Boister notes that a mix of 'international morality shaped by the anti-opium lobby consisting of missionaries, anti-opium societies and welfare organisations' coupled with the 'foreign policy and commercial imperatives' of the United States were central to driving this early stage of drug control.[9] Collins describes this social and political context as one that combined nativism and fears of (non-white) drug users among the white populace, along with 'a latent progressivism that sought to use the state to remove social evils'.[10] As neatly summarised by McAllister,

> Once in place, the control paradigm carried a logic of its own. If some substance appeared to present a danger, demands upon public authorities for regulation were sure to follow. When some user group engendered sympathy or enmity, calls arose for enforcement measures designed to protect innocents and punish perpetrators. Moreover, given the nature of the relationship between demand, supply, and regulation, governmental restrictions inevitably propelled the control impetus into the international arena.[11]

Although 'a recent historiographical trend highlighting the emergence of prohibition in the global peripheries of Asia and Latin America, rather than just the core of the US and Europe'[12] has started to reorient traditional assertions that drug control was strictly an American project,[13] in the shaping of international drug control law the leading role of the United States is clear. As described by Windle, 'the move from national to global prohibition reflects the United States' hegemonic status: the United States saw global prohibition as in its best interest and possessed the

[6] Charles I. Bevans, 'International Conventions in the Field of Narcotic Drugs' (1963–1964) 37 Temple Law Quarterly 41, 41.
[7] Chatterjee (see chapter 1 n 57) 20.
[8] Norman Ansley, 'International Efforts to Control Narcotics' (1959–1960) 50 Journal of Criminal Law and Criminology 105, 106.
[9] Boister, 'Interrelationship' (see chapter 1 n 20) 907.
[10] Collins (see chapter 1 n 5) 30.
[11] McAllister (n 2) 19.
[12] Collins (see chapter 1 n 5) 19.
[13] See, for example, Windle (see chapter 1 n 1), Isaac Campos, *Home Grown: Marijuana and the Origins of Mexico's War on Drugs* (University of North Carolina Press 2012).

influence to affect changes in foreign nations, international organisations, and international law'.[14]

The anti-opium social movement of the period aligned neatly with broader US foreign policy and trade objectives, and in particular provided a strategic opportunity to expand political and economic ties with China while isolating Great Britain, which had a long and controversial history of exporting opium to the country.[15] The British East India Company had enjoyed a monopoly trade in opium from 1773,[16] and attempts by China to stop British opium imports resulted in two Opium Wars being fought between the countries in the mid-1800s.[17] The combination of these social, political and economic factors resulted in the initiative of the United States to convene the first international conference to 'study . . . the opium problem throughout the world'.[18] The International Opium Commission, comprising thirteen States representing major opium producing and consuming nations of the day, met in February 1909.[19] This meeting represented the first truly international initiative on opium suppression and marks the beginning of what Wright terms the second stage of drug control, the early multilateral era.[20] It also brought to the fore the divisions between drug producing and drug consuming States that 'represented the core battles over international drug control through World War II and beyond'.[21]

As a commission of inquiry, the conference was mandated to make recommendations rather than produce law. After four weeks of deliberation, the Opium Commission agreed nine unanimous Resolutions, which have been described as 'the foundation of today's world-wide drug control effort'.[22] In the process, the Commission proposed the creation of two new obligations in international law. The first, under Resolution 4, was that it was 'the duty of all countries to adopt reasonable measures to prevent at ports of departure the shipment of opium, its alkaloids,

[14] Windle (see chapter 1 n 1) 3.

[15] David R. Bewley-Taylor, *The United States and International Drug Control, 1909–1997* (Continuum 1999) 18–19, Collins (see chapter 1 n 5) 30.

[16] Hepburn (see chapter 1 n 4) 321.

[17] Dikotter, Laamann and Zhou (see chapter 1 n 6) Chapter 3.

[18] Hamilton Wright, 'The International Opium Commission, Part 1' (1909) 3/3 American Journal of International Law 648.

[19] The states represented were Austria-Hungary, China, France, Germany, Great Britain, Italy, Japan, The Netherlands, Persia, Portugal, Russia, Siam and the United States.

[20] Wright, 'The Opium Question' (see chapter 1 n 1) 283.

[21] Collins (see chapter 1 n 5) 31.

[22] John J. Cohrerrsen and Lawrence H. Hoover, 'The International Control of Dangerous Drugs' (1974) 9 The Journal of International Law and Economics 63, 81.

derivatives and preparations, to any country which prohibits the entry of any opium, its alkaloids, derivatives and preparations'.[23] Chatterjee states that '[t]he word "duty" in this resolution denotes "obligation"'.[24] The second, in Resolution 5, 'urge[d] strongly on all governments that it is highly important that drastic measures should be taken by each government in its own territories and possessions to control the manufacture, sale and distribution of this drugs, and also of such other derivatives of opium as may appear on scientific inquiry to be liable to similar abuse and productive of like ill effects'.[25] In effect, these two resolutions established the principles that the control and suppression of drugs were both the 'duty' of individual states and the shared responsibility of the international community. As described in an editorial of the American Journal of International Law at the time, 'by the joint action of the interested governments the opium problem had been raised from a national to an international plane',[26] in the process reframing drug control efforts from being primarily a domestic concern to a shared global responsibility. The recommendations also broadly define the focus on internal and external commodity controls that would underpin the international legal regime for the next century, that of import/export controls alongside limitations on domestic manufacturing.

These non-binding Resolutions were given the force of international law three years later when, following a proposal of the United States, these same thirteen governments convened a second International Opium Commission in May 1911 at The Hague in order to incorporate the recommendations into an international treaty. The resulting International Opium Convention, the first multilateral treaty on drug control, was adopted the following year on 23 January 1912.[27] As described by Bevans, the Hague Convention 'embodied a number of general principles that have remained the foundation and mainspring of all drug control'.[28]

> Import or export was to be made only by duly authorized persons. Exportation to countries prohibiting the import of raw opium was to be prevented and export to countries which desired to limit its import was required to conform to the regulations of such countries. The manufacture, internal traffic, and use of prepared opium were to be gradually suppressed, and

[23] International Opium Commission, 'Report of the International Opium Commission: Vol. I - Report of the Proceedings' (North-China Daily News & Herald Ltd 1909) 84.

[24] Chatterjee (see chapter 1 n 57) 38. [25] International Opium Commission (n 23) 84.

[26] 'The International Opium Conference' (1911) 5/2 American Journal of International Law 466, 466.

[27] 1912 Convention (see chapter 1 n 51). [28] Bevans (n 6) 43.

> imports and exports were to be prohibited. The manufacture, sale, and use of morphine, cocaine, and their derivatives, were to be controlled and limited to medicinal and other legitimate uses only. Legal and statistical information was to be exchanged by the parties.[29]

The new convention contained six chapters and twenty-five articles. The ratification process of the treaty was slow, however, as many States were reluctant to voluntarily submit to the new regime. This slow pace of ratification was despite the fact, as described by McAllister, that '[t]he treaty urged much but required little. States inclined to enhance controls found ample justification in the convention's stipulations . . . The treaty's equivocal provisions, however, allowed recalcitrants to avoid enacting substantive measures'.[30] The ratification process all but ground to a halt with the advent of the first World War in 1914.[31] However, a major step towards expanding the regime was made at the end of the war when the victorious powers inserted Article 295 into the Treaty of Versailles. This article committed all High Contracting Parties who were not already parties to the Opium Convention to ratify it within one year, and specified that the signing of the Treaty of Versailles would itself 'be deemed in all respects equivalent to the ratification of the Convention and to the signature of the Special Protocol . . . for bringing the said Convention into force'.[32] Similar clauses were also inserted into the other peace treaties at the conclusion of the war.[33]

2.3 The League of Nations Era and an Enhanced System of Control

The third stage of drug control, as described by Wright, begins with the foundation of the League of Nations in 1920. One of the considered shortcomings of the 1912 Opium Convention was that it established no structures through which drug control efforts could be progressed and monitored.[34] As described by Taylor,

> [O]ne of the Conventions greatest defects was the lack of an organ of administration to supervise or carry out the provisions of the Convention. Fear by the powers of an international body that would infringe on their

[29] Ibid. [30] McAllister (n 2) 39.
[31] Renborg, 'International Control of Narcotics' (n 3) 86.
[32] Peace Treaty of Versailles (see chapter 1 n 14) art 295.
[33] Lande (see chapter 1 n 15) 396.
[34] Quincy Wright, 'The Opium Conferences' (1925) 19/3 American Journal of International Law 559, 561.

> sovereignty prevented even the consideration of this step at the [drafting] conference.[35]

Governments sought to rectify this 'defect' within the League of Nations, and the period is marked by an increased commitment to international cooperation in drug control, and the creation of a 'permanent international control machinery'.[36] This increased commitment is reflected in the foundational document of the organisation, the Covenant of the League of Nations, Article 23(c) of which 'intrust[s] the League with general supervision over the execution of agreements with regard to traffic in . . . opium and other dangerous drugs'.[37] Later, this third stage sees the expansion of multilateral drug control efforts, including the creation of an Advisory Committee on the Traffic in Opium and Other Dangerous Drugs by the Council of the League of Nations, the adoption of new resolutions and a growing number of States entering into the regime. It is also marked by the adoption of new treaties that expanded the scope of international legal obligations in this area, and the creation of new control organs, which would later come to form the foundations of the United Nations regime. As characterised by one State representative in 1925, 'the drug question has entered upon a new period. It is now caught in the day-to-day machinery of the League of Nations. It cannot escape'.[38]

In the two decades following the foundation of the League, three major and two lesser drug treaties were adopted. In describing the progress of the legal regime during this period, Renborg explains that,

> The League of Nations could not advance quicker or further [on drugs] than governments and public opinion were prepared to go. And they were not prepared to go the whole way at once . . . The League had to proceed slowly and gradually, attacking the most important problems first. The various important steps were marked by different conventions concluded one after the other.[39]

The first of the major treaties was the 1925 International Opium Convention,[40] which in effect implemented the proposals put forward in Resolution 4 of the International Opium Commission in 1909.[41] The treaty also expanded the existing scope of control to include coca[42] and

[35] Taylor (see chapter 1 n 11) 109. [36] May (see chapter 1 n 9) 497.
[37] Covenant (see chapter 1 n 17) art 23(c).
[38] M. Zahle of Denmark, cited in Wright, 'The Opium Conferences' (n 34) 561.
[39] Bertil A. Renborg, 'Principles of International Control of Narcotics' (1943) 37 American Journal of International Law 436, 437.
[40] 1925 Convention (see chapter 1 n 19). [41] Chatterjee (see chapter 1 n 57) 38.
[42] 1925 Convention (see chapter 1 n 19) arts 3, 4.

cannabis (termed 'Indian hemp' in the text[43]) and their derivatives. Although this Convention established some greater domestic controls on the manufacture, sale and transport of drugs than those found in the 1912 Opium Convention,[44] its primary contribution to international drug control law was to create systems to regulate international trade in controlled substances. This included requiring mandatory government import and export authorisation certificates for all international transactions of drugs covered within the treaty,[45] a development '[p]redicated on the assumption that it would be much more difficult to misuse narcotics if each act of importation and exportation were subject to government approval'.[46] The 1925 Convention also established a process allowing the scope of international drug control to evolve, based upon advances in medical and scientific knowledge. Through this process, new substances could be included within the treaty, or currently controlled substances removed, based upon the recommendation of the Health Committee of the League of Nations, and an assessment of whether the drug in question was 'liable to similar abuse and productive of similar ill-effects' as other drugs in the treaty.[47]

Perhaps the most significant element in terms of the development of the regime as a whole was the establishment of the Permanent Central Board (also referred to as the Permanent Central Opium Board) as a new supervisory organ, composed of eight independent experts 'who, by their technical competence, impartiality and disinterestedness, will command general confidence'.[48] The Board was empowered to oversee a new system of 'estimates', under which each Contracting Party was required to submit 'estimates of the quantities of each of the substances covered by the Convention to be imported into their territory for internal consumption during the following year for medical, scientific and other purposes'.[49] Parties to the Convention were also obligated to submit statistics on domestic production of raw materials (for example, raw opium or coca leaves), domestic manufacture and consumption of substances covered by the treaty and report stocks on hand.[50] In addition to this data collection function, the Board was bestowed with powers of enforcement. If, based on the statistical data collected, the Board suspected that a State were producing or importing drugs in excess of its estimated legitimate consumption requirements, and that therefore there was 'a danger of the

[43] Ibid Chapter IV. [44] Ibid Chapter III. [45] Ibid Chapter V.
[46] Gregg (n 5) 190. [47] 1925 Convention (see chapter 1 n 19) arts 8, 10.
[48] Ibid art 19. [49] Ibid art 21. [50] Ibid art 22.

country becoming a centre of . . . illicit traffic', the Board was empowered to take actions of varying severity, from requesting additional information of the Government in question, to raising concerns to the Council of the League of Nations to even recommending an international embargo on further exports to the offending State.[51]

With new controls and regulations established on international trade in controlled drugs, the next step taken by the League was to create a system to limit the levels of manufacturing of drugs strictly to that necessary for medical and scientific purposes. Following a similar logic to that underpinning the 1925 Convention, it was considered that controlling production solely to that needed for 'legitimate' need would limit the amount of drugs being diverted into illicit markets. As described by the US Department of State at the time, 'It is foreign overproduction, *i.e.*, total production over and above the amount needed for medical and scientific purposes, which supplies the illicit international traffic.'[52] To this end, the Convention for Limiting the Manufacture and Regulating the Distribution of Narcotic Drugs was adopted in Geneva on 13 July 1931.[53] This treaty operationalised the restrictions on production and manufacture found in the International Opium Commission's Resolution 5.[54] Like the 1925 Convention, the controls in the 1931 Convention were based around a system of estimates of domestic consumption of drugs for medical and scientific purposes.[55] However, unlike the non-binding estimates system established in 1925 Convention, 'under the 1931 Convention estimates were required for total consumption and were binding'.[56] The Convention also created a second international control organ, a Supervisory Body (often called the Drug Supervisory Body) under Article 5.[57] A critical new approach taken under the 1931 Convention was that the belief that drug '[l]imitation could never be effective if there were parts of the world to which the estimate system did not apply'.[58] Therefore, in order to be successful, it was decided that drug control must be universal in application. To address this, Article 2 of the Convention instructed that the Permanent Central Board 'shall request estimates for countries and

[51] Ibid art 24.

[52] United States Department of State Press Release, 15 July 1933. Cited in Quincy Wright, 'The Narcotics Convention of 1931' (1934) 28 American Journal of International Law 475, 477.

[53] 1931 Convention (see chapter 1 n 19).

[54] Chatterjee (see chapter 1 n 57) 38.

[55] 1931 Convention (see chapter 1 n 19) art 4(7).

[56] Bevans (n 6) 46.

[57] 1931 Convention (see chapter 1 n 19) art 5.

[58] Renborg, 'Principles of International Control of Narcotics' (n 39) 438.

territories to which this Convention does not apply',[59] in other words from non-Parties to the treaty. According to Renborg, this represented 'a rather unusual feature which is a novelty in international legislation. Non-parties to a convention are requested to perform a certain act although they have not undertaken an obligation to do so'.[60] The 1931 Convention went beyond merely requesting information from non-Parties. It also created a mechanism subjecting all States to the controls established under the treaty, regardless of whether the States had ratified the instrument or not. This power was found in Article 2 and mandated that in cases where States or territories failed to provide voluntary estimates to the Permanent Central Board, 'the Supervisory Body shall itself, as far as possible, make the estimate'.[61] Estimates carried equal legal authority, whether they were submitted voluntarily by a State or were produced independently by the Supervisory Body. They were also equally binding on the treaty obligations of other States, as the estimates would be the basis for authorising importing/exporting controlled drugs to/from other Parties to the treaty. As a consequence, 'non-parties, who have accepted no obligations whatsoever, are nevertheless limited in their drug supplies by the estimates made by the Supervisory Body'.[62] This development was described by Renborg as being 'probably the most radical feature of the convention'.[63] The Convention also increased the powers of the Permanent Central Board in this regard. Under the 1925 Convention, the power to impose an import/export embargo on an offending State was vested in the Council of the League of Nations, with the Board only having the authority to recommend an embargo for the Council to consider.[64] Under Article 14 of the 1931 Convention, however, the Board was given power to directly impose an embargo itself, without requiring the Council's approval, and to communicate this decision directly with the High Contracting Parties.[65]

The 1925 and 1931 Conventions defined a framework that reflected Resolutions 4 and 5 of the International Opium Commission in 1909, and as such represented significant developments in international drug control law, both in terms of State obligations and the scope of the international supervisory bodies. Taken together, the treaties establish the

[59] 1931 Convention (see chapter 1 n 19) art 2(3).
[60] Renborg, 'Principles of International Control of Narcotics' (n 39) 438.
[61] 1931 Convention (see chapter 1 n 19) art 2(3).
[62] Renborg, 'Principles of International Control of Narcotics' (n 39) 439. [63] Ibid.
[64] 1925 Convention (see chapter 1 n 19) art 24.
[65] 1931 Convention (see chapter 1 n 19) art 14(2).

principles and control measures that still define the commodity control pillar of the regime today. However, as described by Boister, one of the outcomes of codifying a system for limiting the manufacture and trade in drugs to medical and scientific purposes was that it 'marked the line between licit and illicit traffic, thus inviting the international community to endeavour to suppress the illicit traffic'.[66] This created the impetus for the development of a new convention, one establishing State obligations to strengthen the severity of penal sanctions within domestic criminal law, leading to the third and final major drug convention of the League of Nations era,[67] the Convention of 1936 for the Suppression of the Illicit Traffic in Dangerous Drugs.[68]

Few provisions within the previous instruments dealt with the question of domestic criminal laws of Contracting Parties,[69] and the 1936 treaty was the source of many of the penal approaches that underpin the punitive approach of the modern 'war on drugs', in essence making illicit drug trafficking a crime under international law. The preamble states that the objective of the convention is 'to strengthen the measures intended to penalise offences contrary to the provisions' of the previous drug treaties, and 'to combat by the methods most effective in the present circumstances the illicit traffic in the drugs and substances covered by the . . . Conventions'.[70] To pursue these outcomes, the convention obligated Contracting Parties to enact a strict, penal-focussed approach to drugs within their domestic legislation, with a view towards increasing the severity of punishments for drug offences, and harmonising national criminal laws related to drugs in much the same way the previous conventions harmonised domestic administration and control practices. Article 2 created an obligation 'to make the necessary legislative provisions for severely punishing, particularly by imprisonment or other penalties of deprivation of liberty' a wide range of acts including the manufacture, possession, distribution, purchase and sale, transport, import

66 Boister, *Penal Aspects* (see chapter 1 n 57) 32–33.

67 Two additional drug control instruments were also adopted under the League, the Agreements of 1925 and 1931 for the Suppression of Opium Smoking, which were intended to accomplish the gradual elimination of opium smoking in various Asian countries and territories. Agreement concerning the Suppression of the Manufacture of, Internal Trade in, and Use of, Prepared Opium, (signed 11 February 1925) 51 LNTS 337; Agreement concerning the Suppression of Opium Smoking, (signed 27 November 1931) 177 LNTS 375.

68 1936 Convention (see chapter 1 n 19).

69 Boister, *Penal Aspects* (see chapter 1 n 57) 32.

70 1936 Convention (see chapter 1 n 19) preamble.

and export of illicit drugs, as well as participation in such offences or conspiracy to commit them.[71] The convention also included provisions on extradition[72] and mandated the creation of centralised police offices 'for the supervision and co-ordination of all operations necessary'[73] to prevent or prosecute the offences enumerated under Article 2. However, few States ratified the treaty, and the 1936 Convention was largely seen as a failure, as 'many states with negligible or nonexistent illicit narcotic drug traffic have not felt it incumbent on them to ratify a convention that would involve them in complicated legislation and administrative measures'.[74]

2.4 The United Nations Era: The 'Fourth Stage' of Drug Control

The advent of the second World War had a significant impact on the international drug control machinery. Although the League of Nations drug supervisory bodies continued to function, in reality the regime had largely broken down as a result of the hostilities.[75] The Permanent Central Board and the drug Supervisory Body continued to operate, although they were moved to Washington DC where they 'came under increased US influence'.[76] In many cases, the national mechanisms ceased to function altogether, and the Advisory Committee on Traffic in Opium and other Dangerous Drugs did not meet after 1940.[77] Therefore, one of the first tasks of the newly formed United Nations was to re-establish the international systems of control that had deteriorated or collapsed during the war. Indeed, Collins argues that the Second World War and its aftermath 'heavily reshaped international narcotics control in many respects. It achieved what previous conferences and conventions could not: a tangible commitment by colonial powers to prohibit and eradicate most non-medical and non-scientific consumption of opium in their colonies and end the monopolies that supplied them'.[78]

2.4.1 International Drug Control, from Covenant to Charter

As described above, the Covenant of the League of Nations specifically invested the organisation with a drug control mandate under Article 23(c).[79] When the Charter of the United Nations was drafted in 1945, this

[71] Ibid art 2. [72] Ibid arts 7–9. [73] Ibid art 11.
[74] Renborg, 'International Control of Narcotics' (n 3) 102.
[75] Boister, *Penal Aspects* (see chapter 1 n 57) 40. [76] Collins (see chapter 1 n 5) 74.
[77] May (see chapter 1 n 9) 503–504.
[78] Collins (see chapter 1 n 5) 11. [79] Covenant (see chapter 1 n 17) art 23 (c).

specific reference to drug control was not included. However, it would be incorrect to suggest that the elimination of specific reference to drugs in the Charter represented, or was intended by States to be, a weakening of the mandate of the new UN organisation in the area of drug control.[80] In fact the opposite was the case, as this choice of language did not represent a fundamental shift away from the international community's concern for drug control, nor of the central role of international organisations in that effort. Rather, it reflected what was largely seen as the 'unsatisfactory' ability of the League to coordinate international activities on drugs and other areas of social and economic cooperation.[81] To address these concerns, the Charter adopted language allowing for a new, more rigorous and robust system of international oversight and control of drugs to be put in place.

The UN Charter effectively takes the old Article 23 of the Covenant and expands it into six more detailed provisions, Articles 55–60 under Chapter IX,[82] with the result that the specific activity areas identified under Article 23 were subsumed in the more general language of 'international economic, social, health and related problems' under Article 55.[83] This did not represent a shift in concept or content, as under the Covenant drug control was already included within a subset of bilateral and multilateral activities that could be described as relating to social, health and economic needs. Article 23 was not solely concerned with the control of drugs but more broadly addressed the improvement of the social and economic welfare of the populations of the High Contracting Parties. For example, in addition to clause (c) on drugs, other clauses addressed issues including fair and humane labour standards,[84] just treatment of aboriginal peoples,[85] preventing trafficking of women and children,[86] arms

[80] For an example of this perspective, see Daniel Heilmann, 'The International Control of Illegal Drugs and the U.N. Treaty Regime: Preventing or Causing Human Rights Violations' (2011) 19/2 Cardozo Journal of International and Comparative Law 237, 272.

[81] Bruno Simma (ed) *The Charter of the United Nations: A Commentary* (Oxford University Press 1994) 761. See also, for example, comments of the South African and Canadian delegates to the San Francisco Conference. 'Documents of the United Nations Conference on International Organization, San Francisco, 1945', Vol. III 'Dumbarton Oaks Proposals, Comments and Proposed Amendments', United Nations Information Organizations, 1945 vol. 8, 52–53, vol. 10, 21 (Official Records San Francisco).

[82] See, A. Walter Dorn, 'The League Covenant and the UN Charter: A side-by side (full text) comparison' (12 May 2008) Royal Military College of Canada.

[83] Charter of the United Nations (24 October 1945) 1 UNTS XVI, art 55(b) (Charter).

[84] Covenant (see chapter 1 n 17) art 23(a). [85] Ibid art 23(b). [86] Ibid art 23(c).

control[87], commerce[88] and public health.[89] In essence, the UN Charter does not remove drug control as a matter of international concern but rather enshrines a more flexible formulation of wording that allows not only for the inclusion of drug control but also for new and additional areas, as deemed necessary over time by the General Assembly. Indeed, in 1959 the General Assembly specifically recognised that the UN 'exercises responsibilities in the field of narcotic drugs' under Chapter IX of the Charter.[90]

Furthermore, the operational language of Article 23 of the Covenant did little more than mandate States to abide by the terms of existing international instruments, requiring only that Contracting Parties act 'in accordance with the provisions of international conventions existing or hereafter to be agreed upon'.[91] As such, the Covenant created no new obligations towards drug control, other than symbolising the particular significance attributed by the League to this and other identified areas of social and economic activity and encouraging States to meet their treaty obligations in this regard. Indeed, when the inclusion of a clause on narcotics control was proposed by the British delegation, there was specific agreement among the High Contracting Parties that naming these areas of activity in the Covenant would not create legal obligations upon the States that had not ratified the relevant treaties.[92] The British delegation's minutes of the meeting note that 'President Wilson replied that their only obligation would be to see to it that subscribing States kept their obligations thereunder'.[93] Therefore, the clause on drugs had little or no legal significance, as it created no new obligations for States, whether or not they were party to the 1912 Opium Convention. It also did not create any new supervisory bodies under the League as an organisation. As noted by Simma, the Covenant 'did not establish a connection between the promotion of . . . social well-being and the maintenance of international peace and security; consequently it did not provide the League of Nations with the machinery necessary for dealing with social and economic matters'.[94]

87 Ibid art 23(d). 88 Ibid art 23(e). 89 Ibid art 23(f).

90 UN General Assembly, 'Technical assistance in narcotics control' (20 November 1959) UN Doc No A/RES/1395(XIV), para 1.

91 Covenant (see chapter 1 n 17) art 23.

92 David Hunter Miller, *The Drafting of the Covenant*, vol. I (GP Putnam's Sons 1928) 339–341.

93 Ibid 341. 94 Simma (n 81) 760.

The UN Charter, however, commits that '[a]ll Members pledge themselves to take joint and separate action in cooperation with the Organization for the achievement of the purposes set forth in Article 55'.[95] In this context, Article 57 establishes a mechanism allowing the UN to create 'specialized agencies' with 'wide international responsibilities' to deal with the economic, health and social matters identified by the Organization,[96] these 'specialized agencies' to fall under the authority of the newly created Economic and Social Council.[97] These Charter provisions are a reflection of the proposals that emerged from the 1944 Washington Conversations on International Peace and Security Organization, known as the 'Dumbarton Oaks Proposals', where the major powers agreed the framework for a new international organisation to take the place of the League. Part of that new framework was agreement that 'solutions of international economic, social and other humanitarian problems and promot[ing] respect for human rights and fundamental freedoms' was necessary for 'the creation of conditions of stability and well-being which are necessary for peaceful and friendly relations among nations'.[98] In order to promote these aims, the Washington Conference proposed the creation of 'specialized economic, social and other organizations and agencies that would have responsibilities in their respective fields',[99] a proposal that was directly incorporated into the Charter.

Despite the existence of four major, and two lesser, multilateral drug control treaties at the time of the San Francisco Conference, and the specific mention of drug control efforts within the Covenant, there was surprisingly little discussion of drugs during the drafting of the Charter. While Mexico proposed a list of twelve specific areas in which the Economic and Social Council should establish 'permanent organizations', drug control was not included among them.[100] The drafting committee

[95] Charter (n 83) art 56. [96] Ibid art 57. [97] Ibid art 60.

[98] 'Washington Conversations on International Peace and Security Organization. October 7, 1944', Chapter IX, para 1 in *Pamphlet No. 4, Pillars of Peace: Documents Pertaining To American Interest In Establishing A Lasting World Peace: January 1941–February 1946* (Book Department, Army Information School 1946) 45.

[99] Ibid Chapter IX, para 2.

[100] The subject areas proposed by Mexico were Protection of the International Rights of Man; Progress in international economy and commerce; Furtherance and coordination of land, sea, and air communications; Improvement of working conditions and abolition of unemployment; Nutrition and health; Agriculture; Financial and investment problems; Demographic and migration problems; Intellectual cooperation; Child welfare; Protection of countries under mandate; White slavery. 'Official Records San Francisco, Vol. 10' (n 81) 310–311.

did however, by unanimous vote, accept a proposal that the language of the draft Article 'includes international traffic in, and abuse of, opium and other narcotics and dangerous drugs',[101] a decision that was also reflected in the Rapporteur's report of the drafting committee's proceedings.[102] The specific discussion of drug control in this context appears to have been pushed most vigorously by the United States, which issued the only specific document on drug control during the Conference, stating that 'drug control raises issues that can best be met not by an international health, economic and social agency' but instead by 'specialized agencies'.[103] It proposed that the new international organisation 'be entrusted with supervision over the execution of existing or future international agreements' related to drugs, and that there 'be established an advisory body to advise directly the Economic and Social Council in these matters'.[104] The US statement received support from China, Canada and India.[105]

Therefore, the new structures created under the Charter reflect not a retreat from a prioritisation of drug control, but rather an evolution in the scope of international cooperation and collaboration on social, health and economic issues. In 1946, the first sessions of both the General Assembly[106] and the Economic and Social Council[107] considered resolutions to incorporate the League's drug control instruments under UN authority, a fact suggesting the importance placed upon the issue had not diminished. In fact, the adoption of the UN Charter represents a significant evolution of the normative nature of international drug control. Under Article 1 of the Charter, which sets out the four purposes of the United Nations, paragraph three states that a purpose of the organisation is, '[t]o achieve international cooperation in solving international problems of an economic, social, cultural, or humanitarian character, and in promoting and encouraging respect for human rights and for fundamental freedoms for all without distinction as to race, sex, language, or religion'.[108] The drafters regarded Article 55 as a reinforcing and implementing provision for Article 1, in particular Articles 1(2) and

[101] Ibid 127–128, 390. [102] Official Records San Francisco (n 81) vol. 8, 81.

[103] Ibid 98–99, 'Statement by the United States Delegation on the Control of Dangerous Drugs'.

[104] Ibid. [105] Official Records San Francisco (n 81) vol. 10, 197.

[106] UN General Assembly, 'Transfer to the United Nations of powers exercised by the League of Nations under the International Agreements, Conventions and Protocols on Narcotic Drugs' (19 November 1946) UN Doc No A/RES/54(1).

[107] UN Economic and Social Council, 'ECOSOC Official Records, No. 2' (First Year Third Session, 12 and 17 September 1946) 28.

[108] Charter (n 83) art 1(3).

1(3).[109] Simma refers to Articles 55 and 56 as the 'operative parts of the Charter to which Art. 1(3) refer'.[110] Significantly, Article 55 states that promoting 'solutions of international economic, social, health, and related problems' as well as 'universal respect for, and observance of, human rights and fundamental freedoms' are 'necessary' for 'the creation of conditions of stability and well-being which are necessary for peaceful and friendly relations among nations based on respect for the principle of equal rights and self-determination of peoples'.[111] The Charter of the United Nations therefore established the framework for the creation of the legal and administrative tools necessary to enable the new organisation to take a more robust approach to international drug control than was previously possible.

2.4.2 The United Nations Treaty Regime

2.4.2.1 The Pre-Treaty Period: Protocols of 1946, 1948 and 1953

Under the League of Nations, the development of the international legal regime on drugs had 'proceed[ed] slowly, step by step'.[112] The pace of this evolution reflected the evolving 'technical, medical, and social knowledge of the nature of the problem', the slow nature of international treaty-making processes and the lack of enthusiasm of many States to voluntarily enter the new legal regime.[113] As a result, at the time of the founding of the United Nations, the body of international law addressing drugs consisted of an assortment of instruments built up over the course of thirty years. The task before the United Nations was therefore to incorporate these existing conventions into a modern, unified and simplified treaty, supported by the supervisory and technical bodies required to carry out the necessary functions. As described by Collins, Member States needed to agree 'where to draw the line between licit and illicit consumption; how tightly to restrict, regulate and prohibit global supplies; how much interference in national affairs to allow international organisations; and how to deal with existing drug consuming populations'.[114]

The work on this objective was begun by the Economic and Social Council in September 1946, which set about to prepare a protocol

109 Simma (n 81) 760, 762. 110 Ibid 53. 111 Charter (n 83) art 55.
112 Renborg, 'International Control of Narcotics' (n 3) 94. 113 Ibid.
114 Collins (see chapter 1 n 5) 12.

entitled 'Transfer to the United Nations of the powers exercised by the League of Nations in connexion with Narcotic Drugs.'[115] The 'Lake Success Protocol,' as it was known, was adopted by the General Assembly during its first session in November,[116] and served as a model for other UN instruments similarly transferring previous League of Nations powers and functions.[117] Under the protocol, the United Nations assumed supervisory responsibility for all previous conventions and protocols on drugs. Although maintaining the functions of the Permanent Central Board and Supervisory Body, the protocol shifted all other responsibilities to the newly established UN drug control machinery. The role of the Council of the League of Nations was taken over by the Economic and Social Council; that of the Advisory Committee on Traffic in Opium and other Dangerous Drugs was taken over by the UN Commission on Narcotic Drugs; that of the Health Committee of the League was taken over by the World Health Organization.[118]

Two years later in 1948, a second protocol was adopted by the General Assembly. The 'Paris Protocol,'[119] which entered into force on 1 December 1949,[120] extended controls to new drugs and precursors not covered by the 1931 Convention, in order to address 'the progress of modern pharmacology and chemistry', which had 'resulted in the discovery of drugs, particularly synthetic drugs, capable of producing addiction'.[121] This resulted in twenty new substances coming under international control by 1954,[122] a number that increased to over thirty by 1956.[123] A third protocol was agreed in 1953 on limiting and regulating the cultivation of poppies, and

115 UN Economic and Social Council (n 107) 28.

116 UN General Assembly, 'Transfer to the United Nations of powers exercised by the League of Nations under the International Agreements, Conventions and Protocols on Narcotic Drugs' (n 106).

117 May (see chapter 1 n 9) 505.

118 Protocol amending the Agreements, Conventional and Protocols on Narcotic Drugs concluded at the Hague on 23 January 1912, at Geneva on 11 February 1925 and 19 February 1925 and 13 July 1931, at Bangkok on 27 November 1931 and at Geneva on 26 June 1936 (19 November 1946) (Lake Success Protocol).

119 Protocol bringing under international control drugs outside of the Convention of 13 July 1931 for Limiting the Manufacture and Regulating the Distribution of Narcotic Drugs. As amended by the Protocol signed at Lake Success on 11 December 1946 (8 October 1948) (Paris Protocol).

120 May (see chapter 1 n 9) 516.

121 Paris Protocol (n 119) preamble.

122 UN Office on Drugs and Crime, *A Century of International Drug Control* (UN Office on Drugs and Crime 2009) 59.

123 Ansley (n 8) 110.

the manufacture and trade in opium.[124] Under the protocol, only seven countries were authorised to produce opium for export (Bulgaria, Greece, India, Iran, Turkey, Yugoslavia and the Soviet Union).[125] The protocol also bestowed the Permanent Central Board with strong regulatory powers.[126] Described by one source as containing 'the most stringent drug-control provisions that had ever been embodied in international law',[127] Boister notes that these terms were 'a more difficult legal pill to swallow and [the protocol] did not enter force until 1962. This lack of enthusiasm can to some extent be explained by the simultaneous development of . . . the 1961 Single Convention [on Narcotic Drugs]',[128] the first of the UN drug treaties.

2.4.2.2 The United Nations Drug Conventions

The need for a new drug convention that would amalgamate the complicated set of instruments agreed over the previous three decades, and also to update and expand the regime to meet contemporary challenges, had been under consideration since the very earliest years of the UN.[129] As described by one observer at the time, '[b]ecause they were drafted at different times under different sets of circumstances and ratified by different combinations of states in each case, the several [pre-existing] international agreements amounted to a patchwork of obligations and commitments which was not wholly satisfactory'.[130] This process was initiated in 1948 with a request from the Commission on Narcotic Drugs to the Economic and Social Council to invite the Secretary-General to begin the drafting.[131] Formal efforts got underway in 1949, with the objective to 'simplify and improve the existing international instruments . . . on narcotic drugs' as well as to 'contain provisions for the limitation of the production of raw materials'.[132] The task, therefore, was to bring together the content of the pre-existing international drug control instruments, as well as to address new areas of concern, in one single international

[124] Protocol for Limiting and Regulating the Cultivation of the Poppy Plant, the Production of International and Wholesale Trade in, and use of Opium (23 June 1953).

[125] Ibid Chapter XV. This was later changed under the Single Convention on Narcotic Drugs, 1961.

[126] Ibid art 6.

[127] UN Office on Drugs and Crime, *A Century of International Drug Control* (n 122) 60.

[128] Boister, *Penal Aspects* (see chapter 1 n 57) 41. [129] May (see chapter 1 n 9) 518.

[130] Gregg (n 5) 188. [131] May (see chapter 1 n 9) 519.

[132] H. J. Anslinger, 'Report of Progress in Drafting the "Single Convention", a Proposed Codification of the Multilateral Treaty Law on Narcotic Drugs' (1958) 13 Food, Drug, and Cosmetic Law Journal 692, 692.

instrument (hence the eventual title of the treaty, the Single Convention on Narcotic Drugs).[133]

The Single Convention was adopted on 30 March 1961 and entered into force on 13 December 1964.[134] Its fifty-one articles focus primarily on the control of plant-based narcotics: opium, cannabis, coca and their derivatives. It enshrines the basic principles of the League of Nations regime, namely that of limiting the availability and use of controlled drugs solely to medical and scientific purposes through administrative controls placed on manufacture, import, export and distribution. The treaty contextualises this mission in the preamble as being because the Parties are '[c]oncerned with the health and welfare of mankind', because 'adequate provision must be made to ensure the availability of narcotic drugs' for medical purposes and 'the relief of pain and suffering' and because 'addiction to narcotic drugs constitutes a serious evil for the individual and is fraught with social and economic danger to mankind' and therefore 'require[s] co-ordinated and universal action'.[135] To pursue these goals, the treaty adopts the approaches developed under the earlier conventions, including that of indirect control, giving States themselves primary responsibility for implementing control measures within domestic law,[136] and establishes supervisory bodies to monitor progress and treaty implementation. Measures carried forward from the League include the system of import/export authorisation (Article 31), the estimates system (Article 19), licensing regulations (Article 29) and the limitation on manufacturing (Article 21). The Single Convention includes penal provisions under Article 36, obligating that 'each Party shall adopt such measures as will ensure that' a list of offences related to drug cultivation, production, manufacture, possession, distribution, purchase, sale and trafficking 'shall be punishable offences . . . and that serious offences shall be liable to adequate punishment particularly by imprisonment or other penalties of deprivation of liberty'.[137] The penal provisions contained in Article 36 represented a compromise position, and were deemed too mild by some

[133] The Single Convention was intended to replace the following agreements: International Opium Convention 23 Jan 1912 and subsequent protocols; Opium Agreement and Protocol and Final 11 Feb 1925; Convention, Protocol and Final Act 19 Feb 1925 and later protocol; Convention for Limiting the Manufacture and Regulating the Distribution of Narcotic Drugs 13 July 1931; Opium Agreement and Final Act 27 Nov 1931; Convention for the Suppression of Illicit Traffic in Dangerous Drugs 26 June 1936; Protocol to bring under international control drugs outside the scope of the 1932 convention.

[134] Single Convention on Narcotic Drugs, 1961 (30 March 1961) 520 UNTS 151 (1961 Convention).

[135] Ibid preamble. [136] Ibid art 4. [137] Ibid art 36(1)(a).

States.[138] Collins, for example, writes that the perceived weakness of provisions as compared to those in the 1936 Convention led some States Parties to this older treaty to demand that it be kept in force.[139] Bewley-Taylor argues that in its mandatory penalisation of certain behaviours based upon a prohibition of drug use, 'the Single Convention redefined the normative order of the international drug control system'.[140]

The Single Convention also introduced several new provisions that expanded and refined the scope of international drug control law. For example, it represented the first time that controls on the planting, cultivation and harvesting stages of drug production were included in international law.[141] The Convention also marked the first time that the provision of drug treatment for what it termed 'addicts' was codified in international law. Under Article 38, '[t]he Parties shall give special attention to the provision of facilities for the medical treatment, care and rehabilitation of drug addicts', and that, subject to economic resources, 'it is desirable that [States] establish adequate facilities for the effective treatment of drug addicts'.[142] The Single Convention also established a system of 'scheduling', which divided controlled substances into four different categories, each category subject to differing levels of control under Article 2. As was the case with the 1925 Convention, a process was established to enable changes to be made to the schedules based upon advances in medical and scientific knowledge about the substances in question, and recommendations from expert bodies.[143] One particularly significant development was the decision to consolidate the two League of Nations drug supervisory bodies into a single organ.[144] As a result, the Permanent Central Board and the Supervisory Body were dissolved and their respective functions amalgamated into an eleven member International Narcotics Control Board.[145]

The Single Convention was amended by a protocol in 1972.[146] The 1972 Protocol did not modify the terms of the convention in any dramatic way, although it did make a number of changes to the scope of the International Narcotics Control Board.[147] The protocol increased the membership of the Board from eleven to thirteen seats[148] and increased the term of office

[138] Boister, *Penal Aspects* (see chapter 1 n 57) 44. [139] Collins (see chapter 1 n 5) 250.
[140] Bewley-Taylor, *International Drug Control* (n 2) 5. [141] Gregg (n 5) 201.
[142] 1961 Convention (n 134) art 38. [143] Ibid art 3. [144] Ibid art 5.
[145] The functions of the Board will be explored in more detail in section 2.4.3.2 below.
[146] Protocol Amending the Single Convention on Narcotic Drugs, 1961 (25 March 1972) 976 UNTS 3 (1972 Protocol).
[147] Boister, *Penal Aspects* (see chapter 1 n 57) 48. [148] 1972 Protocol (n 146) art 2.

from three to five years,[149] on the basis that longer terms of office would contribute to its independence.[150] In addition, Article 6 of the Protocol amended Article 14 of the Single Convention to bestow the Board with enhanced monitoring and enforcement functions.[151] The Protocol also significantly amended Article 38 of the convention on the provision of drug treatment services, increasing the scope of the treaty to create an obligation to take 'all practicable measures for the prevention of abuse of drugs and for the early identification, treatment, education, after-care, rehabilitation and social reintegration of persons involved'.[152]

The second drug convention adopted under the United Nations system was the 1971 Convention on Psychotropic Substances. The purpose of the treaty was to bring under international control the increasingly diverse group of synthetically-produced, non-plant-based drugs, the use of which had become particularly prevalent in the 1960s.[153] These included synthetically produced stimulants, barbiturates, tranquilisers and hallucinogens, all of which fell outside the scope of the 1961 Convention. Like the Single Convention, the 1971 Convention sought to limit the use of psychotropic substances to medical and scientific purposes,[154] and to pursue this its thirty-three articles largely reflect the template used in the earlier treaty. Like the Single Convention before it, the 1971 Convention codified a four-tiered system of scheduling (Article 2), import and export regulations (Article 12), limitations on manufacture (Article 5), the provision of treatment and rehabilitation (Article 20) and penal sanctions (Article 22). The treaty also falls under the supervision of the International Narcotics Control Board.[155] However, unlike the Single Convention, the 1971 Convention does not employ a system of estimates. According to Cohrerrsen and Hoover, this reflected the fact that, unlike narcotic drugs, the medical use of psychotropic drugs at the time was relatively new, and therefore 'the necessary experience for making estimate projections [was] not available'.[156] However, both Jelsma and McAllister note that during treaty negotiations, Western States with powerful pharmaceutical industries played a key role in ensuring the structures for control of

[149] Ibid art 3.

[150] *Commentary on the Protocol amending the Single Convention on Narcotic Drugs, 1961* (United Nations 1976) 16, para 1.

[151] 1972 Protocol (n 146) art 6. [152] Ibid art 15.

[153] UN Office on Drugs and Crime, *A Century of International Drug Control* (n 122) 64.

[154] 1971 Convention on Psychotropic Substances (21 February 1971) 1019 UNTS 14956, art 5 (1971 Convention).

[155] Ibid arts 16, 18, 19. [156] Cohrerrsen and Hoover (n 22) 101.

psychotropic substances were weaker than that those created under the 1961 Convention for narcotics.[157] As described by Boister, the 1961 and 1971 Conventions 'do not . . . in any significant way depart from the basic assumption upon which the international drug control system by this time had come to rest, viz.: that the best way of dealing with the drug problem was prohibition'.[158]

Similar to the League of Nations evolution, once the administrative systems of commodity control had been established, States sought to create a universal approach to suppressing illicit drug trafficking by harmonising domestic criminal laws and penalties. The first attempt at this, the 1936 Convention, was largely deemed unsuccessful,[159] as few States ratified the treaty and the objective of creating a universal approach to domestic criminal law was far from achieved. However, with increased international concern about drug trafficking in the 1970s and 1980s,[160] as well as increasing political pressures being exerted by the United States,[161] there was renewed momentum among Member States to conclude a trafficking convention. The result was the adoption in December 1988 of the Convention against Illicit Traffic in Narcotic Drugs and Psychotropic Substances, which entered into force on 11 November 1990.[162] As described in Article 2(1), which defines its scope,

> The purpose of this Convention is to promote co-operation among the Parties so that they may address more effectively the various aspects of illicit traffic in narcotic drugs and psychotropic substances having an international dimension. In carrying out their obligations under the Convention, the Parties shall take necessary measures, including legislative and administrative measures, in conformity with the fundamental provisions of their respective domestic legislative systems.[163]

[157] Martin Jelsma, 'The Development of International Drug Control: Lessons Learned and Strategic Challenges for the Future': Working Paper Prepared for the First Meeting of the Global Commission on Drug Policy (24–25 January 2011) 4, McAllister (n 2) 229.
[158] Boister, 'Interrelationship' (see chapter 1 n 20) 911.
[159] Boister, *Penal Aspects*, (see chapter 1 n 57) 36.
[160] See, for example, UN General Assembly, 'International campaign against traffic in drugs' (18 December 1982) UN Doc No A/RES/37/198; UN General Assembly, 'International campaign against traffic in drugs' (16 December 1983) UN Doc No A/RES/38/122; UN General Assembly, 'International campaign against traffic in drugs' (14 December 1984) UN Doc No A/RES/ 39/143.
[161] See Chapter 3.
[162] UN Convention against the Illicit Traffic in Narcotic Drugs and Psychotropic Substances (20 December 1988) 1582 UNTS 27627 (1988 Convention).
[163] Ibid art 2(1).

The convention's thirty-four articles 'provide the structure for an extensive legal regime for the suppression of the illicit drug traffic',[164] one that creates a universal penal approach to drugs worldwide. As described by one commentator, the 1988 Convention represents an 'internationalizing of the war on drugs',[165] while another calls it 'the general extension of international drug control law into every corner of the globe'.[166] According to the Official Commentary, the convention requires that States 'establish a modern code of criminal offences relating to various aspects of illicit trafficking and to ensure that such activities are dealt with as serious offences by each State's judiciary and prosecutorial authorities'.[167] Central to this goal is Article 3,[168] which proscribes a wide range of drug offences at every stage, from cultivation, to production and manufacture, to transport and traffic, to distribution and sale, to purchase and possession, including in some circumstances possession for personal use.[169] Significantly, unlike the previous UN conventions, Article 3 obligates States to makes these acts 'criminal offences'[170] rather than the more vague and flexible terms 'distinct offence'[171] and 'punishable offence'[172] employed in the two previous treaties, and applies them to 'any narcotic drug or any psychotropic substance contrary to the provisions' of the 1961 and 1971 Conventions.[173] In effect, the 1988 Convention criminalises the entire market chain, including not only offences related to controlled substances but also to precursors and money laundering.[174] In this process, the 1988 Convention also has the effect of criminalising large groups of individuals involved in the illicit industry, from farmers and growers, to producers and manufacturers, to large scale traffickers and small scale couriers, to individual retailers and consumers.

The 1988 Convention represents the third leg of the stool of modern international drug control law, augmenting the largely commodity-based

[164] Boister, *Penal Aspects* (see chapter 1 n 57) 59.

[165] David P. Stewart, 'Internationalizing The War on Drugs: The UN Convention Against Illicit Traffic in Narcotic Drugs and Psychotropic Substances' (1989–1990) 18 Denver Journal of International Law and Policy 387, 387.

[166] Boister, 'Interrelationship' (see chapter 1 n 20) 913.

[167] *Commentary on the United Nations Convention against the Illicit Traffic in Narcotic Drugs and Psychotropic Substances 1988* (United Nations 1998) 48, para 3.1.

[168] Ibid. [169] 1988 Convention (n 162) art 3. [170] Ibid art 3(1).

[171] Single Convention on Narcotic Drugs 1961 (as amended by the 1972 Protocol) (30 March 1961) 520 UNTS 7515 (1961 Convention amended) art 36(2)(a)(i); 1971 Convention (n 154) art 22(2)(a)(i).

[172] 1961 Convention amended (n 171) art 36(1)(a); 1971 Convention (n 154) art 22(1)(a).

[173] 1988 Convention (n 162) art 3(1)(a)(i).

[174] UN Commission on Narcotic Drugs, 'Fit for Purpose' (see chapter 1 n 21) 5.

controls of the 1961 and 1971 treaties with strict penal laws and sanctions for those infringing those controls.[175] In addition to the increased focus on penal sanctions, a second significant feature of the fourth stage of drug control is the near universal ratification of the United Nations regime. Whereas the League of Nations drug control system was marked by differing combinations of States ratifying different instruments,[176] and very few States at all agreeing to ratify the 1936 Convention on penal sanctions,[177] the United Nations instruments have received broad support: the Single Convention (as amended by the 1972 Protocol) has been ratified by 184 States; the 1971 Convention has been ratified by 183 States; and the 1988 Convention has been ratified by 188 States.[178] This has the effect of creating international obligations to domestically implement a largely uniform and punitive approach to drug suppression and control.

2.4.3 *The United Nations Machinery*

During the League of Nations period, two different types of bodies were established to advance international drug control: a policy-making body comprised of Member States (the Advisory Committee on the Traffic in Opium and Other Dangerous Drugs), and two independent expert bodies with a mandate to monitor State practice and criticise Governments where necessary (the Permanent Central Board and the Supervisory Committee).[179] This basic structure was incorporated into the drug control machinery of the United Nations. The three primary United Nations organs mandated to supervise and progress international drug control are the Commission on Narcotic Drugs, the International Narcotics Control Board and the United Nations Office on Drugs and Crime. Each has an important role to play in the question of human rights in the fourth stage of drug control, as well as a part in shaping drug control's fifth stage.

2.4.3.1 The Policy-Making Body: Commission on Narcotic Drugs

The primary policy-making body with the United Nations is the Commission on Narcotic Drugs. The Commission also functions as the governing body of the United Nations Office on Drugs and Crime. At the first session

175 Bewley-Taylor, *International Drug Control* (n 2) 3.
176 Gregg (n 5) 188.
177 Only thirteen States ratified the 1936 Convention prior to 1940. United Nations Treaty Collection https://treaties.un.org last accessed 14 May 2014.
178 Ibid. 179 May (see chapter 1 n 9) 493.

of the Economic and Social Council of the United Nations in February 1946, the Council established the Commission on Narcotic Drugs as one of the 'specialized agencies' described under Article 55 of the Charter. The Commission thereby replaced the Advisory Committee on the Traffic in Opium and Other Dangerous Drugs.[180] According to the resolution establishing the Commission, in addition to carrying out the functions of the former Opium Advisory Committee, its mandate includes assisting the Council in supervising international drug control conventions and agreements, advising the Council on all matters pertaining to drug control, drafting international drug conventions and advising on any necessary changes to the UN drug control machinery.[181] As an advisory body to the Economic and Social Council, Commission decisions must be confirmed by the Council, except in those cases where the drug conventions bestow specific authority on the Commission alone.[182] When founded, the Commission was limited to fifteen members serving terms of three years, to be composed of States that were 'important producing or manufacturing countries or countries in which illicit traffic in narcotics constitutes a serious social problem'.[183] However, the membership has expanded over time, alongside the growth of the UN itself, to fifty-three members, with a specific regional distribution.[184]

The Commission has been described by the General Assembly as 'the principal United Nations policy-making body on drug abuse control'.[185] It meets annually at the United Nations headquarters in Vienna, where Members take the opportunity to publicly review their progress towards meeting domestic and international drug control goals, and debate and ratify resolutions on various related topics. In addition to its policy-making role, the Commission is also mandated with normative functions

180 UN Economic and Social Council, 'Resolution of the Economic and Social Council of 16 February 1946 on the establishment of a Commission on Narcotic Drugs' (16 February 1946) UN Doc No E/RES/1946/9(I).

181 Ibid para 2.

182 Renborg, 'International Control of Narcotics' (n 3) 88.

183 UN Economic and Social Council, 'Resolution of the Economic and Social Council of 16 February 1946 on the establishment of a Commission on Narcotic Drugs' (n 180) para 4.

184 UN Economic and Social Council, 'Enlargement of the Commission on Narcotic Drugs' (21 June 1991) UN Doc No E/RES/1991/49. The distribution of seats is eleven each for the African and Asian regions, ten for Latin American/Caribbean States, six for Eastern Europe, fourteen for Western Europe and other States, and one seat that rotates every four years. Members are elected from among those States that have ratified the 1961 Single Convention on Narcotic Drugs.

185 UN General Assembly, 'Preparation of a draft convention against illicit traffic in narcotic drugs and psychotropic substances' (8 December 1988) UN Doc No A/RES/43/120, OP 3.

under the UN drug control treaties, the most significant of these being the authority to make changes in the listing of substances under international control. This authority is exercised through a treaty provision enabling it to amend the schedules to the 1961 and 1971 Conventions, in effect empowering the Commission to modify the terms of the treaties.[186] Taking into account recommendations from the World Health Organization,[187] the Commission has the authority to include a new drug under international control by adding it to the schedules, or change the nature of the controls applied to a currently scheduled substance by raising or lowering its categorisation within the schedules. The 1971 and 1988 Conventions also bestow the same powers on the Commission regarding preparations and precursor chemicals.[188] As the substances included within the schedules of the 1961 and 1971 Conventions are also those to which domestic criminal sanctions must be applied under Article 3 of the 1988 Convention, these powers also directly affect State obligations under that treaty. As a consequence, the Commission may on its own authority list a new substance within the schedules of the 1961 or 1971 Convention, therefore requiring Parties to the 1988 treaty to criminalise it under domestic drug law, without all States Parties explicitly consenting to that treaty amendment and subsequent legislative change. These are the only powers the Commission exercises autonomously, outside of its mandate from the Economic and Social Council, and are ones the Commission exercises routinely at its annual session.[189]

The powers given to the Commission are highly unusual within international law, effectively authorising a subcommittee of States Parties to amend the terms of the treaties without requiring consent of a conference of all other Parties. Under the working practice of the Commission, only a simple majority of Members is required to amend the schedules.

[186] 1961 Convention amended (n 171) art 3; 1971 Convention (n 154) art 2.

[187] Within the UN drug control regime, the World Health Organization takes over the role formerly played by the Health Committee of the League of Nations.

[188] 1971 Convention (n 154) art 3; 1988 Convention (n 162) art 12.

[189] See, for example, UN Commission on Narcotic Drugs, 'Transfer of phenylacetic acid from Table II to Table I of the United Nations Convention against Illicit Traffic in Narcotic Drugs and Psychotropic Substances of 1988' (8 March 2010) CND dec 53/1; 'Inclusion of oripavine in Schedule I of the Single Convention on Narcotic Drugs of 1961 and that Convention as amended by the 1972 Protocol' (14 March 2007) CND dec 50/1; 'Inclusion of amineptine in Schedule II of the Convention on Psychotropic Substances of 1971' (8 April 2003) CND dec 46/1. 'Transfer of acetic anhydride from Table II to Table I of the United Nations Convention against Illicit Traffic in Narcotic Drugs and Psychotropic Substances of 1988' (20 March 2001) CND dec 44/5, among many others.

With a membership of fifty-three States, this means that a group of only twenty-seven governments can make changes to the treaties that affect all of the one hundred and eighty or more States Parties.

Consider this practice against that of the Convention on International Trade in Endangered Species of Wild Fauna and Flora, a treaty that creates similar systems of control to regulate imports and exports of protected species between and among States Parties, and a system of licensing for such trade.[190] Like the 1961 and 1971 drug conventions, which contain four schedules that list and categorise substances under international control, the Convention on International Trade in Endangered Species contains three appendices of species covered under the treaty, 'afford[ing] different levels or types of protection' to each of the three groups.[191] These controls vary from the most rigorous under Appendix I, covering species threatened with extinction, the trade in which is controlled in all countries, to the least restrictive under Appendix III, which covers species protected in at least one State, the government of which has requested the co-operation of the other Parties in curtailing international trade.[192] Unlike the autonomous powers given to the Commission on Narcotic Drugs in relations to scheduling, Appendix I and II of the Convention on International Trade in Endangered Species, which list species subject to the tightest controls, may only be amended at a Conference of State Parties, and then by a two-thirds majority of votes cast.[193] Unlike the drug conventions, States may also enter individual reservations to any of the specific species listed in all three appendices, a practice which is quite widely used among States Parties to the convention.[194] The 1961 and 1971 drug conventions do not allow States to enter reservations on individual substances listed within the treaty schedules.

The Commission on Narcotic Drugs has emerged as a key forum where significant debates of relevance to issues of human rights and drug control have taken place. These debates have exposed many fractures within the international drug control regime, and the differing approaches of States on key human rights issues such as the death penalty and the right to health. Some of these will be explored later in Chapter 4.

[190] Convention on International Trade in Endangered Species of Wild Fauna and Flora (signed 3 March 1973, amended 22 June 1979)(CITES).

[191] 'The CITES Appendices', Convention on International Trade in Endangered Species of Wild Fauna and Flora Web site https://cites.org/eng/app/index.php accessed 10 May 2013.

[192] CITES (n 190) art II(1–3). [193] Ibid art XV.

[194] See 'Reservations entered by Parties', Convention on International Trade in Endangered Species of Wild Fauna and Flora Web site www.cites.org/eng/app/reserve.php accessed 10 May 2013.

2.4.3.2 The Treaty Body: International Narcotics Control Board

The 1925 and 1931 League of Nations Conventions established separate organs to supervise State compliance with their treaty obligations, the Permanent Central Board and the Supervisory Committee. The 1961 drug convention consolidated these two bodies into a single organ, the International Narcotics Control Board (commonly referred to by its acronym, the INCB).[195] As described under Article 9(4),

> The Board, in co-operation with Governments, and subject to the terms of this Convention, shall endeavour to limit the cultivation, production, manufacture and use of drugs to an adequate amount required for medical and scientific purposes, to ensure their availability for such purposes and to prevent illicit cultivation, production and manufacture of, and illicit trafficking in and use of, drugs.[196]

The Board was first appointed in 1968.[197] As a body of independent experts, the Board fulfils a similar role to that of treaty bodies within the UN human rights system, engaging with Governments to ensure their compliance with treaty obligations and monitoring State progress in that regard.[198] Its members, expanded from eleven to thirteen under the 1972 Protocol, sit in an independent capacity, and 'shall be persons who, by their competence, impartiality and disinterestedness, will command general confidence'.[199] Members of the Board are elected by the Economic and Social Council, with ten seats filled by persons nominated by States, and three seats filled by candidates proposed by the World Health Organization.[200]

The Board's functions largely mirror those previously fulfilled by the two League of Nations organs, including responsibility for administering the systems of estimates and statistical returns used to establish national projections of quantities of controlled drugs needed for medical and scientific uses.[201] As was the case under the League of Nations, should the Board feel 'there exists evidence of a serious risk that it may become, an important centre of illicit cultivation, production or manufacture of,

[195] 1961 Convention amended (n 171) art 5. [196] Ibid art 9(4).

[197] Chatterjee (see chapter 1 n 57) 256.

[198] See generally, Damon Barrett, 'Unique in International Relations?: A Comparison of the International Narcotics Control Board and the UN Human Rights Treaty Bodies' (International Harm Reduction Association 2008).

[199] 1961 Convention amended (n 171) art 9(2). [200] Ibid art 9(1).

[201] Ibid arts 12, 13.

or traffic in or consumption of drugs',[202] it has various powers, ranging from opening communications with the Government in question to recommending to States Parties that they impose import/export embargoes on the offending country.[203] This merging of the separate roles of the two previous organs into a single body was not without potential concern. Under the previous system, the Supervisory Body was responsible for overseeing the system of estimates and determining the permitted national and international limits on drug manufacture and stockpiling, while the Permanent Central Board had the power to impose sanctions should States violate these limits. As described by one commentator, by consolidating both these mandates into a single entity, '[t]he International Narcotics Control Board would, thus, in a manner, function as both prosecutor and judge'.[204]

As was the case with the 1931 Convention, the 1961 Convention vests the treaty body with the power to set estimates, and propose sanctions, even on States that have not ratified the treaty. This provision was the source of tension in the drafting, as the 'Soviet bloc delegates pressed the view that international law is violated when nonparties are made the prospective objects of board actions to which they have never given their consent'.[205] However, a vote on the question supported the continuation of the former legal regime established under the 1931 Convention.[206]

In addition to these technical functions, the Board has what Chatterjee describes as a 'remedial and preventive' role,[207] in the sense that it is authorised to take measures where 'the Board has *objective reasons* to believe that the aims of [the 1961] Convention are being seriously endangered by reason of the failure of any *Party*, country or territory to carry out the provisions of [the] Convention'.[208] These measures are essentially communicative in nature, and include raising issues of concern with Governments directly, or, if the matter is not resolved to the Board's satisfaction, 'it may call the attention of the Parties, the [Economic and Social] Council and the Commission [on Narcotic Drugs] to the matter'.[209] Part of this communicative role is achieved via the production of its annual

[202] Ibid art 14(1)(a). [203] Ibid arts 14(1), 14(2).

[204] Renborg, 'International Control of Narcotics' (n 3) 100, see also Gregg (n 5) 198.

[205] Gregg (n 5) 199.

[206] See 'United Nations Conference for the Adoption of a Single Convention on Narcotic Drugs, Official Records Volume I' (24 January–25 March 1961) UN Doc No E/CONF.34/24, 135–141 (1961 Official Records vol. I).

[207] Chatterjee (see chapter 1 n 57) 264. [208] 1972 Protocol (n 146) art 6(1)(a).

[209] Ibid art 6(1)(d).

reports, which the treaties specify that '[t]he Parties shall permit their unrestricted distribution'.[210] As discussed by Bewley-Taylor, over time these annual public reports have become a major source of the Board's political influence, and 'are one of the key mechanisms deployed by the INCB to affect state behaviour and attempt to ensure what it perceives to be compliance to the conventions'.[211]

The Board is mandated with additional functions under both the 1971 and 1988 Conventions. Under the 1971 Convention, the Board holds similar powers as under the 1961 treaty,[212] with the exception of an estimates system, which the 1971 Convention does not create for psychotropic substances. These functions include gathering statistical information, preparing annual reports and engaging with States.[213] As with the Single Convention, the 1971 treaty also empowers the Board with the authority to take various actions against offending States, up to and including recommending import/export embargoes.[214]

The Board's mandate under the 1988 Convention is less extensive than in the previous treaties, and its technical mandate confined to some limited authority to monitor and comment on the control of precursors by States.[215] The degree to which its mandate extends beyond these explicitly technical matters is the source of some debate in the literature. Bewley-Taylor, for example, argues there is 'no mandate . . . given to the INCB to monitor implementation of the 1988 Convention',[216] while Boister concludes 'that the INCB does have general scrutiny powers in respect to the 1988 Convention in areas in which it is competent in other conventions'.[217] The latter perspective finds stronger support within the convention text itself. Article 22(1)(a) states that if 'the Board has reason to believe that the aims of this Convention in matters related to its competence are not being met',[218] it is mandated to undertake in a variety of communicative measures. This provision has the effect of providing the Board with a mandate to monitor the overall implementation of the treaty's broader provisions on suppressing illicit traffic.[219] While the scope and breadth of this mandate is open to debate and interpretation, as is the question of

[210] 1961 Convention amended (n 171) art 15; 1971 Convention (n 154) art 18; 1988 Convention (n 162) art 23.
[211] Bewley-Taylor, *International Drug Control* (n 2) 224.
[212] Boister, *Penal Aspects* (see chapter 1 n 57) 47.
[213] 1971 Convention (n 154) art 18(1).
[214] Ibid art 19.
[215] 1988 Convention (n 162) art 12.
[216] Bewley-Taylor, *International Drug Control* (n 2) 224.
[217] Boister, *Penal Aspects* (see chapter 1 n 57) 488.
[218] 1988 Convention (n 162) art 22(1)(a).
[219] Boister, *Penal Aspects* (see chapter 1 n 57) 488.

what is and is not within the Board's 'competence', the language of Article 22 clearly allows scope for the Board to comment on issues beyond purely technical matters.

Although in many ways the functioning of the Board is akin to human rights treaty bodies, their working procedures differ in significant ways, which have been the source of criticism. One of these is transparency. Whereas human rights treaty bodies engage in their monitoring functions with States Parties in an open fashion, via public hearings and publicly accessible documentation, the Board's engagement with Governments takes place behind closed doors. Unlike human rights treaty bodies, the Board does not invite and embrace the contribution of civil society within its monitoring functions. Both of these factors have resulted in ongoing criticism of the Board's secretive nature and failure to engage openly with broader civil society expertise.[220]

2.4.3.3 The Secretariat: United Nations Office on Drugs and Crime

The final pillar of the United Nations drug control machinery is the UN Office on Drugs and Crime, housed within the UN Secretariat. In 1959, the General Assembly passed a resolution establishing 'a continuing programme of technical assistance in narcotics control within the regular budget of the United Nations'.[221] This resolution initiated the development of a formal programme of activities aimed at supporting States, particularly in developing countries, to meet their international drug control obligations. This effort was expanded in 1970 with the creation of the United Nations Fund for Drug Abuse Control, a fund composed of voluntary contributions from Members States and others to support such technical assistance activities.[222] In 1990, the General Assembly requested that the Secretary-General create a single UN drug control programme, to be called the United Nations International Drug Control Programme. This new body would bring together the previously separate activities of the United Nations Fund for Drug Abuse Control, the secretariat of the International Narcotics Control Board and the functions of the Division

[220] For example, see Joanne Csete and Daniel Wolfe, 'Closed to Reason: The International Narcotics Control Board and HIV/AIDS' (Canadian HIV/AIDS Legal Network/Open Society Institute, 2007), Barrett, 'Unique in International Relations?' (n 199).

[221] UN General Assembly, 'Technical assistance in narcotics control' (20 November 1959) UN Doc No A/RES/1395(XIV), para 1.

[222] UN General Assembly, 'Technical assistance in the field of drug abuse control' (15 December 1970) UN Doc No A/RES/2719(XXV).

of Narcotic Drugs.[223] This same resolution requested the creation of a new senior UN official at the rank of Under-Secretary-General to lead the newly amalgamated Programme.[224]

Established in 1997, the Office on Drugs and Crime was created through a merger of the United Nations International Drug Control Programme[225] and the Crime Prevention and Criminal Justice Programme.[226] As part of the United Nations Secretariat, the Office was 'established to implement the Organization's drug programme and crime programme in an integrated manner',[227] and carries out various activities as directed by the Commission on Narcotic Drugs, the Economic and Social Council and the General Assembly. The Office '[s]erves as the central drug control entity with the exclusive responsibility for coordinating and providing effective leadership on all United Nations drug control activities'.[228]

As the primary technical body providing assistance to States in drug control efforts, there is often significant overlap between the work of the UN Office on Drugs and Crime and human rights issues. For example, the agency provides technical assistance to States in drafting their domestic drugs laws, to ensure those laws meet the obligations within the international treaties.[229] It also coordinates distribution of international drug control aid to recipient States, therefore facilitating the development and implementation of domestic enforcement and interdiction programmes. As has been documented by civil society organisations, in many cases these programmes are being implemented in States that impose extremely harsh penalties on convicted offenders, including capital punishment in some cases, raising concerns about the complicity of both donor Governments and the UN Office on Drugs and Crime with human rights violations.[230]

[223] UN General Assembly, 'Enhancement of the United Nations structure for drug abuse control' (21 December 1990) UN Doc No A/RES/45/179, para 3.

[224] Ibid para 4.

[225] Established by UN General Assembly, 'Enhancement of the United Nations structure for drug abuse control' (n 223).

[226] Established by UN General Assembly, 'Creation of an effective United Nations crime prevention and criminal justice programme' (18 December 1991) UN Doc No A/RES/46/152.

[227] UN Secretariat, 'Secretary-General's bulletin: Organization of the United Nations Office on Drugs and Crime' (15 March 2004) UN Doc No ST/SGB/2006/6, para 2.1.

[228] Ibid para 2.2(a).

[229] See UN Office on Drugs and Crime, 'Model Laws and Treaties' www.unodc.org/unodc/en/legal-tools/model-treaties-and-laws.html accessed 22 October 2015.

[230] See Gallahue, 'The Death Penalty for Drug Offences Global Overview 2011' (see chapter 1 n 25), Patrick Gallahue, Roxanne Saucier and Damon Barrett, 'Partners in Crime: International Funding for Drug Control and Gross Violations of Human Rights' (International Harm Reduction Association 2012).

2.5 Conclusion

This chapter has provided an overview of the historical and normative development of one hundred years of international law in the area of drug control, with a particular focus on the legal instruments and machinery of the fourth stage United Nations era. This history reveals several unusual features of international drug control law as a legal system, including the establishment of treaty obligations for non-Parties, the creation of a mechanism to amend the terms of the treaties outside of a Conference of Parties and the near universal ratification of the treaty regime as a whole. This history also illustrates the increasing use of penal sanctions as a tool of drug control, and the use of international law as a framework to harmonise a universal domestic criminal law approach in the area of drugs. It also summarised the roles and mandates of the three main drug control bodies within the UN system. All of these factors and actors influence the emergence of the negative unintended consequences of the drug control regime in the UN era, as well as considerations of the development of a fifth stage of drug control.

3

Humanitarian or Stigmatising? – The Contradictory Paradigms of International Drug Control

I extend to the Commissioners to-day assembled my good wishes and conviction that their labours will be of the greatest importance towards the general suppression of the opium evil throughout the world.[1]

President Theodore Roosevelt 1909

3.1 Introduction

Writing in 1934 of the League of Nations drug control machinery, Quincy Wright described the international treaty regime of the time as representing 'the first attempt at a world plan for any economic commodity'.[2] Ten years later, another noted commentator described 'the international opium administration' as 'one of the most advanced examples of international control and cooperation in respect of an article of commerce'.[3] However, past and current international attitudes towards drugs and drug use inevitably mean that attempts at regulation occur in a context markedly different than that of most other economic commodities. Indeed, although the controls established in international law during the second and third stages of the regime, incorporated into and expanded during the fourth stage, are in many ways dry and technical systems of licensing production, estimating need, limiting manufacture and controlling imports and exports, the rationales justifying them have been anything but dry and technical. As discussed in Chapter 2, the origins of the anti-opium movement of the late nineteenth and early twentieth century were situated in a context of popular agitation against other

[1] International Opium Commission (see chapter 2 n 23) 14.

[2] Wright, 'The Narcotics Convention of 1931' (see chapter 2 n 52) 475.

[3] Lande (see chapter 1 n 15) 394. Reborg also notes that 'The conventions . . . represent the first concerted attempt by governments to regulate a single industry throughout the world, from the point at which the raw materials enter the international trade to the point at which they finally reach the legitimate consumer.' Renborg, 'International Control of Narcotics' (see chapter 2 n 3)110.

perceived 'moral vices' such as alcohol use and 'white slavery', particularly within the United States.[4] This Western campaign against opium fit neatly alongside prohibitionist projects or histories in other parts of the world, such as Asia and Latin America.[5] It is perhaps unsurprising therefore that the subsequent historical development of international drug control has been intertwined in a complicated mixture of fear and aspiration, of threat and responsibility. It is this mix of apparently conflicting drives that form the context for the human rights abuses evident in the fourth stage of drug control. They also contribute to the challenge of forging a fifth stage of drug control that remedies or prevents these abuses.

In reviewing the past one hundred years of international drug control law, efforts to suppress drugs evolve from interplay between two related yet ultimately contradictory paradigms. The first of these is that 'addiction' to drugs is considered a form of 'evil', one that constitutes a threat not only to individuals but indeed to the fabric of society as a whole. As a result, States have a moral obligation to suppress drugs. The second paradigm is that coordinated international drug control activities, which by definition are morally demanded to fight this 'evil', represent a collective humanitarian mission by the international community, rather than simply an exercise in commodity control or law enforcement. As described by Wright, 'The international conventions to control the use of opium and narcotic drugs have been of interest to the United States . . . primarily from the standpoint of their efficiency in combating an acknowledged evil.'[6] The relationship between these two paradigms is illustrated in the comments of an Iranian delegate during the drafting of the 1961 Single Convention on Narcotic Drugs, who stated that 'drug addiction was like a contagious disease: no country could be certain that it would be spared . . . when a country like Iran at great cost prohibited the cultivation of the poppy to abolish that evil, it was in fact eliminating a source of danger to the health of the whole world and benefiting all mankind'.[7] From the perspective of the international drug control regime, these two paradigms are not only copacetic, they are in fact mutually reinforcing, flowing logically one into the other. Because drug addiction is considered an evil to the individual, and because that evil is a risk of spreading throughout societies like a disease, the shared effort to suppress this 'contagion' is not merely a

[4] Ansley (see chapter 2 n 8) 106.
[5] See Windle (see chapter 1 n 1), Campos (see chapter 2 n 13).
[6] Wright, 'The Narcotics Convention of 1931' (see chapter 2 n 52) 475.
[7] 1961 Official Records vol. I (see chapter 2 n 206) 6.

policy objective of an individual government, it is a moral and altruistic mission of the world community, one pursued for the greater good and protection of humankind.

However, when considered from the perspective of human rights, the assessment is very different, and must take into account the effects on State practice of defining various human activities (drug use, cultivation, manufacturing, trafficking, sale, purchase, etc.) and, by extension, the people who engage in these activities, as being a direct contributor to or enabler of this 'evil', and therefore an existential threat to the greater good. This is particularly relevant as the legal framework of international drug control has always been one of indirect control, based around the domestic laws and administrative practices of States, with the role of the international regime being to standardise and make universal those laws and practices enshrined in the treaties.[8] As a result, these paradigms create and perpetuate an atmosphere of human rights risk, in which the global cause of drug control is framed in a manner whereby activities to suppress drugs (whatever those may entail) are not only considered necessary, they are indeed morally justified by the righteousness of the end goal itself. While Wright's 1934 perspective of the drug control regime as 'the first attempt at a world plan for any economic commodity' is illuminating, in the current period it must be acknowledged that this plan is built upon the stigmatisation, discrimination and demonisation of certain elements of society, and in many cases of individuals who are already vulnerable to exploitation and human rights abuse. This is the challenge inherent to the development of a fifth stage of drug control.

3.2 The Humanitarian Drive for Drug Control

Although perhaps not obvious in the modern context of the 'war on drugs' – and its association with policing, incarceration and even military action – multilateral efforts to control narcotics have, from the beginning, been rhetorically framed as a humanitarian mission, rather than an exercise in law enforcement or commodity regulation. The title of Arnold Taylor's detailed history of the US diplomacy in international drug control between 1900 and 1939, 'A study in international humanitarian reform', reflects this context.[9] During the proceedings of the first International Opium Commission in 1909, the global effort to suppress opium was described as being the contemporary equivalent of the great humanitarian

[8] Gregg (see chapter 2 n 5) 192. [9] Taylor (see chapter 1 n 11).

movement of the previous century, that to abolish slavery.[10] In his closing address to the conference delegates, for example, the Commission President, Bishop Charles Brent, stated,

> Just as slavery reached a point when among its opponents it was no longer a mere question of morals or academic theory but 'an actual perplexing problem continually appearing in every direction and in various forms,' so has it come to be with the evil before us, and we have, we trust, not wholly failed in carrying the problem a stage nearer to its final solution.[11]

Speaking on behalf of the delegation of the United States, Dr Hamilton Wright described the growing international consensus in support of the suppression of opium.

> The slavery question agitated the civilised world for a century. No more emotion was expended, no greater misconception of facts occurred, no greater stubbornness of opinion was shown in the initial stage of the solution of that problem, than has been shown in the initial stages of the opium question . . . During the last few years our people have watched with admiration a repetition of history.[12]

In the International Opium Convention of 1912, drug suppression was conceptualised as a noble enterprise and measures of control as tools for promoting the greater public good. For example, the preamble specifically described 'the gradual suppression of the abuse of opium, morphine, and cocaine' and their derivatives as a 'humanitarian endeavour'.[13]

This humanitarian paradigm also influences the development of the third stage of drug control. The Covenant of the League of Nations, under Article 23(c), invested the League with 'the general supervision over the execution of agreements with regard to the traffic in . . . opium and other dangerous drugs'.[14] This clause was inserted at the request of the British delegation, and was described by David Hunter Miller, in his definitive 1928 account of the drafting history of the Covenant, as being 'in the line of extending the humanitarian activities of the League'.[15] In fact, 'Humanitarian Activities of the League' is the characterisation Miller uses to describe Article 23 and its subclauses.[16] The subsequent

[10] See, for example, the statement of the Commission President, International Opium Commission (see chapter 2 n 23) 82.
[11] Ibid 82. [12] Ibid 44. [13] 1912 Convention (see chapter 1 n 51) preamble.
[14] Covenant (see chapter 1 n 17) art 23(c).
[15] Hunter Miller, vol. 1 (see chapter 2 n 92) 220.
[16] David Hunter Miller, *The Drafting of the Covenant*, vol. 2 (GP Putnam's Sons 1928) 850.

drug convention of 1925 similarly describes international cooperation to control the trade in and use of drugs as a 'humanitarian effort'.[17]

This humanitarian framing of drug control is also evident in the foundations of the fourth stage United Nations drug control regime. As explored in Chapter 2, unlike the Covenant of the League of Nations, the Charter of the United Nations does not explicitly reference drug control within its text. The Charter in effect expands the mandate of the League under Article 23 into five related articles, 55–60, under Chapter IX on International Economic and Social Cooperation.[18] The basis for Article 55, which gives the United Nations a mandate to 'promote . . . solutions of international economic, social, and health related problems'[19] originates in the Dumbarton Oaks Proposals, which laid the foundational framework for the Charter and served as the basis for the drafting debates. Chapter IX, Section A of the Proposals, entitled 'Arrangements for International Economic and Social Cooperation', proposed that

> With a view to the creation of conditions of stability and well-being which are necessary for peaceful and friendly relations among nations, the Organization should facilitate solutions of international economic, social and other humanitarian problems and promote respect for human rights and fundamental freedoms.[20]

The structure of what evolved into the UN drug control regime can be seen in these original documents, as Chapter IX proposed the creation of 'various specialized economic, social and other organizations and agencies [that] would have responsibilities in their respective fields'.[21] These 'specialized organizations and agencies' were to be coordinated by, and were to report to, an Economic and Social Council under the authority of a General Assembly.[22] One of the first of these 'specialized agencies' to be created by the new United Nations was the Commission on Narcotic Drugs.[23] Therefore, although not specifically named within the text of the Charter, the fourth stage of international drug control clearly continues

[17] 1925 Convention (see chapter 1 n 19). preamble.

[18] The relationship between Article 23 of the Covenant and Articles 55–60 of the Charter on the question of drug control is explored in Chapter 2.

[19] Charter (see chapter 2 n 83) art 55(b).

[20] The United Nations Conference on International Organization. 'The United Nations Dumbarton Oaks Proposals for a General International Organization', Doc. 1, G/1, p. 18 in Official Records San Francisco (see chapter 2 n 81).

[21] Ibid. [22] Ibid 18–19.

[23] UN Economic and Social Council, 'Resolution of the Economic and Social Council of 16 February 1946 on the establishment of a Commission on Narcotic Drugs' (chapter 2 n 180).

to address drugs within the context of the humanitarian activities of the organisation.

The influence of this humanitarian ethos is more explicit within the work of the United Nations drug control bodies themselves. For example, during the first session of the Commission on Narcotic Drugs held in Lake Success, New York in 1946, the French delegate to the Commission made a rather grand statement to this effect.

> Confucius . . . had advocated the establishment, under the name of the 'Great Union' of a vast association of peoples who 'would extend the conception of welfare not only to include all nationals, of which each State was inclined to cherish its own, but also all individuals without distinction.' Twenty-five centuries had passed. The "Great Union" so earnestly desired by Confucius had been brought into being, not at Peking, but at Geneva and later at Lake Success and now its first care had been to fight the scourge of opium which afflicted above all the populations of the Far East. The dream of Confucius had thus become a reality.[24]

During the preliminary drafting stages of the Single Convention of Narcotic Drugs in 1950, the UN Secretary-General specifically suggested that the new treaty highlight these same principles, asking that '[i]f it is decided that the new single convention should have a preamble it might refer . . . to the social and humanitarian motivation of international co-operation in the field'.[25] This humanitarian drive to establish an effective international drug control regime was reiterated throughout the 1961 Plenipotentiary Conference that concluded the drafting of the Single Convention. For example, the representative of Lebanon stated that, 'one of the purposes of the United Nations was to achieve international co-operation in solving international problems of an economic, social, cultural or humanitarian character; the control of narcotic drugs was one of the most important of those problems'.[26] Ghana,[27] the USSR,[28] Czechoslovakia[29] and the United States[30] all made reference to the 'humanitarian purpose' of the new Convention, while India spoke of the 'great humanitarian objectives' of the treaty.[31] Bulgaria expressed its belief 'that the Convention had been drafted on the basis of humanitarian principles'[32] and

24 'Report to the Economic and Social Council on the First Session of the Commission on Narcotic Drugs held at Lake Success New York, from 27 November to 13 December 1946' (11 December 1946) UN Doc. No. E/C.S.7/55, p 14.

25 Economic and Social Council of the United Nations, 'Commentary on the Draft Single Convention: Note by the Secretary-General' (March 1950) UN Doc. No. E/CN.7/AC.3/4, p 8.

26 1961 Official Records vol. I (see chapter 2 n 206) 7. 27 Ibid 83. 28 Ibid 156.

29 Ibid 157. 30 Ibid 158. 31 Ibid 156. 32 Ibid 162.

that 'every step towards the elimination of that social evil was regarded by [the] government as having great humanitarian importance'.[33] The representative of Afghanistan noted how that country's 'interest in narcotic drugs had . . . always been humanitarian rather than commercial'.[34] The representative of the Vatican expressed that '[t]he Holy See, which had always been concerned with the welfare of mankind and of civilization, was therefore happy to lend its moral support to the humanitarian aims of the Conference'.[35] The delegate of the United Arab Republic stated that '[e]very country was under a moral obligation to make the Convention an effective instrument serving the interests of the entire world. On behalf of mankind, therefore, his delegation urged all States to give it their full and whole-hearted support'.[36] For some delegations, the humanitarian imperative driving drug control was so significant as to limit national self-interest. China, for example, encouraged other delegations to agree that, '[f]or humanitarian reasons, every State should be willing to make greater sacrifices of national sovereignty and to co-operate more closely with others in preventing the abuse of narcotics'.[37] Guatemala argued that '[p]rogress in the control of narcotic drugs would only be made if the international and humanitarian aspects of the problem were given precedence over national interests'.[38] The humanitarian paradigm evident during the drafting conference was eventually reflected in the opening lines of the preamble of the 1961 Single Convention on Narcotic Drugs.

> *The Parties,*
>
> *Concerned with the health and welfare of mankind,*
>
> *Recognizing that the medical use of narcotic drugs continues to be indispensable for the relief of pain and suffering and that adequate provision must be made to ensure the availability of narcotic drugs for such purposes*[39]

When States met again in 1971 to conclude the drafting of the Convention on Psychotropic Substances, the second of the three UN drug treaties, this humanitarian purpose was again reiterated by some. The USSR noted that its support for international narcotics control measures was based on 'humanitarian reasons',[40] while Mexico noted 'the humanitarian purposes

[33] Ibid 12. [34] Ibid. [35] Ibid 216. [36] Ibid 6.
[37] Ibid 13. [38] Ibid. [39] 1961 Convention amended (see chapter 2 n 171) preamble.
[40] 'United Nations Conference for the Adoption of a Single Convention on Narcotic Drugs, Official Records Volume II' (24 January–25 March 1961) UN Doc No E/CONF.34/24/Add. 1, 7 (1961 Official Records vol. II).

to be served by the proposed international instrument'.[41] The preamble to the Convention on Psychotropic Substances reaffirms the concern for the health and welfare of mankind expressed in the Single Convention, while also '[n]oting with concern the public health and social problems resulting from the abuse of certain psychotropic substances'.[42]

3.3 The Concept of 'Evil' in International Drug Control Law

This notion of the international control of drugs as an historic humanitarian mission, rather than a technical exercise in commodity control, was made possible only by the second paradigm driving the development of the regime: that drugs constitute a form of 'evil', and that the activities related to their use, cultivation, manufacture and trade constitute a tangible threat to health, morality and stability of society. As stated by Bishop Charles Brent, President of the 1909 International Opium Commission, '[b]ehind the raw statistics and cold sentences of our deliberative language and of most of our resolutions stand the pitiable army of moral slaves, in whose behalf we have been labouring in order that they may gain the greatest of all gifts – moral freedom'.[43] In this context, international efforts to suppress drugs become part humanitarian mission, part protective intervention and part moral crusade, all underpinned by an international legal framework. Absent this context, drug control looks a rather uninspiring and technical system of licensing, manufacturing/import/export controls and law enforcement measures: one lacking the necessary urgency to merit the construction of a huge international suppression regime. In this regard, the concept of a common humanitarian mission, shared by all countries of the world for the betterment and protection of the world community, had a functional outcome. The sense of shared purpose was critical to expanding support for the regime, particularly in the early stages of the international system when States, many of which did not themselves have any domestic interest or concern in drug issues, were being asked to voluntarily enter a new treaty framework and submit their domestic systems to international control. As described by one League of Nations official, as 'the drug smuggler has no respect for national frontiers . . . only concerted international action could bring any hope of eradicating drug smuggling or

[41] Ibid 10. [42] 1971 Convention (see chapter 2 n 154) preamble.
[43] International Opium Commission (see chapter 2 n 23) 82.

reducing it to a minimum and thereby gradually eliminating drug addiction as a social evil'.[44] In 1950, the United Nations Bulletin of Narcotics described

> the close interdependence of nations and the need of their association for the accomplishment of an object of importance to each one of them separately, and therefore to all of them as a group. It is because no one country could protect itself against the evils of addiction that they found it necessary to associate themselves in limiting the spread of a habit which all regarded as an evil. There was thus the strong motive of a national interest which moved the governments and which has held them together in the fight against one of the great curses of the human race.[45]

A particularly insightful perspective in this regard is offered by May, who observed in 1951 that 'the national interest of the various countries in the maintenance of international control of narcotic drugs is not equally strong'.[46] As a result, the sense of shared common purpose was critical to the maintenance of the regime.

> There is a definite danger that if an organization separate from the United Nations were charged with such control a considerable number of countries might fail to join it. The cooperation of states which believe that they have a comparatively minor interest in narcotic drugs, can, however, be secured within the framework of the United Nations if this Organization is charged with the campaign against the drug evil. It is, therefore, vital that international control of narcotic drugs be entrusted not to a separate organization but to a general international organization such as the United Nations, representing mankind as a whole.[47]

Taylor describes the main principle behind US engagement in international drug control efforts during the early twentieth century as being based on the position that 'the use of opium and other narcotic substances for other than strictly medical and scientific purposes [w]as a moral and social evil'.[48]

In a review of anti-narcotic campaigns in the United States between 1920 and 1940, Susan Speaker finds that the characterisation of drugs as an 'evil', a 'menace' or a threat was standard fare within the propaganda of the US anti-drugs movement of the period. According to Speaker, 'After about 1918 . . . these negative images expanded enormously: drug use was increasing characterized . . . as a monstrous, immensely powerful,

[44] Renborg, 'Principles of International Control of Narcotics' (see chapter 2 n 39) 436.

[45] United Nations 'Bulletin of Narcotics' (July 1950) vol. H, no 3, 4. Cited in May (see chapter 1 n 5) 535.

[46] May (see chapter 1 n 9) 494. [47] Ibid 494–495. [48] Taylor (see chapter 1 n 11) 330.

civilization-threatening evil, perhaps the worst menace in all history'.[49] She continues,

> During the 1920s and 1930s, newspaper and magazine accounts of the 'narcotics problem'... consistently used the same stock images and ideas to construct an intensely fearful rhetoric about drugs. Authors routinely described drugs, users, and sellers as 'evil' and often implied that there was a sinister conspiracy at work to undermine American society and values through drug addiction... According to most of these accounts, addiction was spreading rapidly and would soon engulf the country... Such was the danger to civilization that there could be no compromise measures: drug use and drug trafficking would have to be completely eradicated, no matter what it cost or how long it took.[50]

While the use of such 'apocalyptic' language, to use Speaker's assessment,[51] is perhaps understandable and expected within the realm of social or political agitation, it becomes of more serious concern when that same language moves outside of popular media and anti-drugs campaigning literature, and becomes reflected in broader discourse. However, this is precisely the case with drugs, and the use of this type of language was common in the professional legal and medical literature of the time. A 1909 article in the American Journal of International Law, for example, described the 'widespread evil' of opium smoking,[52] and a 1911 editorial in that same journal welcoming the second International Opium Conference stated:

> It may be said that there is no such thing as an evil wholly national in its incidence. Where an evil appears amongst one people, it is generally the reflex or concomitant of a similar evil amongst other peoples. This being so, few evils can be eradicated by national action alone. National action may be incentive, but finally there must be international action. The suppression of the opium and allied evils has on these principles been raised from the plane of sporadic national effort to the higher and more certain ground of international cooperation. The honor roll of international action for the settlement of the opium and allied problems is as follows: America, Austria-Hungary, China, France, Germany, Great Britain, Italy, Japan, Netherlands, Persia, Portugal, Russia and Siam.[53]
>
> (n.b. the thirteen countries at the first International Opium Convention in 1909)

[49] Susan L Speaker, '"The Struggle of Mankind against its Deadliest Foe": Themes of Counter-Subversion in Anti-Narcotics Campaigns, 1920–1940' (2001) 34/3 Journal of Social History 591, 592.

[50] Ibid 591. [51] Ibid.

[52] Wright, 'The International Opium Commission' (see chapter 1 n 13) 670.

[53] 'The International Opium Conference' (see chapter 2 n 26) 472.

The medical literature of the era was also rife with similar characterisations. The British Medical Journal, for example, published many articles describing drugs, drug use or drug trafficking as 'evil' in the 1920s and 1930s.[54] However, such characterisations of drug use are not mere historical curiosities. For example, a 2015 opinion piece by the Director of the US National Institute on Drug Abuse stated that 'because of drug use, a person's brain is no longer able to produce something needed for our functioning and that healthy people take for granted, *free will*',[55] in effect mirroring Bishop Brent's 1909 call to delegates at the first Opium Commission to restore the 'moral freedom' of those 'slaves' to drug use.

Apocalyptic language and provocative analogies about drugs are also evident in the work of some modern legal scholars. Professor Yehuda Z. Blum, for example, in his comparative analysis of extradition for terrorism and drug trafficking, includes drug offences among those categories of crimes that 'represent an attempt . . . to subvert the existing social order'. These crimes 'are aimed at the fundamental human rights of life and liberty of a person, as well as his physical integrity. As such, they must be viewed as violating not only the domestic laws of the target State but also as being directed against mankind in general'.[56] Blum therefore argues that drug crimes constitute *delicta juris gentium*, those grave crimes that shock the conscience of nations, often applied in the context of crimes against humanity and genocide.[57] In a similar vein, Cherif Bassiouni has proposed, in discussing codification of international offences, that 'drug offences' should be included in the same category of 'seriousness' as slavery and slave-related practices, torture, unlawful human experimentation, aircraft hijacking, taking of civilian hostages and theft of nuclear weapons.[58]

[54] See, for example, 'The Traffic in Narcotic Drugs' (1923) 2/3283 British Medical Journal 1053, 'The Opium Evil' (1924) 2/3328 British Medical Journal 678, 'Control Of Dangerous Drugs' (1930) 2/3639 British Medical Journal 572, 'The Traffic in Narcotic Drugs' (1933) 2/3795 British Medical Journal 618.

[55] Nora Volkow, 'Addiction is a Disease of Free Will', *The Huffington Post* (12 June 2015).

[56] Yehuda Z. Blum, 'Extradition: A Common Approach to the Control of International Terrorism and Traffic in Narcotic Drugs' (1978) 13 Israeli Law Review 194, 197.

[57] For example, in the judgement in *Israel v Adolf Eichmann*, the Court found 'The abhorrent crimes defined in this Law are crimes not under Israeli law alone. These crimes which offended the whole of mankind and shocked the conscience of nations are grave offences against the law of nations itself ("delicta juris gentium").' *Attorney-General of the Government of Israel v Adolf Eichmann* (District Court, Jerusalem) [11 December 1961] Criminal Case No 40/61, para 12.

[58] M. Cherif Bassiouni, 'A Comprehensive Strategic Approach on International Cooperation for the Prevention, Control and Suppression on International and Transnational

The language of drugs as 'evil' can be found in the discourse of States in the early stages of fashioning domestic approaches to drug control. Windle's historiography of drug prohibition in Asia illustrates the roots of the concept of drugs as 'evil' within many countries in the region, and its links to ruling elites.

> [T]he religious leaders of many Buddhist societies had viewed all intoxicants, including opium, as an obstacle to concentration. That is, opium was viewed as an impediment to the primary goal of the monkhood. Buddhist kings and elites followed their religious leaders' prohibitions. In other words, Buddhist elites throughout Asia had prohibited opium before the West had started routinely trading the drug.[59]

Entering the twentieth century, an Imperial Decree of the Chinese Government published in the *Peking Gazette* on 6 September 1906 stated

> The opium smoker wastes time and neglects work, ruins his health, and impoverishes his family, and the poverty and weakness which for the past few decades have been daily increasing amongst us are undoubtedly attributable to this cause. To speak of this arouses our indignation, and, at a moment when we are striving to strengthen the Empire, it behooves us to admonish the people, that all may realize the necessity of freeing themselves from these coils, and thus pass from sickness into health.
>
> It is hereby commanded that within a period of ten years the evils arising from foreign and native opium be equally and completely eradicated.[60]

In China, the language of evil moved quickly from the realm of political statement to that of domestic law when Article 1 of the eleven measures published in November of that same year to implement this edict described its objective as being, '[t]o restrict the cultivation of the poppy in order to remove the root of the evil'.[61] A Second Imperial Decree issued in February 1907 similarly noted that 'it is even more necessary to forbid the cultivation of the poppy, in order to sweep away the source of evil'.[62] In September 1908, the King of Siam declared it to be 'unquestionable that opium had an evil effect upon its consumers and casts degradation upon

Criminality, including the Establishment of an International Criminal Court' (1991) 15 Nova Law Review 353, 362–363. Bassiouni categorises these and a number of other offences as International Delicts, or 'those offenses which offend basic human values, but which do not affect the peace and security of humankind, and which are not the product of state action or state policy'.

59 Windle (see chapter 1 n 1) 5.

60 Cited in Hamilton Wright, 'The International Opium Commission' (1909) 2/4 American Journal of International Law 828.

61 Ibid. 62 Ibid 836.

every country where the inhabitants are largely addicted to the habit of opium smoking. There is no reason to doubt that the most earnest desire of nearly every country in the world is to suppress this noxious habit'.[63]

This language is omnipresent in the work of international drug control organs, and within the drafting of international instruments, dating back to the first International Opium Commission when a telegram from US President Theodore Roosevelt extended to delegates 'my good wishes and conviction that their labours will be of the greatest importance towards the general suppression of the opium evil throughout the world'.[64] Throughout the official record of the Commission's work, the characterisation of opium as an 'evil' features regularly among the statements of various delegations,[65] although this language is not ultimately reflected in the resolutions that emerged from the meeting. The codification of this language in law would not occur until drug control's fourth stage.

3.4 The Legacy of Language on Law: 'Evil' and the Fourth Stage of Drug Control

It would be tempting to dismiss such use of language as a relic of a previous time, and not relevant to the modern era where medical knowledge of drugs and drug use is advanced, and international law on this subject exists on a contemporary footing. However, to do so would ignore the legacy of such language in the historical development of international drug control law, its currency in the modern legal regime and its continuing influence on the human rights violations occurring in this fourth stage. Indeed, one of the main justifications for punitive, prohibitionist policies towards drugs – including strict enforcement measures and severe punishments – has been on the 'moral' grounds[66] that drug use is intrinsically wrong, evidence of moral inadequacy and should therefore be harshly penalised.[67] From this context emerges the discourse that is now common to the drugs debate around the world, where pronouncements are made about the 'social evil caused by drug trafficking'[68] and the 'global menace' of

[63] Ibid 851. [64] International Opium Commission (see chapter 2 n 23) 14.

[65] Ibid. See, for example, statements of delegates of Great Britain (p 27), China (p 32), France (see chapter 1 n 37) and United States (see chapter 1 n 42).

[66] M. T. Aoyagi, 'Beyond Punitive Prohibition: Liberalizing the Dialogue on International Drug Policy' (2005) 37 NYU Journal of International Law and Policy 555, 585.

[67] Ibid 561, Gilmore (see chapter 1 n 44) 384.

[68] *Ong Ah Chuan v Public Prosecutor* [1981] AC 648 (PC), para 64.

the drug trade.[69] Persons involved in the drug trade are 'merchants of death',[70] 'engineers of evil'[71] or 'peddlers of death'.[72] In a major address on drugs in June 2014, Pope Francis stated that '[d]rug addiction is an evil, and with evil there can be no yielding or compromise'.[73]

As is evident from the Pope's comments, the end of the League of Nations did not mean an end to the morality-based paradigm of drug control, and the language of drugs as 'evil' common to the second and third stages of drug control also carries over into the fourth. Such language is evident in the very first session of the UN Commission on Narcotic Drugs in 1946, which was presented with a resolution of the US Congress speaking of 'freeing the world of an age-old evil', noting that 'the only effective way to suppress the demoralizing use of opium and its derivatives (heroin, morphine, and so forth) was to control the source of the evil by limiting cultivation of the poppy plant'.[74] Speaking at Commission's second session, the Chairman noted that 'addicts derived real pleasure from inducing others to follow the same vice; in this way they increased the number of their potential sources of supply. A criminal addict was no more useful to the community than a case of smallpox'.[75] The third session of the Commission in 1948 went so far as to agree a resolution to the Economic and Social Council stating 'that narcotic drugs constituted, and may constitute in the future, a powerful instrument of the most hideous crime against mankind' and urging the Council to 'ensure that the use of narcotics as an instrument of committing a crime of this nature be covered by the proposed Convention on the prevention and

[69] A. H. Geraghty, 'Universal Jurisdiction and Drug Trafficking: A Tool for Fighting one of the World's Most Pervasive Problems' (2004) 16 Florida Journal of International Law 371, 374.

[70] M. Hor, 'Singapore's Innovations to Due Process' (International Society for the Reform of Criminal Law Conference on Human Rights and the Administration of Justice, Johannesburg, December 2000) www.isrcl.org/Papers/Hor.pdf accessed 13 May 2014, 9.

[71] Malaysia Chief Justice Azlan Shah. Cited in S. L. Harrington, 'Death, Drugs and Development: Malaysia's Mandatory Death Penalty for Traffickers and the International War on Drugs' (1991) 29 Columbia Journal of Transnational Law 365, 380.

[72] Ibid.

[73] James Mackenzie, 'Pope Francis warns on "evil" of drugs, opposes legalization' *Reuters* (20 June 2014).

[74] UN Commission on Narcotic Drugs, 'Limitation of the Production of Raw Materials (Opium and Coca Leaf) used in the manufacture of narcotic drugs: Documents Transmitted by the Government of the United States of America' (26 November 1946) UN Doc No E/C.S.7/8, 6.

[75] UN Commission on Narcotic Drugs, 'Summary Records of the Second Session' (7 January 1948) UN Doc No E/CN.7/106, 124.

punishment of genocide'.[76] This attempt by a UN drug control body to have drug offences codified alongside the most heinous of international crimes was seen again half a century later in 1996, when the International Narcotics Control Board urged the inclusion of drug trafficking within the remit of the International Criminal Court.[77] The language of 'evil' remains a common feature of drug policy political discourse within the Commission on Narcotic Drugs in the twenty-first century.[78]

While the characterisation of drugs as 'evil' has been omnipresent throughout the era of international drug control at a rhetorical level, the fourth stage of drug control is unique and significant for the fact that it is within the United Nations period that the language of evil moves from the realm of political discourse or newspaper editorial to codification within the core international legal instrument. The preamble of the 1961 Single Convention on Narcotic Drugs reads,

> *Recognizing that addiction to narcotic drugs constitutes a serious evil for the individual and is fraught with social and economic danger to mankind,*
>
> *Conscious of their duty to prevent and combat this evil,*
>
> *Considering that effective measures against abuse of narcotic drugs require co-ordinated and universal action* [. . . ?][79]

In the context of international treaty law, this wording is notable for a number of reasons, all of which have the effect of undermining, if not outright conflicting with, the humanitarian aspirations of the regime. Whatever the intended appeal to a greater humanitarian mission expressed in the Single Convention's opening line, 'Concerned with the health and welfare of mankind', such sentiments are compromised, if not negated, by those describing 'addiction to narcotic drugs' as a form of 'evil'. It is interesting to consider in this context the Spanish and French translations of the Single Convention, in which the opening preambular statement

[76] UN Commission on Narcotic Drugs, 'Summary Records of the Third Session Lake Success New York, 3–22 May 1948' (16 February 1949) UN Doc No E/CN.7/155, 161.

[77] International Narcotics Control Board, 'Report of the International Narcotics Control Board for 1996' (1997) UN Doc E/INCB/1996/1, para 14.

[78] See, for example, Antonio Maria Costa, 'Speech by Antonio Maria Costa, Executive Director of UNODC, to the 50th Session of the Commission on Narcotic Drugs, Vienna' (12 March 2007), Zhanat Suleimenov, 'Statement by Mr. Zhanat Suleimenov, Chairman of the Anti-Drugs Control Committee of the Ministry of Internal Affairs of Kazakhstan, at the high-level segment of the Fifty-Second Session of the UN Commission on Narcotic Drugs' (11 March 2009), 2.

[79] 1961 Convention amended (see chapter 2 n 171) preamble.

refers not to promoting the health and welfare of mankind, but instead promoting the 'physical and moral health of mankind'.[80]

As the international drug control regime necessarily regulates human activities – whether those be drug production, manufacturing, cultivation, trafficking, selling/purchase or use – the Single Convention labels, by extension, those who engage in these activities as being, if not evil themselves, then at least purveyors of evil deeds or collaborators in the threat drugs pose to the established order. It is useful here to consider Conor Gearty's thoughts on the use of similar language in the context of the 'war on terror', where human rights violations also occur in the name of, and are often justified by, the drive to suppress an existential 'evil' or 'threat'. In assessing the negative impact of anti-terrorism rhetoric on public and political discourse, Gearty notes,

> There are many things worryingly wrong about this perspective when viewed through a human rights lens. First, it reintroduces into international affairs the language of evil, when one of the primary achievements of the international legal order has been to remove such tendentious and highly inflammatory absolutist talk from the conduct of nation states.[81]

However, in the context of drug control, the international legal order, rather than 'remov[ing] such tendentious and highly inflammatory absolutist talk', actually enshrines it within the core international instrument. The use of such language, as Gearty notes, is highly unusual, and the unique nature of its use is particularly glaring when considered alongside other treaties addressing matters that the international community considers abhorrent. For example, neither slavery,[82] apartheid[83] nor torture[84] are described as being 'evil' in the relevant international conventions that prohibit them. Nuclear war is not described as being 'evil' in the treaty that seeks to limit the proliferation of atomic weapons, despite the recognition in the preamble that 'devastation that would be visited upon all

80 The Spanish version states 'Preoccupadas for la salud fisica y moral de la humanidad' while the French version states 'Soucieuses de santé physique et morale de l'humanité'; 1961 Convention amended (see chapter 2 n 171) preamble.

81 Conor A. Gearty, 'Terrorism and Human Rights' (2005) European Human Rights Law Review 1, 3.

82 Convention to Suppress the Slave Trade and Slavery (signed 25 September 1926, entered into force 9 March 1927) 60 LNTS 253, registered no 141.

83 UN General Assembly, 'International Convention on the Suppression and Punishment of the Crime of Apartheid' (30 November 1973) UN Doc No A/RES/3068(XXVIII).

84 Convention Against Torture and Other Cruel, Inhuman or Degrading Treatment or Punishment (adopted 10 December 1984, entered into force 26 June 1987) 1465 UNTS 85.

mankind' by such a conflict.[85] Perhaps the closest one finds to the language contained in the preamble to the Single Convention to describe drugs is that found in international instruments in the context of genocide. For example, in describing the crimes committed during the Second World War, the Universal Declaration of Human Rights uses the term 'barbarous acts',[86] while the Genocide Convention uses the term 'odious scourge'.[87] Although genocide itself is still not described as 'evil' within the treaty.

The framing of drugs in this manner is not without broader legal impacts and can be found in the reasoning of domestic constitutional courts, and even international human rights mechanisms, the bodies charged with upholding and defending the rights of individuals against the State. For example, drugs have been characterised as a 'social evil' by the Supreme Court of Singapore.[88] Persons involved in the drug trade have been described as 'engineers of evil' by the former Chief Justice of the Malaysian Supreme Court.[89] The House of Lords in Great Britain has characterised drug trafficking as a 'notorious social evil'[90] and the Irish High Court has described 'the growing evil associated with drug dealing'.[91] In a dissent to a 1986 judgement in the Argentina Supreme Court, a group of dissenting Justices stated that 'the current spread of drug use is a plague'.[92] In a 2006 speech, the then Chief Justice of the Supreme Court of India stated

> Drug abuse is a social evil . . . Just as any virus, use of drugs and drug trafficking knows no bonds or limitations. It spreads all over a country; from nation to nation; to the entire globe infecting every civilized society irrespective of caste, creed, culture and the geographical location.[93]

85 Treaty on the Non-Proliferation of Nuclear Weapons (adopted 12 June 1968, entered into force 5 March 1970) 729 UNTS 161.
86 UN General Assembly, 'Universal Declaration of Human Rights' (10 December 1948) UN Doc No A/RES/217 A (III).
87 UN General Assembly, 'Convention on the Prevention and Punishment of the Crime of Genocide' (9 December 1948) UN Doc No A/RES/260, preamble.
88 *Ong Ah Chuan* (n 68) para 64. 89 Harring (n 71) 380.
90 *R v Lambert (Steven)* [2001] UKHL 37; [2001] 3 WLR 206; [2001] 3 All ER 577, HL para 156.
91 *Director of Public Prosecutions v Farrell* [2009] IEHC 368 (HC), para 16.
92 Original Spanish reads 'la actual difusión del consumo de drogas es una verdadera plaga'. Fallo 'Bazterrica, Gustavo Mario' (29 August 1986) LL 1986-D-582, dissenting opinion, para 15.
93 Y. K. Sabharwal, 'Keynote Address' (National Seminar and Training Programme on Narcotic Drugs and Psychotropic Substances', 25 March 2006, New Delhi) www.supremecourtofindia.nic.in/speeches/speeches_2006/ndps.pdf accessed 14 June 2014, 1.

Even the European Court of Human Rights has referred to 'the scourge of drug trafficking'.[94]

The presence of such 'tendentious and highly inflammatory absolutist talk', to use Gearty's phrase, within discourse of both UN drug control bodies as well as domestic courts is not only worrying, but contributes to an environment in which human rights violations in the name of drug control flourish. It can be argued that this rhetoric of 'evil' goes so far as to provide ideological justification for, and defence of, such abuses. As noted by Room, it is this language of drugs as 'evil' that 'serves as a justification of the . . . Convention regime of control and coercion'.[95]

In addition to enshrining drugs as evil within its core international instrument, a second element observed in the fourth stage of drug control, one again with an impact on the human rights environment, is the evolution of the notion of drugs as 'evil' to drugs as 'threat'. As discussed earlier, the concept of drug use as a threat to the individual and the fabric of society has always been a component of what one might call the 'morality-based' paradigm of the regime. As noted by Speaker, at the birth of the League of Nations era 'negative images expanded enormously: drug use was increasingly characterized as not just a serious medical or social problem, but as a monstrous, immensely powerful, civilization-threatening evil, perhaps the worst menace in all history'.[96] During the drafting of the 1961 Single Convention, Harry J. Anslinger, chairman of the US delegation, notably stated that '[n]arcotic drugs have taken more lives than hydrogen bombs ever would', a statement to which one observer noted '[n]one of the other 72 delegations in the meeting voiced any exception'.[97] However, from the early 1970s onwards, it is possible to observe a tangible shift in the emphasis of the language UN system, with a decreasing emphasis on drugs as a moral or subversive 'evil', which dominated the discourse in the second and third stages of drug control, to an emphasis on drugs as a real and present danger to the State and the international community as a whole, one that if not suppressed vigorously threatens the future of humankind.

The political context for this shift was the US-driven 'war on drugs', initiated by President Richard Nixon in 1969.[98] The United States has

[94] *Phillips v United Kingdom* App no 41087/98 (ECHR, 5 July 2001), para 52.

[95] Robin Room, 'Addiction Concepts and International Control' (2006) 20 The Social History of Alcohol and Drugs 282.

[96] Speaker (n 49) 592. [97] Bevans (see chapter 2 n 6) 41.

[98] Boister, *Penal Aspects* (see chapter 1 n 57) 49. Campos argues that, in practice, 'Nixon merely intensified an anti-drug crusade that formally began in the United States (and Mexico) in the early twentieth century.' Campos (see chapter 2 n 13) 4.

always been a leading force driving international drug control, dating back to the beginnings of the regime, when the Opium Commissions of 1909 and 1912 were convened at the urging of the United States.[99] However, under the new 'war on drugs' approach, the United States, 'sceptical about the international community's willingness and ability to implement strict drug prohibition',[100] took an increasingly active unilateral role in pressing a supply reduction and law enforcement-centred approach to drug control, through actions including financial support and training to foreign States and the concluding of thirty bilateral treaties on drug control.[101] As described by Boister, this US-led agenda influenced the UN to follow a similar approach, if for no other reason than the desire of many States to try and rein in the unilateral actions of the United States.[102] As a result, '[t]he UN was the agent for the transformation of this new approach into general international consciousness'.[103] Windle concurs, stating that 'the United States saw global prohibition as in its best interest and possessed the influence to affect changes in foreign nations, international organisations, and international law'.[104]

This transformation is apparent when reviewing the proceedings of the UN General Assembly. Prior to 1970, language typically adopted in General Assembly resolutions on drug control tended to be of a more technical and less rhetorical nature. However, beginning around 1970 there is a noticeable shift. For example, General Assembly resolutions passed in 1970 state that 'on the whole addicts in all countries constitute a danger to society at large'[105] and note 'with grave concern the spread of drug abuse in many parts of the world and its disastrous impact on individuals and nations';[106] in 1971 'that the abuse of dependence-producing drugs represents an especially serious threat to the youth of the world';[107] in 1972 that drugs represent a 'threat to human dignity and society';[108] in 1974 that 'the abuse and illicit traffic in narcotic drugs have transcended national boundaries and affect the well-being and health of mankind as a

99 May (see chapter 1 n 9) 491. 100 Boister, *Penal Aspects* (see chapter 1 n 57) 49.
101 Ibid 48–52. 102 Ibid 50. 103 Ibid. 104 Windle (see chapter 1 n 1) 3.
105 UN General Assembly, 'Technical assistance in the field of narcotic drugs' (15 December 1970) UN Doc No A/RES/2720(XXV).
106 UN General Assembly, 'Technical assistance in the field of drug abuse control' (see chapter 2 n 217).
107 UN General Assembly, 'Youth and dependence-producing drugs' (20 December 1971) UN Doc No A/RES/2859(XXVI).
108 UN General Assembly, 'International instruments relating to drug abuse control' (18 December 1972) UN Doc No A/RES/3013(XXVII).

whole... [and] that the misuse of narcotic and psychotropic substances presents an actual as well as a potential danger to the health and future of mankind';[109] and in 1975 'the growing threat caused by the spread of drug abuse in certain parts of the world'[110] and 'the continuing serious menace of drug abuse'.[111] Although such language would seem commonplace today, viewed in the historical context of the General Assembly's statements on drugs, these early 1970s resolutions demonstrate a subtle shift in the paradigm, one which would become more extreme over the following decade.

UN General Assembly Resolution 32/124, adopted in 1977, was the first detailed example of the lengths to which the shift to a threat-based paradigm had progressed, and an indication of where it would develop in the future. Rather than individual references to danger, as was evidenced in the resolutions noted above, Resolution 32/124 describes a worldview in which drugs are a central menace threatening all aspects of society.

> *Recognizing* the growing threat caused by the spread of drug abuse in many parts of the world, the impact of this situation on social and economic development, agriculture and many other areas, and the resultant increase in crime and corruption,
>
> *Aware* that drug abuse has serious adverse effects on the quality of life of individuals and upon the societies in which they live,
>
> *Concerned* by the fact that drug trafficking exploits every individual with which it comes into contact,
>
> *Realizing* that the concerted effort of States is required in dealing with this problem, and that the international effort in this respect should be strengthened,
>
> ...
>
> *Recognizing* the urgent need to make individuals and Governments more aware of the dangers of drug abuse and the need for increased attention in the field of prevention, treatment and rehabilitation.[112]

109 UN General Assembly, 'Abuse of and illicit traffic in narcotic drugs' (10 December 1974) UN Doc No A/RES/3279(XXIX).

110 UN General Assembly, 'Adequate priority for narcotics control' (9 December 1975) UN Doc No A/RES/3445(XXX).

111 UN General Assembly, 'United Nations Fund for Drug Abuse Control' (9 December 1975) UN Doc No Res 3446(XXX).

112 UN General Assembly, 'International co-operation in the field of narcotic drugs relating to treatment and rehabilitation' (16 December 1977) UN Doc No A/RES/32/124.

To examine the content of this resolution in its constituent parts, the first two sentences paint drugs as a threat to social and economic development, agriculture and the environment, community safety and good governance, the life and health of individuals and the fabric of society. Sentence three characterises this threat as being contagious, affecting 'every individual with which it comes into contact'. Importantly for the threat-based paradigm, sentence four indicates the need for 'strengthened' international efforts, while sentence five highlights 'the urgent need to make individuals and Governments more aware of the dangers of drug abuse'. Taken together, these sentences suggest an international response that is insufficiently robust, and an international community that is largely ignorant of, and therefore vulnerable from, the menace confronting it. In essence, the resolution describes a threat that is growing and spreading, one that threatens essentially every aspect of life and society, to which the international response is insufficient, and States not properly aware of the danger facing them. In 1998, this threat-based paradigm would find ultimate expression in the opening preamble of the UN Political Declaration on the world drug problem.

> Drugs destroy lives and communities, undermine sustainable human development and generate crime. Drugs affect all sectors of society in all countries; in particular, drug abuse affects the freedom and development of young people, the world's most valuable asset. Drugs are a grave threat to the health and well-being of all mankind, the independence of States, democracy, the stability of nations, the structure of all societies, and the dignity and hope of millions of people and their families.[113]

In 2012, the annual General Assembly resolution on 'International cooperation against the world drug problem' stated that 'the world drug problem continues to constitute a serious threat to public health and safety and the well-being of humanity . . . and to the national security and sovereignty of States'.[114] In the contemporary context, the only area of international concern in which language approximates this is found in the context of the 'war on terror'. Consider, for example, the language of the 1998 Political Declaration with that found in UN Security Council Resolution 1377 in 2001, which '[u]nderlines that acts of terrorism endanger innocent lives and the dignity and security of human beings

[113] UN General Assembly, 'Political Declaration' (21 October 1998) UN Doc No A/RES/S-20/2, 1.

[114] UN General Assembly, 'International cooperation against the world drug problem' (3 April 2012) UN Doc No A/RES/66/183, preamble.

everywhere, threaten the social and economic development of all States and undermine global stability and prosperity',[115] or that of the Council of Europe in 2002, that 'terrorism seriously jeopardises human rights, threatens democracy, and aims notably to destabilise legitimately constituted governments and to undermine pluralistic civil society'.[116] Given this parallel, Gearty's work on terrorism and human rights again provides useful insights when considering the impact of such a threat-based approach to public policy-making.

> [T]his approach asserts that the danger facing our democracies and our culture of human rights is so great, so evil that we are entitled, indeed morally obliged, to fight back, and that in defending ourselves in this way it may well be that we ourselves have to commit evil acts, to commit harms that run counter to our fundamental principles, but that these actions are nevertheless justified, both as necessary (to save ourselves) and as less evil than what our opponents do.[117]

Although writing in the context of terrorism, Gearty's analysis slips easily into a discussion of international drug control, where the 'evil threat' posed by drugs is similarly a driving rationale for the international response, and the use of extreme measures in waging that response.

3.5 Conclusion

When considering a framework for the development of a fifth stage of drug control, unpacking the implications of this evolution is critical, as the reality, or perhaps the unintended consequence, of the UN era is that the two historical paradigms driving drug control have gone from being mutually reinforcing to being in open conflict. At the heart of this conflict is human rights. As Boister writes, 'most commentators ignore the fact that the drug conventions fail to adequately protect the human rights of those individuals subject to the system, whether they are offenders, alleged offenders or innocent third parties'.[118] However, as this chapter has illustrated, the drug control regime not only fails to fulfil a protective human rights function, it contributes to a political and legal environment that heightens human rights risk.

Although the similarities explored above between the discourse on drug control and that on terrorism are illuminating, there is at least one clear

[115] UN Security Council Res 1377 (12 November 2001) UN Doc No S/RES/1377.

[116] COE, *Guidelines on human rights and the fight against terrorism* (adopted by the Committee of Ministers 11 July 2002) preamble, para a.

[117] Gearty (see chapter n 81) 1.

[118] Boister, *Penal Aspects* (see chapter 1 n 57) 524.

point of difference in the approach that is relevant in this context. From the very early years of the most recent 'war on terror' post 11 September 2001, the international community has recognised and understood the risk that the threat-based paradigm poses to human rights. Beginning in 2003, the General Assembly has adopted a resolution each year on the 'Protection of human rights and fundamental freedoms while countering terrorism', stating in its preambular section that the General Assembly '[d]eeply deplor[es] the occurrence of violations of human rights and fundamental freedoms in the context of the fight against terrorism, as well as violations of international refugee and humanitarian law', and that 'all measures used in the fight against terrorism . . . must be in compliance with obligations of States under international law, including international human rights, refugee and humanitarian law'.[119] The resolution continues in its operational paragraphs to urge States to comply with human rights obligations in specific areas including the right not to be subjected to torture, cruel, inhuman or degrading treatment or punishment;[120] the rights of persons deprived of liberty;[121] the rights of due process;[122] the right to privacy;[123] the protection of economic, social and cultural rights;[124] and non-refoulement.[125]

When the threat of drugs is painted in the type of extreme terms described above, a threat not only to the individual but to the nation itself, it creates an atmosphere where the risk of abusive measures against people involved in these activities is heightened. As described by Boister, 'the drug conventions . . . provide a broad framework and introduce a no-holds-barred ethos into domestic drug control'.[126] The paradigm that paints drug suppression as a collective campaign against an evil threat has had the effect of creating a legal and policy environment in which millions of people worldwide are stigmatised and criminalised, and their vulnerability to both health problems and human rights abuses increased as a consequence. It has served to justify the application of abusive laws and policies, and the imposition of severe penalties, resulting in the incarceration of millions of people for drug offences,[127] often in overcrowded and inhumane conditions, and the execution of perhaps one thousand

[119] UN General Assembly, 'Protection of human rights and fundamental freedoms while countering terrorism' (30 March 2012) UN Doc No A/RES/66/171, preamble.

[120] Ibid para 6(a). [121] Ibid paras 6(b), 6(c), 6(e). [122] Ibid paras 6(d), 6(f).

[123] Ibid para 6(g). [124] Ibid para 6(h). [125] Ibid para 6(j-l).

[126] Boister, *Penal Aspects* (see chapter 1 n 57) 527.

[127] See, for example, Dave Bewley-Taylor, Mike Trace and Alex Stevens, 'Incarceration of drug offenders: costs and impacts' (Beckley Foundation Drug Policy Programme 2005).

people annually for drug crimes.[128] Although the same abuses identified in the 2003 General Assembly resolution human rights and terrorism have also been documented in the context of drug control, there has yet to be a similar resolution on protecting human rights and fundamental freedoms while countering drugs.

Although the threat-based discourse used in drug policy and terrorism is similar, there is still little official recognition of the human rights impacts of this in the area of drug control. Such negative human rights outcomes cannot be considered anything other than a direct contradiction to the historical claim to a humanitarian basis of the international drug control project. Indeed, it is fair to say that in the modern reality of efforts to suppress drugs, the threat paradigm has become the sole driving force behind the regime, to the point that few would imagine that an expressly humanitarian paradigm exists in the regime at all. Developing a framework for a fifth stage of drug control can occur only if this situation is reversed, and promoting 'the health and welfare of mankind' becomes the engine of drug policy, to the extent that the moralistic paradigm of 'evil' is abandoned as an historical curiosity.

[128] Gallahue, 'The Death Penalty for Drug Offences Global Overview 2011' (see chapter 1 n 25) 5.

4

Drug Control and Human Rights

Complementarities, Conflicts and Tensions between the Regimes

4.1 Introduction

The previous chapter explored the historic internal tensions peculiar to the development of international drug control law: the competing drive to pursue humanitarian objectives on the one hand, while viewing drug use and the drug trade as an 'evil' to be suppressed and eradicated on the other hand. During the United Nations era, the inherent strains between these two moral and philosophical concepts have been amplified, in both law and in practice, in the engagement between international drug control law and international human rights law.

As mentioned previously, there are three key elements of the fourth stage, United Nations era, of drug control that differentiate it from its predecessors. The first is the increased use of penal sanctions as a tool of drug suppression. As described by Bewley-Taylor,

> While the pre-1961 foundational treaties were in essence 'restrictive commodity agreements', the Single Convention [on Narcotic Drugs] was a stricter and wider-ranging multilateral instrument which, although still addressing the concerns of its predecessors, became more prohibitionist in tenor; including an increased focus upon individual drug users.[1]

The second element is the near universal ratification of the core drug control instruments. While the pre-United Nations drug control regime was characterised by a patchwork of treaties and numbers of States Parties to them, the modern conventions have achieved near unanimous support, resulting in this penal-focussed approach to drug control being incorporated into domestic law in almost every country of the world. The increasingly punitive nature of drug control has contributed to what the United Nations Office on Drugs and Crime calls the negative 'unintended consequences' of the regime. As described in a 2008 report from its Executive Director, '[l]ooking back over the last century, we can see

[1] Bewley-Taylor, *International Drug Control* (see chapter 2 n 2) 5.

that the control system and its application have had several unintended consequences – they may or may not have been *unexpected*, but they were certainly *unintended*.[2] The unintended consequences identified by the Executive Director include the creation of 'a huge criminal black market', the prioritising of law enforcement in government policy and expenditure at the expense of public health and the destabilising effects of the drug trade on producer and transit countries.[3] The notion that there are unintended negative consequences resulting from punitive approaches to drug control is not a new one. Writing of the domestic situation in the United States almost fifty years earlier, Makowski observed,

> It is evident . . . that present controls leave much to be desired. International attempts have failed to stifle illicit drug traffic at its sources. In spite of severe penalties and spirited enforcement existing domestic policies have failed to weaken a billion-dollar American black market in drugs. Narcotism in America remains an embarrassing social problem. This dark state of affairs has cast doubt not only upon present legislation but also upon the entire fabric of concepts and attitudes which gave rise to it . . . Severe penalties where the addict has no legal access to drugs merely elevates black market prices rendering it impossible for him to alleviate his suffering by lawful means. Such penalties even where rendered fall heavily only upon 'pushers' and other unimportant violators many of whom are addicts themselves driven to such employment by the high cost of drugs . . . Incarceration of addicts has proved entirely without merit.[4]

The third element differentiating the fourth stage of drug control from those that came before is that the modern legal instruments developed in parallel to an increasingly robust system of international human rights treaty law. This international legal terrain has led to another negative unintended consequence of the fourth stage of international drug control, one alluded to by Makowski, namely the multiple human rights violations documented around the world occurring as a result of drug enforcement efforts. In many cases, these human rights violations are excused or justified on the basis that the abusive policies or practices are supported under international drug control law, or are implemented as part of fulfilling drug treaty obligations. This has created, in effect, a situation where one branch of international law is used as a rationale to ignore, erode or limit the effect of another – the phenomenon of 'parallel universes' described by Professor Paul Hunt.[5]

[2] UN Commission on Narcotic Drugs, 'Fit for Purpose' (see chapter 1 n 21) 10.
[3] Ibid 10–11. [4] Makowski (see chapter 1 n 2) 317. [5] Hunt (see chapter 1 n 29) 9.

This chapter will explore the engagement between these two legal regimes, and the negative human rights consequences that often emerge as a result of the parallel universes. It is not intended as a comprehensive listing of the multiple areas in which human rights are affected by drug control, nor an exhaustive treatment of any one particular issue. Rather, the purpose is to illustrate the often strained nature of the relationship between these two legal regimes, highlighting examples of tensions and conflicts within this broader field of concern. In doing so, this chapter will lay the foundations for a later discussion of treaty interpretation, and the development of an approach that bridges the parallel universes in a manner that ensures protection and fulfilment of human rights.

4.2 Franco, Drug Control and the Historical Background to Fourth Stage Conflicts and Tension

In February 1946, the First Session on the UN General Assembly was held in London. On the agenda during that inaugural meeting of the UN's highest policy-making body was the question of the new organisation's relationship with Spain. While the defeat of the Axis powers less than twelve months earlier had precipitated the fall of fascist regimes across Europe, the government of General Francisco Franco was an anomaly. Franco had seized power in Spain some ten years earlier in a military coup, overthrowing a democratically elected civilian government, and throwing the country into civil war. Franco's victory in that civil war was in no small way attributable to the assistance of both Hitler's Germany and Mussolini's Italy. Franco, in turn, was an active supporter of the Axis powers during World War II, although, unlike in Germany and Italy, the Allied victory did not result in toppling his regime.

At the very first session of the UN General Assembly, Panama put forward a resolution proposing that the UN and its Member States have no relations with Franco's government, and neither diplomatically recognise nor support the regime.[6] The Panamanian proposal was based upon positions agreed at the Potsdam Conference at the end of World War II, and at the San Francisco Conference that led to the drafting of the Charter of the United Nations.[7] At those meetings, it was agreed that membership 'cannot apply to States whose regimes have been installed with the help of

[6] UN General Assembly, 'Relations of Members of the United Nations with Spain' (12 December 1946) UN Doc No A/RES/39(I).

[7] Ibid para 1.

armed forces of countries which have fought against the United Nations, so long as these regimes are in power'.[8] As explained by the delegate of Panama in proposing the resolution, 'all the members of the San Francisco Conference who approved this resolution had in mind exactly the country to which it really was referring; that is, the regime now in power in Spain'.[9] The resolution specifically recommended that Franco's Spain be 'debarred from membership in international agencies established by or brought into relationship with the United Nations'. It further recommended that it be banned from 'participation in conferences or other activities which may be arranged by the United Nations or by these agencies'.[10]

The Panamanian resolution received wide support from other Member States. Speaking in support of the resolution, the delegation of Czechoslovakia noted that '[t]he United Nations are met in London to lay the foundations of a just and democratic world order'. Franco's regime 'came into power through crimes against humanity and justice, such are to-day on trial in Nuremberg'.[11] The delegate continued, '[n]either democracy in Czechoslovakia, nor the democratic system in any other countries, can consider itself safe so long as, even in a far distant country, the fact of being a democrat means prison or the concentration camp. Not only is peace indivisible, but liberty and democracy too'.[12] The delegation of Mexico expressed its belief that the Franco regime should 'not be granted, by this Organization nor by any one of our countries, the international status of a government representing the Spanish nation. Our only demand is that we should refrain from having diplomatic relations with a spurious regime'.[13] Uruguay stated that 'if we are not to be in flagrant opposition to the origins and purposes of our Organization . . . this resolution should be carried with the whole-hearted and unanimous support of the Assembly'.[14] The Byelorussian Soviet Socialist Republic concurred, stating that the people of Spain were 'still under the yoke of a dictatorship'.[15] According to the Byelorussian delegate, '[t]hat situation is like a nightmare. There is terror; there is bloodshed; there are no laws. This is entirely in contradiction with the principles adopted by the United Nations . . . The Franco regime

[8] Official Records of the First Part of the First Section of the General Assembly, Plenary Meetings of the General Assembly Verbatim Record (10 January–14 February 1946), para 352. (Official Records: First Section).

[9] Ibid.

[10] UN General Assembly, 'Relations of Members of the United Nations with Spain' (n 6) 9.

[11] Official Records: First Section (n 8) 354. [12] Ibid 355. [13] Ibid.

[14] Ibid 357. [15] Ibid 359.

must not enjoy any help or support whatever from the States Members of the United Nations'.[16] Other governments speaking in support of the resolution included France, Norway, Venezuela, Yugoslavia and the United Kingdom. When put to the General Assembly for a decision, the resolution was passed by a vote of forty-six to two.[17]

Just over six months after the General Assembly's decision that the newly formed United Nations would neither recognise nor have diplomatic relations with fascist Spain, the UN Economic and Social Council (ECOSOC) convened its Third Session in Lake Success, New York. At its ninth meeting on 26 September 1946, ECOSOC members heard a report from the Drafting Committee on Narcotic Drugs. The Committee had been tasked by ECOSOC and the General Assembly to draft a new protocol that would 'transfer to the United Nations the activities, powers and functions formerly exercised by the League of Nations in the field of narcotics control'.[18] At this meeting, the question of UN relations with Spain was again on the agenda for debate. At issue was a proposal put forward jointly by the governments of China, Czechoslovakia and the USSR that the new protocol on drug control include a clause which would have the effect of excluding Franco's Spain from being invited to become a party to the new narcotics instrument, this based upon the resolution of the General Assembly in February and the previous decisions made at Potsdam and at the San Francisco Conference. According to the Soviet delegate who presented the proposal, 'to invite Franco to sign the Protocol would be contrary to the decisions taken regarding Spain'.[19]

Despite the clear direction from the General Assembly that the UN and its Member States should neither recognise nor engage with the fascist regime in Spain in its activities, the proposed clause to the new drugs protocol provoked surprising debate among ECOSOC members. For some, the crimes of the Spanish regime and the resulting General Assembly decision should not prevent the UN from working with Franco when it came to matters of narcotics control. The United Kingdom, which had spoken in favour of the General Assembly resolution seven months earlier, 'did not want to exclude Franco from the Protocol', arguing that to prevent Spain from becoming a party to the Protocol 'could only weaken

[16] Ibid 359–360. [17] Ibid 361.

[18] UN Commission on Narcotic Drugs, First Session Agenda (27 November 1946) UN Doc No E/C.S.7/2/Rev.2, 3.

[19] UN Economic and Social Council, Official Records No. 5, First Year: Third Session, Ninth and Tenth Meetings (26 and 27 September 1946) 57.

the international [drug] control system'.[20] Canada, which had also voted in favour of the General Assembly resolution excluding Spain, reasoned that the objective of narcotics control demanded a different approach. According to the Official Records of the session,

> As regards Spain, the representative of Canada realized that the advantages and privileges of the United Nations should not be accorded to a nation which was not qualified to enter the Organization, but found it difficult to exclude a signatory to the [drug] Conventions from control, whoever he might be. In [Canadian delegate] Mr. Martin's opinion, no political problem was involved in this case, and he therefore declared himself against the exclusion of Spain.[21]

Other States argued in favour of the exclusion clause. Czechoslovakia, one of the proposal's co-sponsors, stated simply that '[t]he principle of entertaining no relations with Franco had been admitted. To accept the participation of the Franco Government in the Protocol would mean denying that principle'.[22] Similarly, Chile 'was in favour of excluding Franco Spain on the basis of the attitude adopted at San Francisco and London'.[23] The Ukrainian Soviet Socialist Republic argued that 'if the Secretary-General sent an invitation to Franco in order to settle any problem whatever, it would be tantamount to recognizing Franco's signature'.[24] Therefore, Spain should be excluded from the protocol. In the end, the proposal to exclude Franco's Spain was adopted by ECOSOC. Only the United Kingdom voted against the proposal. Five others – Canada, Colombia, France, Greece and Peru – abstained from the vote.[25] Interestingly, all six of these countries had voted in favour of the General Assembly resolution against UN engagement with Franco earlier that same year.[26]

This history is interesting not only for the light it sheds on the politics of international relations in the months following the end of the Second World War, and the emerging East-West factionalism that would come to define much of the UN's work during the ensuing decades of the Cold War. It also reveals the tensions within the United Nations between concern for human rights on the one hand and the desire to control illicit drugs on the other, and the question of whether human rights violations should be considered relevant in decisions on fighting drugs. Although set in a specific historical context, the debates over the UN's relations with fascist Spain on drug control are not at all unique in either content or reasoning. Rather, they provide a vivid illustration that these tensions and conflicts

[20] Ibid. [21] Ibid 58. [22] Ibid. [23] Ibid. [24] Ibid 60. [25] Ibid 61.
[26] Official Records: First Section (n 8) 361.

within the United Nations system are as old as the institution itself, and have remained at the heart of the international community's approaches to human rights and drug control over the next seventy years.

4.3 Complementarities, Tensions and Conflicts

In his work, *General Theory of Norms*, Hans Kelsen argues that norms in international law reflect four general functions – commanding norms, permitting norms, derogating norms and empowering norms.[27] Pauwelyn summarises these four categories of norms as being:

1. Those that impose upon a State an obligation to do something, that is, to take some form of action – norms that impose positive obligations.
2. Those that impose an obligation on a State not to do something, that is, norms that impose negative obligations.
3. [Those that] grant the right to States not to do something, also known as an exemption [derogation] obligation.
4. [Those that] grant the right to a State to do something, or permissive norms.[28]

Types 1 and 2 impose *obligations* on States, and from these obligations other States or individuals derive rights. Types 3 and 4 grant rights to States, and therefore create obligations on other States or individuals.[29]

In general terms, a norm of international law can interact with another, separate norm, in one of two ways. The norms can either *accumulate* or they can *conflict*.[30] Norms accumulate when the rights or obligations contained within them complement each other, therefore adding to or reinforcing the normative content of each. They may also have an accumulative relationship where the rights or obligations of one norm confirms that of the other, without creating any additionality in terms of content.[31] In general, norms accumulate or are *complementary* where they either deal with different subject matters, or where they do not share any common States Parties.[32] However, norms may also form a complementary relationship when they share common subject matter and/or States Parties where one norm adds new rights or obligations to the existing norm without contradicting it.[33]

[27] Hans Kelsen, *General Theory of Norms* (Michael Hartney tr, Clarendon Press 1991) 96–114.
[28] Pauwelyn (see chapter 1 n 55) 158. [29] Ibid. [30] Ibid 161.
[31] Ibid 161–162. [32] Ibid.
[33] Hans Kelsen, *General Theory of Law and State* (Anders Wedberg tr, Harvard University Press 1949) 38–39.

It is also possible for two norms to be in conflict. According to Jenks, in his influential 1953 treatise on the subject, '[a] conflict of law-making treaties arises only where simultaneous compliance with the obligations of different instruments is impossible'.[34] There are a number of preconditions that must be met in order for a conflict of norms to exist. Therefore, one of the key issues in considering conflicts of norms between human rights and drug control, and resolving them, is to ascertain whether the preconditions for a conflict exist to begin with. This territory is not uncontested, particularly by mechanisms of the international drug control regime, which have traditionally been reluctant to embrace the relevance of human rights within their mandates.[35]

There are a number of preconditions that must be met in order for a conflict of norms to exist – an overlap of *ratione personae*,[36] *ratione materiae* and *ratione temporis*.[37] In essence, in order for a conflict to exist, the norms in question must overlap in terms of States concerned, the subject matter involved and must exist at the same point in time (whether a single unique event or over a prolonged period). There can be little doubt that the thresholds of both *ratione personae* and *ratione temporis* are met in this case. Given that nearly all States have ratified at least one of the three drug conventions, it would be highly unusual that a State Party to any human rights treaty would not also be Party to at least one drug convention. Similarly, the obligations placed upon States by both the drug conventions and the UN human rights treaties exist contemporaneously. One set of obligations does not switch on, and another switch off. Therefore, in assessing any potential or actual conflicts of norms, the threshold of *ratione temporis* is also clearly established. On the third question of *ratione materiae*, there is little to suggest that there is not at least some overlap – and indeed in some cases significant overlap – between the human rights and drug control regimes. Even if one were to consider drug control a purely technical matter, and that the subject matter in that sense does not overlap with that of human rights, the activities that States undertake to

[34] C. Wilfred Jenks, 'The Conflict of Law-Making Treaties' (1953) 30 British Yearbook of International Law 401, 451.

[35] See generally Barrett and Nowak (see chapter 1 n 24), Hunt (see chapter 1 n 29).

[36] 'If two treaties are concluded by totally different parties, no conflict of obligations is possible. At least one party must be common to both treaties.' Hans Kelsen, *The Law of the United Nations* (Stevens & Sons Ltd 1950) 122.

[37] For discussion on necessary conditions for a conflict of norms to occur, see Karl Wolfram, 'Conflicts Between Treaties' in R. Bernhardt (ed) *Encyclopedia of Public International Law* (1984) vol. VII, 467, Pauwelyn (see chapter 1 n 55) 165.

fulfil their obligations under the drug control regime – whether those be related to matters of supply reduction, demand reduction or treatment – clearly overlap with or engage human rights norms. Subjects addressed within the drug treaties – such as health, law enforcement, incarceration and extradition, to name but a few – all engage elements of international human rights law. Therefore, the necessary preconditions exist to enable a consideration of conflicts between the two regimes.

In addition to the traditional categories of complementary and conflicting norms described above, Barrett proposes a third category when considering the specific relationship between international drug control law and international human rights law, which he calls *tensions*.[38] Tensions are instances where drug control policy, law or practice is implemented in a manner that undermines human rights protections. However, unlike an outright conflict, a tension is not the consequence of explicit treaty obligation in the drug conventions but rather results from the manner in which a State or other body interprets that obligation within domestic practice. In effect, going further than is required under the drug control treaties to a point where the activities encroach on human rights safeguards. Jenks proposes a similar category in general international law, which he terms 'divergences'. He states that

> A divergence between treaty provisions dealing with the same subject or related subjects does not in itself constitute a conflict. Two law-making treaties with a number of common parties may deal with the same subject from different points of view or be applicable in different circumstances, or one of the treaties may embody obligations more far-reaching than, but not inconsistent with, those of the other. A conflict in the strict sense of direct incompatibility arises only where a party to the two treaties cannot simultaneously comply with its obligations under both treaties.[39]

Tensions or divergences compose the vast majority of instances where human rights are violated in the name of drug control, which in many ways reflects the relationship of indirect control that suppression regimes such as drug control establish. This chapter will review the question of complementarities, tensions and conflicts between the two legal regimes, and in doing so identify areas where human rights risk occurs, and where a process of interpretation is required in order to minimise or eliminate that risk.

[38] Damon Barrett, 'Intersections between the International Legal Regimes for Drug Control and Human Rights' (Human Rights and Drugs Conference, Human Rights Centre, University of Essex, 8 February 2014).

[39] Jenks (n 34) 425–426.

4.4 Regime Complementarities

Complementary norms within international narcotics control law itself are common, for example those existing within provisions of the 1961 and 1971 Conventions. In large part, the 1971 Convention simply expands the control measures established for plant-based narcotics under the 1961 Convention to also include synthetic psychotropic substances. Therefore, for example, Article 5 of the 1971 Convention, which calls upon States to limit to medical and scientific purposes of the psychotropic substances listed in that treaty, complements the General Obligation in Article 4(c) of the 1961 Convention 'to limit exclusively to medical and scientific purposes the production, manufacture, export, import, distribution of, trade in, use and possession of drugs'.[40] In this context, the 1971 treaty provision complements that of the 1961 Convention by expanding the scope and nature of the norm to include a new class of drugs. Norms may also be considered to be accumulating when one norm *confirms* the rights or obligations of another, pre-existing norm without adding to or expanding it.[41] For example, Article 17(1) of the 1988 drug convention, which stipulates that '[t]he Parties shall co-operate to the fullest extent possible to suppress illicit traffic by sea, in conformity with the international law of the sea',[42] confirms Article 108(1) of the 1982 UN Convention on the Law of the Sea, which creates obligations upon States to 'cooperate in the suppression of illicit traffic in narcotic drugs and psychotropic substances engaged in by ships on the high seas contrary to international [drug] conventions'.[43]

Complementary or accumulating norms are also evident in the relationship between international drug control law and international human rights law. Perhaps the clearest example is found in the issue of access to controlled drugs for medical purposes. As stated within the preamble of the 1961 Single Convention, the Parties

> *Concerned with the health and welfare of mankind,*
>
> *Recognizing that the medical use of narcotic drugs continues to be indispensable for the relief of pain and suffering and that adequate provision must be made to ensure the availability of narcotic drugs for such purposes*[44]

[40] 1971 Convention (see chapter 2 n 154) art 5(1); 1961 Convention amended (see chapter 2 n 171) art 4(c).

[41] Pauwelyn (see chapter 1 n 55) 162.

[42] 1988 Convention (see chapter 2 n 162) art 17(1).

[43] UN General Assembly, 'Third United Nations Convention on the Law of the Sea' (14 December 1983) UN Doc No A/RES/38/59, art 108(1).

[44] 1961 Convention amended (see chapter 2 n 171) preamble.

Here the preamble engages concepts central to modern discourse on economic, social and cultural rights, specifically Article 12 of the International Covenant on Economic, Social and Cultural Rights.[45] The Single Convention's context of 'the health and welfare of mankind' suggests that the treaty and its provisions are intended to advance, or be considered within, this broader concept of the right to health. The specific recognition in the preamble of the importance of the 'adequate provision' of medicines, and the need for States to 'ensure the availability of narcotic drugs' for the purpose of 'the relief of pain and suffering', further engages State obligations vis-à-vis the right to health. For example, the Committee on Economic, Social and Cultural Rights considers that the fulfilment of the right to health involves the provision of a number of elements, including access to essential drugs.[46] Indeed, the Committee includes such access among the Core Obligations of States under Article 12.[47]

The failure of States to provide access to medicines to alleviate pain and suffering has prompted critical comment from the UN Special Rapporteurs on the right to health[48] and on torture and other cruel, inhuman or degrading treatment or punishment.[49] The recognition by the States Parties to the Single Convention of the importance of ensuring access to medicines clearly engages the obligation 'to take positive measures that enable and assist individuals and communities to enjoy the right to health'.[50] Similarly, ensuring access to controlled drugs for medical purposes is a core element of the mandate and activities of the International Narcotics Control Board,[51] which since 1989[52] has become

[45] International Covenant on Economic, Social and Cultural Rights (adopted 16 December 1966, entered into force 3 January 1976) 993 UNTS 3, art 12.

[46] UN Committee of Economic, Social and Cultural Rights 'General Comment No. 14: The right to the highest attainable standard of health' (11 August 2000) UN Doc No E/C.12/2000, paras 12(a), 17.

[47] Ibid para 43(c).

[48] Special Rapporteur Health 2010 (n 30) 13; UN Human Rights Council, 'Report of the Special Rapporteur on the right of everyone to the enjoyment of the highest attainable standard of physical and mental health, Anand Grover, on access to medicines' (1 May 2013) UN Doc No A/HRC/23/42.

[49] UN Human Rights Council, 'Nowak Report' (see chapter 1 n 41) paras 68–70.

[50] UN Committee on Economic, Social and Cultural Rights, 'General Comment No. 14' (n 46) para 37.

[51] International Narcotics Control Board, 'Mandate and Functions' www.incb.org/incb/en/about/mandate-functions.html accessed 17 February 2014.

[52] International Narcotics Control Board, 'Demand for and supply of opiates for medical and scientific needs: Report of the International Narcotics Control Board for 1989' (1989) UN Doc No E/INCB/1989/1/Supp.

more active raising this as an issue of concern in its annual reports.[53] The importance of providing access to controlled medicines is acknowledged in the preambular section of the 'outcome document' of the 2016 United Nations General Assembly Special Session on drugs.[54] Promoting access to controlled medicines has also been the subject of resolutions of the Economic and Social Council in 2005,[55] the Commission on Narcotic Drugs in 2010 and 2011[56] and the UN Human Rights Council in 2013.[57]

Therefore, the State obligation to ensure access to essential medicine is one that is reflected in, and reinforced between, the two legal regimes. Yet despite these reinforcing norms, the issue of access (or lack thereof) to controlled medicines for medical purposes remain a global human rights challenge. The International Narcotics Control Board estimated in 2015 that 'approximately 5.5 billion people, or three quarters of the world's population, live in countries with low levels of, or non-existent, access to medicines containing narcotic drugs and have inadequate access to treatment for moderate to severe pain'.[58] This global health gap has been linked to barriers created within the drug control regime, including the system of estimates within the 1961 Convention, and general political context in which the drive to suppress illicit use is prioritised over systems to ensure medical accessibility.[59] Clearly, human rights violations occurring in the

[53] See, for example, International Narcotics Control Board, 'Report of the International Narcotics Control Board on the Availability of Internationally Controlled Drugs: Ensuring Adequate Access for Medical and Scientific Purposes' (2011) UN Doc No E/INCB/2010/1/Supp.1.

[54] UN Commission on Narcotic Drugs, 'Special session of the General Assembly on the world drug problem to be held in 2016' (22 March 2016) UN Doc No E/CN.7/2016/L.12/Rev.1, Annex.

[55] Economic and Social Council of the United Nations, 'Treatment of pain using opioid analgesics' (22 July 2005) UN Doc No E/2005/INF/2/Add.1, 70.

[56] UN Commission on Narcotic Drugs, 'Promoting adequate availability of internationally controlled licit drugs for medical and scientific purposes while preventing their diversion and abuse' (2010), res 53/4; UN Commission on Narcotic Drugs, 'Promoting adequate availability of internationally controlled narcotic drugs and psychotropic substances for medical and scientific purposes while preventing their diversion and abuse' (2011) res 54/6.

[57] UN Human Rights Council, 'Access to medicines in the context of the right of everyone to the enjoyment of the highest attainable standard of physical and mental health' (11 June 2013) UN Doc No A/HRC/23/L.10/Rev.1.

[58] International Narcotics Control Board, 'Report of the International Narcotics Control Board for 2014' (2015) UN Doc No E/INCB/2014/1, 3.

[59] See, for example, Global Commission on Drug Policy, 'The Global Crisis of Avoidable Pain: Drug Control's Negative Impact on Public Health', September 2015.

context of international drug control law are not limited solely to those where conflicts of law are evident.

4.5 Regime Tensions

Tensions or divergences between the drug control and human rights regimes are common and are at the root of some of the most widespread and egregious human rights abuses resulting from drug policy and enforcement. As described above, a tension exists where the implementation of drug control law, policy or enforcement breaches human rights protections, without an explicit treaty obligation upon States to undertake such actions. In effect, it is where a State or an international body interprets the requirements of international drug control law as being broader or more severe than what is codified in the drug conventions, and the resulting outcomes exceed the requirements of treaty obligations. Given the framework of indirect control the drug treaties create, where implementing criminal legislation and punishment is devolved to States without human rights guidance, the space for such tensions to emerge is broad. This section will explore three illustrative examples of tensions or divergences between international drug control law and international human rights law.

4.5.1 Death Penalty for Drug Offences

One example of tensions between the regimes is the issue of the death penalty for drug offences. In the mid-1980s, the death penalty for drug-related offences was in force in twenty-two States. By 1995, this number had increased to twenty-six, and by the end of 2000 at least thirty-four countries had enacted legislation providing for capital punishment for drug crimes.[60] It is estimated today that as many as thirty-three countries and territories have enacted capital laws for drug offences, and although most do not actually carry through the penalties allowed in legislation, it is still thought that as many as one thousand people annually are executed for drug offences.[61] In a number of these States, drug offences can carry a mandatory sentence of death.[62]

[60] See generally, Lines, 'A "Most Serious Crime"?' (see chapter 1 n 34) 21–28.

[61] Patrick Gallahue and Rick Lines, 'The Death Penalty for Drug Offences: Shared Responsibility and Shared Consequences' in P. Hodgkinson (ed) *The International Library of Essays on Capital Punishment, Volume III: Policy and Governance* (Ashgate 2013) 559.

[62] Hood and Hoyle (see chapter 1 n 36) 138, Gallahue, 'The Death Penalty for Drug Offences: Global Overview 2011' (see chapter 1 n 25) 11.

The growth in the number of States applying the death penalty for drug offences, particularly in the years since the adoption of the 1988 drug convention, is remarkable for two reasons. The first is that it stands in stark contrast to the overall international trend towards the abolition of the death penalty.[63] The second is that capital drug laws are not required under any of three drug conventions. In effect, the growth in the application of the death penalty for drug offences did not emerge as the result of a positive obligation in the drug conventions to enact capital punishment laws, but instead by the manner in which States chose to implement the penal drug laws defined in those treaties, often based on the sense of existential threat or paradigm of 'evil' explored in Chapter 2. The Government of Singapore, for example, has defended its use of capital punishment because 'tough anti-drug laws have worked well in Singapore's context to deter and punish drug traffickers' and are 'necessary legislation to help us keep our country drug-free'.[64] In a written statement made at the March 2009 session of the Human Rights Council, Singapore's delegation defended itself from criticism over the use of the death penalty for drug offences by claiming that '[t]he death penalty has deterred major drug syndicates from establishing themselves in Singapore'.[65] In 2006, the Malaysian Prime Minister Datuk Seri Abdullah Ahmad Badawi defended the use of death penalty is the 'right kind of punishment' given the menace that drugs pose to society.[66]

However, the death penalty for drug offences raises serious human rights concerns. Under the International Covenant on Civil and Political Rights, the application of capital punishment, while not prohibited, is restricted in important ways. One key restriction is found in Article 6(2), which states that, '[i]n countries which have not abolished the death penalty, sentence of death may be imposed only for the most serious crimes'.[67] From the perspective of the UN human rights system, there

63 UN Economic and Social Council, 'Capital punishment and the implementation of the safeguards guaranteeing protection of the rights of those facing the death penalty-Report of the Secretary-General' (18 December 2009) UN Doc No E/2010/10, 139.

64 Government of Singapore, 'Letter dated 27 June 1997 from the Permanent Mission of Singapore to the United Nations Office at Geneva addressed to the Special Rapporteur on Extrajudicial, Summary or Arbitrary Executions' (5 December 1997) UN Doc No E/CN.4/1998/113, para 4.

65 'Statement by Singapore during the interactive dialogue at the 10th session of the Human Rights Council on 10 March 2009' (copy on file with author).

66 M. Hussein, 'Abdullah Defends Death Penalty For Drug Traffickers' *Bernama Malaysian National News Agency* (22 February 2006).

67 International Covenant on Civil and Political Rights (adopted 16 December 1966, entered into force 23 March 1976) 999 UNTS 171, art 6(2).

is little to support the suggestion that drug offences meet the threshold of 'most serious crimes'. The Human Rights Committee, which holds the mandate to monitor State compliance with the Covenant, has stated definitively that drug offences do not meet this threshold. In its 2005 Concluding Observations on Thailand, the Committee noted 'with concern that the death penalty is not restricted to the "most serious crimes" within the meaning of article 6, paragraph 2, and is applicable to drug trafficking'.[68] The Committee repeated this interpretation in its 2007 Concluding Observations on The Sudan, raising concern at '[t]he imposition in the State party of the death penalty for offences which cannot be characterized as the most serious, including embezzlement by officials, robbery with violence and drug trafficking'.[69] The Special Rapporteur on Extrajudicial, Summary or Arbitrary Executions has also stated that drug offences do not meet the threshold of 'most serious crimes', concluding in 1996 that:

> [T]he death penalty should be eliminated for crimes such as economic crimes and drug-related offences. In this regard, the Special Rapporteur wishes to express his concern that certain countries, namely China, the Islamic Republic of Iran, Malaysia, Singapore, Thailand and the United States of America, maintain in their national legislation the option to impose the death penalty for economic and/or drug-related offences.[70]

The conclusion that drug-related offences fall outside the scope of 'most serious crimes' was reaffirmed in the Special Rapporteur's 2006 Annual Report.[71] The Special Rapporteur on torture and other cruel, inhuman or degrading treatment or punishment has also reached this same conclusion. As stated in his 2009 Report to the Human Rights Council, 'drug offences do not meet the threshold of most serious crimes. Therefore, the imposition of the death penalty on drug offenders amounts to a violation of the right to life, discriminatory treatment and possibly... also their right to human dignity'.[72] In its 2015 study on the human rights impacts

[68] UN Human Rights Committee, 'Concluding observations: Thailand' (8 July 2005) UN Doc No CCPR/CO/84/THA, para 14.

[69] UN Human Rights Committee, 'Concluding observations: The Sudan' (29 August 2007) UN Doc No CCPR/C/SDN/CO/3, para 19.

[70] UN Commission on Human Rights, 'Report by the Special Rapporteur, Mr. Bacre Waly Ndiaye, submitted pursuant to Commission on Human Rights resolution 1996/74' (24 December 1996) UN Doc No E/CN.4/1997/60, para 91.

[71] UN Human Rights Council, 'Report of the Special Rapporteur on extrajudicial, summary or arbitrary executions, Philip Alston' (29 January 2007) UN Doc No A/HRC/4/20, paras 51–52.

[72] UN Human Rights Council, 'Nowak Report' (see chapter 1 n 41) para 66.

of drug control, the Office of the United Nations High Commissioner for Human Rights concludes that 'The right to life of persons convicted of drug-related offences should be protected and, in accordance with article 6 of the International Covenant on Civil and Political Rights and the jurisprudence of the Human Rights Committee, such persons should not be subject to the death penalty.'[73]

Here then is a prime example of tension, where State interpretation of how it implements its drug control obligations creates a breach of international human rights law. This breach is not one created by virtue of an explicit drug treaty obligation to impose capital punishment, but instead how a Government chooses to interpret the offences and sanctions within the drug treaties. Interestingly, this tension can be found even within the drug control regime itself. In recent years, the UN Office of Drugs and Crime has taken an unequivocal position that the death penalty is not a justifiable sanction.[74] The International Narcotics Control Board, on the other hand, refused to take a stand against the death penalty until 2014, traditionally adopting the position that the 'determination of sanctions applicable to drug-related offences remains the exclusive prerogative of each State and therefore lies beyond the mandate . . . [of] the Board'.[75] In a case before the Indian Supreme Court in 2013, the Government cited the Board's failure to reject to the death penalty for drugs as evidence that 'the body mandated to ensure compliance of the UN Drug Conventions has no objection to the presence of capital punishment . . . It is, therefore, wrong to say that such provisions are contrary to the UN Conventions'.[76]

Importantly, the issue of the death penalty for drug offences, and the tensions between drug control and human rights obligations, extends

73 Office of the UN High Commissioner for Human Rights, 'Study on the impact of the world drug problem on the enjoyment of human rights' (4 September 2015) UN Doc No A/HRC/30/65, para 63.

74 See, for example, UN Office on Drugs and Crime, 'Contribution of the Executive Director of the United Nations Office on Drugs and Crime to the high-level review of the implementation of the Political Declaration and Plan of Action on International Cooperation towards an Integrated and Balanced Strategy to Counter the World Drug Problem, to be conducted by the Commission on Narcotic Drugs in 2014' (6 December 2013) UN Doc No UNODC/ED/2014/z, para 52(c).

75 Secretariat, International Narcotics Control Board, Correspondence with Harm Reduction International (29 February 2012) www.hrw.org/news/2012/03/12/letter-international-narcotics-control-board-capital-punishment-drug-offences accessed 27 July 2014.

76 Supreme Court of India, *Indian Harm Reduction Network v Union of India and Ors*, Special Leave Petition (Criminal) No 114 of 2012, 'Affidavit in Reply on behalf of Respondent No. 1&2' (11 November 2013), para 4(v).

beyond the actions of retentionist States themselves and involves the actions and human rights responsibilities of both Western donor States (many of them abolitionist in their domestic laws) and the UN Office on Drugs and Crime. Since 2010, several reports[77] have exposed links between international drug enforcement aid programmes from European Union and other governments going to support programmes in retentionist States, resulting in death sentences and even executions as a consequence of those programmes. In many cases, this aid from Western donor governments is administered though the UN Office on Drugs and Crime, therefore also involving a UN agency in programmes driving human rights abuses. This aid is routinely explained as reflecting 'the principle of a common and shared responsibility, including by means of enhanced and better coordinated technical and financial assistance' among and between Member States.[78] However, as described in one investigative report, 'many wealthy donor states . . . eagerly provide funding to help others live up to their international drug control obligations without ensuring that there are appropriate human rights safeguards in place',[79] which often results in executions for drug offences. 'While some governments openly criticise such human rights violations . . . they continue to supply funds and material resources to foreign governments committing those same human rights violations.'[80]

4.5.2 *Compulsory Detention in the name of 'Drug Treatment'*

As described in Chapter 2, the United Nations era marked the first time that the provision of drug treatment was codified as a State obligation in international drug control law. According to Article 38 of the Single Convention on Narcotic Drugs, '[t]he Parties shall give special attention to the provision of facilities for the medical treatment, care and rehabilitation of drug addicts', and, subject to economic resources, 'it is desirable that [States] establish adequate facilities for the effective treatment of drug addicts'.[81] The 1972 Protocol to the 1961 Convention significantly amended Article 38 in this regard, increasing the scope of the treaty to

77 See, for example, Gallahue and Lines (n 61), Gallahue, Saucier and Barrett (see chapter 2 n 230).

78 UN Commission on Narcotic Drugs, 'Political declaration and plan of action on international cooperation towards an integrated and balanced strategy to counter the world drug problem' in report on the fifty-second session (14 March 2008 and 11–20) UN Doc No E/CN.7/2009/12, p 40, para 12.

79 Gallahue, Saucier and Barrett (see chapter 2 n 230) ii.

80 Ibid iii.

81 1961 Convention (see chapter 2 n 134) art 38.

create an obligation to take 'all practicable measures for the prevention of abuse of drugs and for the early identification, treatment, education, after-care, rehabilitation and social reintegration of persons involved'.[82] Similar provisions on drug treatment are found at Article 20 of the 1971 Convention,[83] while the 1988 Convention specifies that drug treatment is an acceptable alternative or additional sanction within the context of penal provisions for offences related to the possession of drugs for personal use.[84]

However, while such obligations are clearly intended to introduce less punitive, health-based options for drug offences into treaty obligations, some States' approaches to providing drug treatment have created another regime tension, particularly the practice of the forcible detention and compulsory 'drug treatment' of people who use (or who are suspected of using) illegal drugs. This practice has been documented in numerous States in Asia, including China, Vietnam, Cambodia, Thailand, Russia, Malaysia, Lao PDR and India.[85] Detention and compulsory drug treatment, often operated by private or religiously affiliated organisations rather than by the State, have also been documented in a number of Latin American countries, including Brazil,[86] Peru,[87] Guatemala[88] and Mexico.[89]

[82] Ibid art 15. [83] 1971 Convention (see chapter 2 n 154) art 20.

[84] 1988 Convention (see chapter 2 n 162) art 3(4)(d).

[85] See, for example, International Harm Reduction Development Program, 'Human Rights Abuses in the Name of Drug Treatment: Reports From the Field', Public Health Fact Sheet (March 2009); Human Rights Watch, 'The Rehab Archipelago Forced Labor and Other Abuses in Drug Detention Centers in Southern Vietnam' (2011); Human Rights Watch, '"Skin on the Cable," The Illegal Arrest, Arbitrary Detention and Torture of People Who Use Drugs in Cambodia' (2010); Nick Thompson, 'Detention as Treatment: Detention of Methamphetamine Users in Cambodia, Laos, and Thailand' (International Harm Reduction Development Program 2010); Elliott, Lines and Schleifer (see chapter 1 n 26); Richard Pearshouse, 'Compulsory Drug Treatment in Thailand' (Canadian HIV/AIDS Legal Network 2009); World Health Organization Western Pacific Region, 'Assessment of Compulsory Treatment of People Who Use Drugs in Cambodia, China, Malaysia and Viet Nam: An Application of Selected Human Rights Principles' (2009).

[86] Human Rights Council, 'Report of the Working Group on Arbitrary Detention' (10 July 2015) UN Doc No A/HRC/30/3, 17. (WGAD 2015).

[87] Daniel Wolfe and Denise Tomasini-Joshi, 'Drug Users Burned by the System in Peru', *Open Society Foundation Voices* (13 May 2012) www.opensocietyfoundations.org/voices/drug-users-burned-system-peru accessed 22 October 2015.

[88] Linda Pressly, 'The rehab centres that lock up addicts against their will', *BBC Radio* 4 (27 August 2014) www.bbc.co.uk/news/magazine-28934795 accessed 22 October 2015.

[89] Roxanne Saucier, Daniel Wolfe, Kathleen Kingsbury and Paul Silva (eds) 'Treated with Cruelty: Abuses in the name of Drug Rehabilitation' (Open Society Foundations 2011) 21.

In total, it is estimated that perhaps half a million people worldwide are arbitrarily detained on any given day for the purpose of 'drug treatment', many of them held for months or even years at a time, without being charged with any criminal offence, being brought before a court or otherwise allowed to challenge the legality of their detention.[90] In many cases, these 'treatment' centres are run by military or police personnel rather than medical staff, and numerous investigations into the conditions of these centres include reports of physical and sexual abuse and humiliation, beatings, forced labour and denial of medical services.[91] The situation clearly raises numerous human rights concerns, including questions of inhuman or degrading treatment or punishment, the right to consent or to refuse treatment and of forced labour. It also raises serious concerns about illegal or arbitrary detention, prohibition of which is integrally linked to the broader right to liberty.[92]

As in the case of the death penalty, the question of compulsory drug detention exposes tensions within the drug control regime itself. While the UN Office on Drugs and Crime has been clear in rejecting compulsory detention for drug use,[93] the International Narcotics Control Board has been far more equivocal, at times commending countries with compulsory systems in its Annual Reports. The Board's 2001 Report, for example, recognises without comment the 'significant increase' in the population of China's compulsory drug detention centres to 360,000.[94] It also 'welcome[d]' Vietnam's approach to drug treatment, which includes widespread use of compulsory detention, while also 'encourag[ing] the Government to reinforce and support existing facilities'.[95]

Muddying the waters considerably in this context is the fact that the Board, although traditionally eschewing any suggestion its mandate should be responsive to human rights concerns,[96] has asserted that there

[90] Ralf Jurgens and Joanne Csete, 'In the name of treatment: ending abuses in compulsory drug detention centers' (2012) 107/4 Addiction 689.

[91] Ibid; UN Human Rights Council, 'Mendez Report' (see chapter 1 n 43) paras 40–44.

[92] International Covenant on Civil and Political Rights (n 67) art 9(1); Human Rights Committee 'General Comment No. 8: Right to liberty and security of the person (Art. 9)' (30 June 1982) UN Doc No HRI/GEN/1/Rev.1. See also Fiona de Londras, 'The Right to Challenge the Lawfulness of Detention: An International Perspective on US Detention of Suspected Terrorists' (2007) 12/2 Journal of Conflict and Security Law, 223, 238.

[93] See, for example, International Labour Organisation, et al. (see chapter 1 n 40).

[94] International Narcotics Control Board, 'Report of the International Narcotics Control Board for 2011' (2012) UN Doc No E/INCB/2011/1, para 583.

[95] Ibid para 117.

[96] Joanne Csete, 'Overhauling Oversight: Human Rights at the INCB' in J. Collins (ed) *Governing The Global Drug Wars LSE Ideas: Special Report* (LSE Ideas 2012) (Overhauling Oversight).

exists a human right to be 'free from drug addiction'.[97] As early as 1998, the President of the Board was stating in United Nations fora that '[t]he right to be free of drug abuse and the right to be protected from drug abuse . . . should be respected by all people'.[98] This claim to a right to be drug free, coupled with the State obligations within the drug conventions to provide drug treatment, creates an environment of human rights risk. As has been pointed out by one non-governmental organisation, such claims 'could easily lead to a justification of forced treatment, claiming that it is aimed at the realisation of human rights'.[99]

This is not simply a theoretical risk, as this rationale underpins some troubling defences of compulsory drug detention within parts of the human rights and medical literature. Takahashi, for example, advances the position in *Human Rights Quarterly* that 'drug addiction . . . destroys – or at least suspends – the free will of the addict',[100] and therefore that '[i]t is disingenuous to pretend that the "decision" not to undergo treatment is an entirely free one . . . [as] [d]ecisions made under the influence of drugs are not decisions of free will'.[101] A similar perspective is advanced by Zunyou Wu of the Chinese Centre for Disease Control and Prevention in a 2013 publication of the World Health Organization. Like Takahashi, Wu questions the ability of people who are drug dependent 'to make rational decisions, provide informed consent for treatment or participate completely in their own due process', in effect suggesting that the rights violations involved are either minimal, non-existent or legitimate as being done in the best interests of the individual.[102] Although not discussing compulsory treatment *per se*, Director of the US National Institute on Drug Abuse, Dr Nora Volkow, has supported these same arguments, writing in 2015 that 'because of drug use, a person's brain is no longer able to produce something needed for our functioning and that healthy people take for granted, *free will*'.[103] Wu further argues that 'the rights of entire communities' [presumably to be drug free] need to be balanced with, or

97 International Narcotics Control Board 2011 (n 94) iii.

98 'Statement by Professor Hamid Ghodse, President of the International Narcotics Control Board' delivered at the Economic and Social Council (28 July 1998). See also Statement by Professor Hamid Ghodse, President of the International Narcotics Control Board', Statement delivered at the 20th Special Session of the General Assembly on the World Drug Problem, 8–10 June 1998.

99 Harm Reduction International, 'Commanding General Confidence? Human Rights, International Law and the INCB Annual Report for 2011' (2012) 8.

100 Takahashi (see chapter 1 n 46) 775.

101 Ibid.

102 Zunyon Wu, 'Arguments in favour of compulsory treatment of opioid dependence' (2013) 91/2 Bulletin of the World Health Organization 142.

103 Volkow (see chapter 3 n 55).

even take priority over, the rights of the individual in question.[104] Takahashi takes a similar position, stating that '[s]ociety has a strong interest in ensuring that persons who are addicted to drugs undergo treatment for their condition and . . . [t]o exclude completely the possibility of any level of coercion would be in many cases to exclude the possibility of the addict overcoming his addiction'.[105]

The issue of compulsory detention for drugs has become an increasing concern among non-governmental organisations and United Nations human rights bodies.[106] As described in 2013 by the UN Special Rapporteur on Torture,

> Compulsory detention for drug users is common in so-called rehabilitation centres. Sometimes referred to as drug treatment centres or "reeducation through labor" centres or camps, these are institutions commonly run by military or paramilitary, police or security forces, or private companies. Persons who use, or are suspected of using, drugs and who do not voluntarily opt for drug treatment and rehabilitation are confined in such centres and compelled to undergo diverse interventions.[107]

International human rights law also offers significant guidance specifically on the question of arbitrary detention in the context of drug treatment, none of it supportive of the notion that people who use drugs or are drug dependent surrender the right to liberty or security of the person, or the right to informed consent.[108] For example, in its General Comment on Article 9 of the International Covenant on Civil and Political Rights, the Human Rights Committee notes that the protections enshrined in the treaty should not be narrowly interpreted to apply only to arrest and detention in the context of criminal cases. Rather, Article 9 'is applicable to all deprivations of liberty, whether in criminal cases or in other cases such as, for example . . . drug addiction'.[109] Similarly, the Working Group on Arbitrary Detention considers Article 9 protections to be engaged in

[104] Wu (n 102). [105] Takahashi (see chapter 1 n 46) 775.

[106] International Labour Organisation, et al. (see chapter 1 n 40).

[107] UN Human Rights Council, 'Mendez Report' (see chapter 1 n 43) 40.

[108] See Rick Lines, '"Treatment in Liberty" - Compulsory Detention for Drug Use and Human Rights' (2016) 3 Journal of International Law and Drug Policy (in press).

[109] UN Human Rights Committee, 'General Comment No. 8' (n 92) para 1. The Committee on the Rights of the Child has similarly noted that the rights of children deprived of their liberty apply with respect to children in conflict with the law and 'to children placed in institutions for the purposes of care, protection or treatment, including mental health, educational, drug treatment, child protection or immigration institutions'. See UN Committee on the Rights of the Child, 'General Comment No. 10 – Children's rights in juvenile justice' (9 February 2007) UN Doc No CRC/C/GC/10, fn 1.

matters related to drugs. In its 2003 Report, the Working Group noted that it had been

> [I]nformed by several sources that, in some countries, the disabled, drug addicts and people suffering from AIDS are detained in places that are incompatible with their state of health, sometimes without treatment and without it having been established that their detention is justified on medical or public health grounds. The Group is concerned because it is vulnerable persons that are involved, people who are often stigmatized by social stereotypes; but it is concerned above all because often such administrative detention is not subject to judicial supervision.[110]

In his 2009 report to the General Assembly, the UN Special Rapporteur on the right to the highest attainable standard of health raised specific concerns about consent to treatment for people who use drugs, noting they 'are often perceived as being dangerous to themselves and unable to make the "right" decision. Prohibitions against their behaviour threaten their ability to refuse testing and treatment'.[111] The Special Rapporteur's report in 2010 was entirely dedicated to exploring issues of drug use and drug policy as they affect the right to health, and the report addressed the question of compulsory detention and treatment.[112] In a clear rebuke of the position argued by Takahashi, Volkow and Wu, he concluded that '[p]eople who use or are dependent on drugs do not automatically lack the capacity to consent to treatment. A presumption of incapacity based on drug use or dependence creates significant potential for abuse'.[113] The Special Rapporteur also found that the type of mass detention and treatment described above were inconsistent with established human rights safeguards governing when such committal is legal. According to the report, '[d]ecisions regarding capacity and competence, and the need to obtain informed consent, must be made on a case-by-case basis. Treatment *en masse* prima facie fails to meet this requirement'.[114] Based upon the findings of previous UN human rights mechanisms, a 2015 report of the Office of the High Commissioner for Human Rights recommended that '[c]ompulsory detention centres should be closed'.[115]

[110] UN Working Group on Arbitrary Detention, 'Report of the Working Group on Arbitrary Detention' (15 December 2003) UN Doc No E/CN.4/2004/3, para 74; See also WGAD 2015 (n 86).

[111] Ibid para 88.

[112] UN General Assembly, 'Special Rapporteur Health 2010' (see chapter 1 n 28).

[113] Ibid para 39. [114] Ibid para 38.

[115] Office of the UN High Commissioner for Human Right (n 73) para 62.

4.5.3 *Harm Reduction*

A third example of tensions between the drug control and human rights regimes is found on the question of harm reduction. 'Harm Reduction' is an approach to providing services to people who are active drug users that seeks to minimise the health harms related to their drug use, rather than end the use of drugs itself.[116] In effect, acknowledging that drugs can be used in ways that are either more safe or less safe for the individual consumer, and that the role of public health interventions should be to encourage and provide the necessary paraphernalia to encourage and enable safer use, and thereby reducing the potential harm. Examples of harm reduction programmes are the distribution of sterile syringes and other injecting paraphernalia, on the basis that using sterile equipment to inject minimises or eliminates the risk of the transmission of blood-borne viruses such as HIV among networks of people who inject as a result of sharing used syringes.[117] Another example is the provision of opioid substitution treatments, such as methadone and buprenorphine. These prescribed medicines are ingested orally, enabling the heroin-dependent individual to cease injecting and therefore end the need to acquire drugs from illicit sources. Although patients are still dependent on an opiate, evidence has demonstrated the numerous health and social benefits that emerge when people move from illicit injectable opiates onto pharmaceutical, non-injectable opiates administered through a physician.[118] Within the drug control system, harm reduction interventions have often been seen as controversial because they do not abide by the dominant paradigm of abstinence from the 'evil' of drug 'addiction', and instead accept the reality of drug use and seek to design health interventions for people who choose to use illegal substances.

Since 2006, a growing body of international human rights jurisprudence and commentary has emerged supporting harm reduction programmes as a component element of the right to the highest attainable standard of health, and United Nations human rights monitors have been specifically critical of a number of States for the failure to provide

[116] International Harm Reduction Association, 'What is Harm Reduction?' (International Harm Reduction Association 2009).

[117] World Health Organization, 'Effectiveness of Sterile Needle and Syringe Programming in reducing HIV/AIDS among Injecting Drug Users' (World Health Organization 2004).

[118] World Health Organization, UN Office on Drugs and Crime and UNAIDS, 'Position Paper: Substitution maintenance therapy in the management of opioid dependence and HIV/AIDS prevention' (World Health Organization 2004).

access to such services. For example, the Special Rapporteur on the Right to Health's 2007 report was critical of Sweden for the poor availability of harm reduction services, stating that 'the Government has a responsibility to ensure the implementation . . . of a comprehensive harm-reduction policy, including counselling, advice on sexual and reproductive health, and clean needles and syringes'.[119] The Committee on the Rights of the Child has called upon Austria to implement 'specialized and youth-friendly drug-dependence treatment and harm reduction services for children' under Article 24 (the right to health) within the Convention on the Rights of the Child.[120] The Committee on Economic, Social and Cultural Rights has been critical of Tajikistan[121] for lack of needle and syringe exchange programme and of Ukraine for lack of access to opioid substitution therapy, therefore falling short of State obligations under Article 12 of the International Covenant on Economic, Social and Cultural Rights.[122]

In its 2011 Concluding Observations on the Russian Federation, the Committee expressed concern about the 'growing epidemic of HIV/AIDS [and] hepatitis C' among people who inject drugs, as well as for 'the continued ban on the medical use of methadone and buprenorphine for treatment of drug dependence and the fact that the Government does not support opioid substitution therapy (OST) and needle and syringe programmes'. The report concluded by stating that '[t]he Committee urges the State party to apply a human rights-based approach to drug users so that they do not forfeit their basic right to health'.[123]

The issue of harm reduction is not simply one that has emerged within the context on individual State human rights obligations. It has also been a major issue of contention and debate within the drug control regime itself. Bewley-Taylor has written in detail on the tension over harm reduction within the international drug control system, in particular intense debates among Member States, and the strains the issue has created within

[119] UN Human Rights Council, 'Report of the Special Rapporteur on the right of everyone to the enjoyment of the highest attainable standard of physical and mental health, Paul Hunt, Mission to Sweden' (28 February 2007) UN Doc No A/HRC/4/28/Add.2, para 62 (Hunt Sweden Report).

[120] UN Committee on the Rights of the Child, 'Concluding observations: Austria' (3 December 2012) CRC/C/AUT/CO/3–4, para 51.

[121] UN Committee on Economic, Social and Cultural Rights, 'Concluding Observations: Tajikistan' (24 November 2006) UN Doc No E/C.12/TJK/CO/1, para 70.

[122] UN Committee on Economic, Social and Cultural Rights, 'Concluding Observations: Ukraine' (23 November 2007) UN Doc No E/C.12/UKR/CO/5, para 28.

[123] UN Committee on Economic, Social and Cultural Rights, 'Concluding Observations: Russian Federation' (1 June 2011) UN Doc No E/C.12/RUS/CO/5, para 29.

and among the UN drug control bodies, especially within the UN Commission on Narcotic Drugs.[124] He notes these debates 'reflected divergent perspectives on the [drug control] regime's fundamental principles and norms concerning punitive prohibition'.[125] Much of this debate, at least from those States that supported the harm reduction approach, was driven by public health imperatives in the face of a growing HIV crisis among people who inject drugs. However, given the centrality of human rights advocacy within the international response to HIV,[126] it was inevitable that human rights concerns also became an element of the harm reduction debate.

The approach of the relevant UN bodies illustrates this tension. Within the UN human rights system, harm reduction approaches have increasingly received explicit endorsement from key actors, including the Committee on Economic, Social and Cultural Rights,[127] the Committee on the Rights of the Child,[128] the Office of the High Commissioner for Human Rights[129] and the Special Rapporteurs on Health[130] and on Torture.[131] However, within the drug control regime, the situation is much different. The International Narcotics Control Board has historically been reluctant to enthusiastically embrace harm reduction approaches. At best, the Board has offered qualified acceptance of these programmes, for example stating in its 1993 Annual Report that,

124 Bewley-Taylor, *International Drug Control* (see chapter 2 n 2) Chapters 2, 3.

125 Ibid 101.

126 See, for example, Office of the UN High Commissioner for Human Rights, 'International Guidelines on HIV/AIDS and Human Rights, 2006 Consolidated Version' (2006) UN Doc No E.06.XIV.4.

127 See, for example, UN Committee on Economic, Social and Cultural Rights, 'Concluding Observations: Tajikistan' (n 121) para 70; 'Concluding Observations: Ukraine' (n 122) para 28.

128 UN Committee on the Rights of the Child, 'Concluding observations: Ukraine' (21 April 2011) UN Doc No CRC/C/UKR/CO/3–4, para 60(a); UN Committee on the Rights of the Child, 'Concluding observations: Albania' (7 December 2012) UN Doc No CRC/C/ALB/CO/2–4, para 63(b); UN Committee on the Rights of the Child, 'Concluding observations: Austria' (3 December 2012) CRC/C/AUT/CO/3–4, para 51.

129 Office of the UN High Commissioner for Human Rights, 'High Commissioner calls for focus on human rights and harm reduction in international drug policy', statement of 10 March 2009; 'Study on the impact of the world drug problem on the enjoyment of human rights: Report of the United Nations High Commissioner for Human Rights (4 September 2015) UN Doc No A/HRC/30/65, paras 11–20; Office of the UN High Commissioner for Human Rights (n 73).

130 UN Human Rights Council, Hunt Sweden Report (n 119) para 60; UN General Assembly, 'Special Rapporteur Health 2010' (see chapter 1 n 28) paras 50–61.

131 UN Human Rights Council, 'Nowak Report' (see chapter 1 n 41) para 74(a-c).

> The Board acknowledges the importance of certain aspects of 'harm reduction' as a tertiary prevention strategy for demand reduction purposes. The Board considers it its duty, however, to draw attention of Governments to the fact that 'harm reduction' programmes are not substitutes for demand reduction programmes.[132]

In 2000, the Board lamented that Government investment in HIV prevention services for people who inject drugs were, in its estimation, being diverting money from drug prevention activities, stating that

> The fact that harm reduction programmes should constitute only one element of a larger, more comprehensive strategy to reduce the demand for illicit drugs has been neglected. The Board regrets that the discussion on drug injection rooms and some other harm reduction measures has diverted the attention (and, in some cases, funds) of Governments from important demand reduction activities such as primary prevention or abstinence-oriented treatment.[133]

In its 2004 Annual Report, the Board encouraged States to address the spread of HIV, yet at the same time qualified this statement with the caution that '[m]easures to prevent the spread of infectious diseases must not be seen as facilitating or even promoting drug abuse, which is, after all, the root of the problem'.[134] Despite the fact that the Board's mandate gives it responsibility for monitoring, and ensuring availability of, internationally controlled opioid replacement medicines for people who are heroin dependent, 'the Board's Reports and associated public statements have demonstrated at best a lukewarm support for the interventions and use of methadone and buprenorphine'.[135]

At other times, the Board has expressed outright hostility to, and denunciation of, harm reduction programmes. The most glaring example of this is in the case of safe injecting facilities, or 'drug injection rooms' to use the Board's own phrase. Such facilities are health clinics established in some urban centres into which people are allowed to bring illicit drugs and inject under sterile, clinical conditions, and under the supervision of medical personnel. Although established in only a handful of countries, these facilities have proved very effective at not only reducing HIV

[132] International Narcotics Control Board, 'Report of the International Narcotics Control Board for 1993' (1994) UN Doc No E/INCB/1993/1, para 29.

[133] International Narcotics Control Board, 'Report of the International Narcotics Control Board for 2000' (2001) UN Doc No E/INCB/2000/1, p 60, para 446.

[134] International Narcotics Control Board, 'Report of the International Narcotics Control Board for 2004' (2005) UN Doc No E/INCB/2004/1, p iv.

[135] Bewley-Taylor, *International Drug Control* (see chapter 2 n 2) 232.

transmission and fatal overdoses but also in ensuring homeless or underhoused people are not injecting publicly, for example in parks and alleys, which has additional residual benefits for the individuals and the broader community.[136]

Safe injecting facilities have often been the source of some domestic controversy in the countries where they have been established. Most notably, the only such facility established in North America – 'Insite' in Vancouver, British Columbia – was the cause of a series of court challenges in which the Federal Government of Canada sought to force the city and province to shut the clinic down.[137] These challenges culminated in the Supreme Court in 2011, where the justices ruled unanimously in favour of Insite and against the attempts of the Canadian Government to close it.[138] However, despite the verdict of the Supreme Court, the International Narcotics Control Board has vocally criticised both Canada and the Court in its reports, calling the existence of the facility and others like it a violation of international law.[139] In a 2014 report to the Commission on Narcotic Drugs, for example, the Board stated that safe injecting facilities 'promote social and legal tolerance of drug abuse and drug trafficking and therefore contravene the international drug control treaties'.[140] The Board's public criticism of Canada in this regard is in stark contrast with its approach on the death penalty for drug offences, where it refused for many years to take a position on the basis of what it considered to be an internal matter for States.[141] It is also at odds with the drug control treaties themselves, which explicitly place constitutional caveats and exceptions

136 Dagmar Hedrich, Thomas Kerr and Françoise Dubois-Arber, 'Drug consumption facilities in Europe and beyond' in T. Rhodes and D. Hedrich (eds) *Harm reduction: evidence, impacts and challenges* (Publications Office of the European Union 2010).

137 *PHS Community Services Society v Attorney General of Canada* [2008] BCSC 661 (B.C. Supreme Court); *PHS Community Services Society v Canada (Attorney General)*, [2010] BCCA 15 (B.C. Court of Appeal).

138 *Attorney General v PHS Community Services Society*, [2011] SCC 44 (Supreme Court of Canada).

139 International Narcotics Control Board 2011 (n 94) para 289.

140 International Narcotics Control Board, 'Contribution of the INCB to the high-level review of the implementation by Member States of the Political Declaration and Plan of Action on International Cooperation towards an Integrated and Balanced Strategy to Counter the World Drug Problem' (2014) p 41, para 7.

141 The Board's inconsistent behaviour in this regard has been described as 'selective reticence' by some observers. See International Drug Policy Consortium, 'The International Narcotics Control Board: Current Tensions and Options for Reform', International Drug Policy Consortium Briefing Paper (February 2008).

for the obligation in question.[142] Article 3(1)(c) of the 1988 Convention, the subclause to which the Board is referring in its criticism, is expressly '[s]ubject to [the State's] constitutional principles and the basic concepts of its legal system'.[143]

The Board's public position is also at odds with its own internal legal advice on the matter. In 2002, and at the specific request of the Board, the Legal Affairs Section of the UN Drug Control Program (the forerunner of the Office on Drugs and Crime) produced a restricted opinion on the legal position of harm reduction approaches under the international drug conventions.[144] The conclusion of the Legal Affairs Section on the question of safe injecting facilities was that 'the intention of governments is to provide healthier conditions for IV drug abusers, thereby reducing their risk of infection with grave transmittable diseases and ... reaching out to them with counselling and other therapeutic options'.[145] The opinion concluded that '[i]t would be difficult to assert that, in establishing drug-injection rooms, it is the intent of Parties to actually *incite* or *induce* the illicit use of drugs, or even more so, to associate with, aid, abet or facilitate the *possession* of drugs', and therefore 'it would ... fall far from the intent of committing an offence as foreseen in the 1988 Convention'.[146] Given this legal opinion from within the UN drug control system itself, as well as the constitutional caveats within the convention noted above, the Board's criticism of Canada in this case appears less based on sound legal grounds, and more reflective of what Bewley-Taylor calls the Board's 'fears for the defence of the status quo regarding drug prohibition than any broader concerns for the "health and welfare of humankind" as laid out under the conventions'.[147]

4.6 Regime Conflicts

Although human rights violations resulting from regime tensions are perhaps the most obvious and widespread, there also exist examples of clear conflicts between explicit treaty obligations within the drug control and human rights conventions, situations where fulfilling the obligation

142 See, for example, 1988 Convention (see chapter 2 n 162) art 3.

143 Ibid art 3(1)(c). The Supreme Court of Canada's judgement in the Insite case will be examined in more detail in Chapter 8.

144 Legal Affairs Section, UN Drug Control Program, 'Flexibility of Treaty Provisions as Regards Harm Reduction Approaches' (20 September 2002) UN Doc No E/INCB/2002/W.13/SS.5.

145 Ibid para 28.

146 Ibid paras 27–28.

147 Bewley-Taylor, *International Drug Control* (see chapter 2 n 2) 230.

of one would necessarily cause a breach of the other. As explained by Jenks, '[a] conflict in the strict sense of direct incompatibility arises only where a party to the two treaties cannot simultaneously comply with its obligations under both treaties'.[148] While few in number, these instances are also important to highlight as they will create a separate yet significant interpretive challenge.

4.6.1 Traditional Uses of Coca

The cultivation and use of the coca leaf has been a part of traditional indigenous communities in the Andean region of South America for hundreds of years. Typically chewed or brewed into tea, coca acts as a mild stimulant, useful for suppressing hunger and fatigue, and overcoming the effects of living and working at high altitudes. Coca is also considered a sacred plant within some indigenous cultures in the region.[149] However, coca is also the plant that serves as the raw material from which cocaine is produced, and as such is considered among the 'plants containing narcotic or psychotropic substances',[150] subject to the strictest controls of the 1961 drug convention.[151] Article 49 of the convention recognises the existence of traditional coca use in some States at the time of the treaty's adoption and requires that '[c]oca leaf chewing must be abolished within twenty-five years from the coming into force of this Convention'.[152]

The obligation contained in Article 49 of the 1961 Convention is perhaps the clearest example of regime conflict between the drug control and human rights legal systems, as it has the effect of creating a State obligation to eradicate a traditional practice of cultural significance to indigenous peoples. In 2007, for example, the International Narcotics Control Board called upon Bolivia to 'initiate action without delay with a view to eliminating uses of coca, including coca leaf chewing'.[153] While the 1961 Convention obligates States to eradicate the practice, multiple human rights instruments – including the Universal Declaration of Human Rights,[154] the International Covenant on Civil and Political

148 Jenks (n 34) 426.

149 Tom Blickman, 'A beginner's guide to coca' (Transnational Institute 2011).

150 1988 Convention (see chapter 2 n 162) art 14(2).

151 1961 Convention amended (see chapter 2 n 171) schedule 1; See also, 1988 Convention (see chapter 2 n 162) art 3.

152 1961 Convention amended (see chapter 2 n 171) art 49(2)(e).

153 International Narcotics Control Board, 'Report of the International Narcotics Control Board for 2007' (2008) UN Doc No E/INCB/2007/1, p 108, rec 7.

154 Universal Declaration of Human Rights (see chapter 3 n 86) art 27.

Rights,[155] the International Covenant on Economic, Social and Cultural Rights,[156] the International Covenant on the Elimination of All forms of Racial Discrimination[157] and the United Nations Declaration on the Rights of Indigenous Peoples[158] – obligate States to protect the traditional cultural practices of indigenous peoples, creating a clear conflict of norms between the two regimes. The UN Permanent Forum on Indigenous Issues has called for 'those portions of the [1961 Single] Convention regarding coca leaf chewing that are inconsistent with the rights of indigenous peoples to maintain their traditional health and cultural practices... be amended or abolished'.[159] Furthermore, as has been pointed out by Barrett, '[t]he ban on both coca chewing as a cultural practice and cultivation as an economic activity rooted in cultural heritage was implemented... without consultation with indigenous communities', having the effect of undermining the principle of free prior and informed consent that is now widely accepted as a norm of international human rights law.[160]

This conflict has been brought into the open in recent years by Bolivia, where the country's first indigenous President, Evo Morales, made the criminalisation of this cultural practice by the drug conventions a national priority issue in UN drug control fora, noting that the ban is not only in conflict with the State's international human rights obligations but is also in violation of Bolivia's new constitution, ratified in 2009. After failing to achieve an amendment to the 1961 Convention in 2011,[161] the State took the unusual step of denouncing the treaty effective January 2012,[162] and re-acceding with a reservation on Article 49 twelve months later in

155 International Covenant on Civil and Political Rights (n 67) art 27.

156 International Covenant on Economic, Social and Cultural Rights (n 45) art 15.

157 UN Committee on the Elimination of All Forms of Racial Discrimination, 'General Recommendation XXIII' (18 August 1997) UN Doc No A/52/18, annex V, paras 4–5.

158 UN General Assembly, 'United Nations Declaration on the Rights of Indigenous Peoples' (2 October 2007) UN Doc No A/RES/61/295, art 31.

159 Permanent Forum on Indigenous Issues, 'Report of the Eighth Session of the UN Permanent Forum on Indigenous Issues' (18–19 May 2009) UN Doc No E/2009/42-EC/C.19/2009/14, para 89.

160 Damon Barrett, 'Backgrounder: Bolivia's concurrent drug control and other international legal commitments' (International Centre on Human Rights and Drug Policy 2011), p 2.

161 Permanent Mission of Bolivia to the United Nations, 'Single Convention on Narcotic Drugs, 1961, as amended by the Protocol amending the Single Convention on Narcotic Drugs, 1961: Proposal of Amendments by Bolivia to Article 49 paragraphs 1(c) and 2(e)' (12 March 2009) UN Doc No C.N.194.2009.TREATIES-2 (Depositary Notification).

162 Permanent Mission of Bolivia to the United Nations, 'Single Convention on Narcotic Drugs, 1961, as amended by the Protocol amending the Single Convention on Narcotic

January 2013.[163] Indeed, Bolivia already had a similar reservation to a similar article on traditional uses of coca in the 1988 drug convention.[164] Despite the objections of fifteen States Parties to this legal manoeuvre,[165] and the outrage of the International Narcotics Control Board, which said the reservation 'would undermine the integrity of the global drug control system',[166] the reservation stood and Bolivia again became a Party to the 1961 Convention.

4.6.2 *Application of 'More Severe Measures'*

Traditionally, the concept of conflict of norms has been limited only to consideration of those norms that create either positive obligations or negative prohibitions[167] – instances in which it is impossible for a State to 'simultaneously comply with . . . obligations under both treaties'.[168] The other two categories of norms – exempting/derogating norms and permissive norms – have not been considered within this context. However, Vranes argues that '[t]he problem with this strict definition is that it does not recognize that a permissive norm may conflict with an obligation or a prohibition'.[169] This point is of particular relevance to examining conflicts between drug control and human rights, as evidence of a conflict of obligations between the regimes is found in a permissive obligation common to all three drug treaties.

As was explored in Chapter 2, the UN drug regime requires the application of penal sanctions to the various categories of offences the treaties identify, as well as suggest a 'minimum level of measures to be taken by all

Drugs, 1961: Denunciation' (30 June 2011) UN Doc No C.N.421.2011.TREATIES-26 (Depositary Notification).

163 Permanent Mission of Bolivia to the United Nations, 'Single Convention on Narcotic Drugs, 1961, as amended by the Protocol amending the Single Convention on Narcotic Drugs, 1961: Accession' (22 January 2013) UN Doc No C.N.94.2013.TREATIES-VI.18 (Depositary Notification).

164 1988 Convention (see chapter 2 n 162) art 14(2).

165 Multilateral Treaties Deposited with the Secretary-General, United Nations, New York (ST/LEG/SER.E) https://treaties.un.org/Pages/ParticipationStatus.aspx accessed 17 February 2014.

166 International Narcotics Control Board, 'International Narcotics Control Board Regrets Bolivia's Denunciation of the Single Convention on Narcotic Drugs' (5 July 2011) UN Doc No UNIS/NAR/1114.

167 Erich Vranes, 'The Definition of "Norm Conflict" in International Law and Legal Theory' (2006) 17/2 The European Yearbook of International Law 395, 395.

168 Jenks (n 34) 426.

169 Vranes (n 167) 395–396.

parties' as sanctions for such offences.[170] However, each of the three drug conventions also contains a specific article permitting States Parties to adopt 'more strict or severe measures' than those required in the treaties themselves.[171] For example, under Article 24 of the 1988 Convention, '[a] Party may adopt more strict or severe measures than those provided by this Convention if, in its opinion, such measures are desirable or necessary for the prevention or suppression of illicit traffic'.[172]

According to the traditional perspective on conflict of laws described by Jenks, '[t]here is no conflict if the obligations of one instrument are stricter than, but not incompatible with, those of another, or if it is possible to comply with the obligations of one instrument by refraining from exercising a privilege or discretion accorded by another'.[173] However, in each of the three drug treaties, this article is enshrined without safeguards or limitations, in effect creating a permissive obligation that opens up scope for potential conflict with international human rights obligations. This conflict is perhaps most clear in the matter of penal sanctions for drug offences, and the licence it may appear to give to States to impose harsh punishments for drug offences that conflict with the protections the human rights treaties embody. For example, the Official Commentaries on both the 1961 and 1971 drug conventions[174] specifically cite the applications of the death penalty for drug offences as an example where States Parties might invoke this permissive obligations to implement 'more strict and severe' measures within domestic legislation. According to the Official Commentary on the 1961 Convention, '[p]ermissable substitute controls would be... the imposition of the death penalty in place of "imprisonment or other penalties of deprivation of liberty"'.[175] It is interesting that the human rights conflicts and tensions inherent in the regime may also be discerned even within the Official Commentary. Although the text suggests that 'substitute measures should clearly be "more strict and severe" to prevent any such doubts' about the legitimacy of the

[170] *Commentary on the United Nations Convention Against Illicit Traffic in Narcotic Drugs and Psychotropic Substances 1988* (see chapter 2 n 167) p 391, para 24.3.

[171] 1961 Convention amended (see chapter 2 n 171) art 39; 1971 Convention (see chapter 2 n 154) art 23; 1988 Convention (see chapter 2 n 162) art 24.

[172] 1988 Convention (see chapter 2 n 162) art 24.

[173] Jenks (n 34) 451.

[174] *Commentary on the Single Convention on Narcotic Drugs, 1961* (United Nations 1973) 448–449; *Commentary on the Convention on Psychotropic Substances* (United Nations 1976) 370.

[175] *Commentary on the Single Convention on Narcotic Drugs, 1961* (n 174) 448–449.

alternative sanction,[176] a cautionary footnote states that '[t]he reference to the "death penalty" . . . does not imply any position as to the admissibility of this penalty on moral or other legal grounds'.[177]

This conflict is not simply theoretical, and the article has been cited to defend human rights violations in the name of drug control by a State. In 2007, the Indonesian Constitutional Court heard a case challenging the death penalty for drug offences.[178] The Court invoked Article 24 of the 1988 Convention as legal justification for the Government to impose this penalty, despite its clear illegality under human rights law. According to the judgement,

> [I]f according to Indonesia, more severe measures are needed to prevent and eradicate such crimes, such measures are not contradictory to but rather are justified and suggested instead by the Convention. This means that Indonesia as a state party adopting the system of capital punishment against the certain Narcotics criminals has the right to determine capital punishment to the Narcotics criminals.[179]

Furthermore, the Court ruled that the 1988 drug convention held a higher status in law than did the UN human rights mechanisms' jurisprudence on the question of 'most serious crimes'.[180]

The human rights implications of this permissive obligation are not limited to penal provisions and can also be evident in its application to administrative procedures. For example, Russia has used Article 39 of 1961 Convention in its response to a series of cases before the European Court of Human Rights on the question of access to opioid substitution treatment (methadone and buprenorphine).[181] The plaintiffs argue that the absolute ban of these substances under domestic law violates the prohibition of torture (Article 3), the right to private and family life (Article 8) and the prohibition of discrimination (Article 14). Specifically citing Article 39 in defence of its 'most stringent controls' on these drugs, the government argues in documents submitted to the European Court that '[t]he prohibition of methadone and buprenorphine use of opioid

176 Ibid 448.

177 Ibid 449. A similar footnote is found in the Official Commentary on the 1971 Convention. *Commentary on the Convention on Psychotropic Substances* (n 174) 370.

178 *Edith Yunita Sianturi, Rani Andriani (Melisa Aprilia), Myuran Sukumaran, Andrew Chan, Scott Anthony Rush* [2007] 2–3/PUU-V/2007 IDCC 16.

179 Ibid p 103, para i.

180 Ibid para j.

181 *Kurmanayevskiy v Russia* App no 62964/10 (case pending 2016); *Abduysheva v Russia* App no 58502/11 (case pending 2016); *Anoshkin v Russia* App no 55683/13 (case pending 2016).

"substitution therapy" for drug addiction treatment is consistent with the international obligations of the Russian Federation'.[182]

These examples illustrate the limitations of the narrow construction of conflict of norms, at least when such conflicts are interpreted within a domestic high court, and underlines the value of calls for 'a broader definition of conflict in public international law'.[183] Vranes,[184] for example, supports Pauwelyn's more flexible approach, where two norms are 'in a relationship of conflict if one constitutes, has led to, or may lead to, a breach of the other'.[185] Using this more flexible definition, it is clear that the permissive norms enshrined in the drug treaties above are in conflict with international human rights law.

4.7 Conclusion

Chapter 4 set out to begin the exploration of the engagement between international human rights law on the one hand and international drug control law on the other. As is evident above, there are multiple examples of complementarities, tensions and conflicts between the regimes, in some cases resulting in drug control efforts creating increased human rights risk, or outright human rights violations. In the case of tensions and conflicts, the question then becomes how to resolve them, and determine an approach to interpreting the engagement between the legal regimes that ensures human rights abuses do not occur as the result of drug control activities. These questions will be explored in the subsequent chapters.

[182] Representative of the Russian Federation at the European Court of Human Rights, 'application no. 62964/10 *Kurmanayevskiy v Russia*, no. 58502/11 *Abduysheva v Russia*, no. 55683/13 *Anoshkin v Russia*: Observations of the Government of the Russian Federation in Respect to the Third-Parties' Submissions in the Above Cases' (2 March 2015) paras 4, 202.

[183] Vranes (n 167) 407. [184] Ibid. [185] Pauwelyn (see chapter 1 n 55) 175–176.

5

The Object and Purpose of the International Drug Control Regime

5.1 Introduction

The modern drug control regime is built upon more than a century of international treaty law, and its core norms and mechanisms predate not only the development of international human rights law, but the foundation of the United Nations itself. The core UN drug control instrument, the 1961 Single Convention on Narcotic Drugs, is itself more than half a century old. This has led some to question the relevance of the drug control regime in the context of twenty-first century challenges.[1] Even the United Nations Office on Drugs and Crime, a staunch defender of the drug control status quo, has identified the need 'to make the conventions fit for purpose and adapt them to a reality on the ground that is considerably different from the time they were drafted'.[2] At the same time, the growing recognition of human rights violations linked to drug laws, policies and enforcement practices – examples of which were explored in Chapter 4 – raises the further question of how States should reconcile their concurrent obligations under these two international legal regimes, and what is to be done when the regimes, or their implementation by States, come into conflict. How do these two treaty regimes engage with one another in cases of human rights violations linked to drug control or enforcement? How are real or apparent conflicts between drug control obligations on the one hand and human rights obligations on the other resolved in a manner in which a State maintains its adherence to both bodies of law? In international law terms, the challenge becomes how 'to redefine the meaning of a treaty without altering its nature [as] . . . . [i]n many cases the very survival of the agreement and its applicability to

[1] See, for example, David Bewley-Taylor and Martin Jelsma, 'Fifty Years of the 1961 Single Convention on Narcotic Drugs: A Reinterpretation' (Transnational Institute Series on Legislative Reform of Drug Policies Nr 12 2011).

[2] UN Commission on Narcotic Drugs, 'Fit for Purpose' (see chapter 1 n 21) 13.

present-day concerns are at stake'.[3] Chapter 5 will begin an exploration of the challenges of treaty interpretation within international drug control law. Using guidance provided within the Vienna Convention on the Law of Treaties, as well as other legal and historical sources, it will explore the object and purpose of the international drug control law regime, which will be critical to later questions of treaty interpretation and adjudication of regime conflicts.

5.2 Background to the Interpretation of Treaties

The process of interpretation of international treaties is one which has been characterised as 'occup[ying] a prime position on the crossroads between law and politics'.[4] This is certainly an appropriate characterisation of the context of treaty interpretation in international drug control law, a regime which, as explored in Chapter 3, has historically evolved through the interplay of two often conflicting paradigms, paradigms often complicated not only by questions of politics but also morality and religion.

General rules of treaty interpretation are found under Articles 31–33 of the Vienna Convention on the Law of Treaties[5] and are seen as providing authoritative guidance in these matters.[6] In particular, Articles 31 and 32 are generally agreed to reflect customary international law.[7] Article 31(1) of the Vienna Convention states that '[a] treaty shall be interpreted in good faith in accordance with the ordinary meaning to be given to the terms of the treaty in their context and in the light of its object and purpose'.[8] Therefore, a key initial challenge in any process of interpreting

[3] Pierre-Marie Dupuy, 'Evolutionary Interpretation of Treaties: Between Memory and Prophecy' in E. Cannizzaro (ed) *The Law of Treaties: Beyond the Vienna Convention* (Oxford University Press 2011) 110. Richard Gardiner, 'The Vienna Convention Rules on Treaty Interpretation' in D. B. Hollis (ed) *The Oxford Guide to Treaties* (Oxford University Press 2012) 125 (Vienna Convention Rules).

[4] Jean-Marc Sorel and Valerie Bore Eveno, 'Article 31: General Rule of Interpretation' in O. Corten and P. Klein (eds) *The Vienna Convention on the Law of Treaties: A Commentary, Vol. I* (Oxford University Press 2011) 807.

[5] Vienna Convention on the Law of Treaties (done at Vienna on 23 May 1969, entered into force on 27 January 1980) UNTS vol. 1155, p 331, arts 31–33 (Vienna Convention).

[6] See, for example, *Golder v United Kingdom* App no 4451/70 21 (ECtHR, 21 February 1975) paras 29–30 ;*Witold Litwa v Poland* App no no. 26629/95 (ECtHR, 4 April 2000) paras 57–64; *Johnston and Others v Ireland* (1986) Series A no 112, para 51; *Lithgow and Others v the United Kingdom* (1986) Series A no 102, paras 47–48.

[7] Fragmentation Report (see chapter 1 n 54) 215, para 427.

[8] Vienna Convention (n 5) art 31(1).

the international drug control conventions in the context of international human rights law is the identification of an 'object and purpose' test for the legal regime the drug conventions establish. Identifying the object and purpose is an essential element when considering broader questions of legal interpretation and is a key element in making an assessment of the 'ordinary meaning' that is to be given to treaty terms.[9] However, doing so is not a straightforward task for several reasons, both legal and political.

In legal terms, the first challenge is that a treaty's object and purpose is itself open to interpretation. Many scholars agree that the concept is somewhat adaptable in practice, if not also in intent, as this provides some flexibility in international relations and in international law.[10] As described by Klabbers, 'the notion of object and purpose cannot have a single fixed meaning: its precise meaning in any given context must be determined on a case by case basis, depending on the treaty concerned and the circumstance in which the notion is invoked'.[11] However, it would be incorrect to suggest, as have some commentators,[12] that because the object and purpose test is open to interpretation that it is irrelevant, or impossible to define, in the context of the drug conventions.

The second challenge is the nature of interpretation itself which, despite the rules articulated in the Vienna Convention, is very much a subjective process. As described by the International Law Commission in 1966, 'the interpretation of documents is to some extent an art, not an exact science'.[13] In discussing Articles 31 to 33 of the Vienna Convention, Gardiner notes that 'the difficult part of the art of treaty interpretation involves going beyond the rules themselves, that is the evaluation and judgement required in applying the rules to a particular treaty to produce an actual interpretation'.[14] Villiger further notes that 'the process of eliciting the different meanings – and in particular the "correct" meaning – from the terms of a treaty is altogether a creative process leaving room for extralegal

[9] Mark E. Villiger, 'The Rules on Interpretation: Misgivings, Misunderstandings, Miscarriage? The "Crucible" Intended by the International Law Commission' in E. Cannizzaro (ed) *The Law of Treaties: Beyond the Vienna Convention* (Oxford University Press 2011), 110 (Rules on Interpretation); Gardiner, 'Vienna Convention Rules' (n 3) 480–481.

[10] See, for example, Jan Klabbers, 'Some Problems Regarding the Object and Purpose of Treaties' (1997) 8 Finnish Yearbook of International Law 160.

[11] Ibid 141.

[12] Robin Room and Sarah MacKay, *Roadmaps to Reforming the UN Drug Conventions* (Beckley Foundation Press 2012) 21–22.

[13] International Law Commission, 'Yearbook of the International Law Commission, vol II' (1966) UN Doc No A/CN.4/SER.A/1966/Add.1, p 218, para 4 (Yearbook vol. II).

[14] Gardiner, 'Vienna Convention Rules' (n 3) 477.

considerations such as one's personal or cultural background'.[15] Gardiner concurs, noting that treaty interpretation is not a mechanical exercise, but one where 'the person giving meaning to the terms of a treaty introduces elements of subjectivity and creativity. Thus judgement is a necessary component of the process'.[16]

In political terms, a further complicating factor is that the international drug control regime is wedded in public consciousness, if not in domestic and international discourse and politics, to law enforcement, criminalisation and prohibition: the paradigm of drugs as 'evil' and 'threat' explored in Chapter 3. As a consequence, it is difficult to engage the question of the 'purpose' of drug control in a context other than one in which prohibition and criminalisation – the suppression of 'evil' – are presumed to be the *raison d'être* of the regime. Japan, for example, in a 2013 objection to a Bolivia's reservation on traditional uses of coca to the 1961 Convention, stated its opinion that the object and purpose of the treaty was 'to prevent the illicit production, manufacture and trafficking of cocaine'.[17] Bewley-Taylor writes that respecting the object and purpose of the drug treaties requires that States 'must adhere to the central prohibitive norm of the global drug control system'.[18] However, while the regime established under the conventions is clearly prohibitionist in nature,[19] the matter of the object and purpose of the treaties is a more nuanced discussion, and on that must be anchored the relevant interpretive sources.

Modern legal discourse on the question of the object and purpose of international treaties begins in 1951 with the Advisory Opinion on Reservations to the Genocide Convention by the International Court of Justice.[20] In that opinion, the Court's assessment of object and purpose derives primarily from its consideration of 'the objects pursued by the General Assembly and the contracting parties', based upon General Assembly resolutions, as well as by reference to the treaty preamble.[21] The European Court of Human Rights has also placed significance on the preambular section of a treaty, noting it 'is generally very useful for

[15] Villiger, 'Rules on Interpretation' (n 9) 106.
[16] Gardiner, 'Vienna Convention Rules' (n 3) 478.
[17] Permanent Mission of Japan to the United Nations, 'Japan: Objection to the Reservation contained in the in the communication by the Plurinational State of Bolivia' (15 January 2013) 1.
[18] Bewley-Taylor, *International Drug Control* (see chapter 2 n 2) 7.
[19] See generally Nadelmann (see chapter 2 n 4).
[20] International Court of Justice, 'Reservations to the Convention on the Prevention and Punishment of the Crime of Genocide: Advisory Opinion of May 28th, 1951'.
[21] Ibid 23. See also Klabbers (n 10) 156.

the determination of the "object" and "purpose" of the instrument to be construed'.[22]

As it is used within the context of international law, the phrase 'object and purpose' is considered a single term.[23] For example, the European Court of Human Rights takes an approach that under 'the general rule of interpretation laid down in Article 31 [of the Vienna Convention] . . . the process of discovering and ascertaining the true meaning of the terms of the treaty is a unity, a single combined operation'.[24] However, this single term can be considered to refer to two separate concepts. The first of these could be described as utilitarian, that is, the normative content of the treaty, or the rights and obligations to which it gives expression.[25] The second is what might be described as the ultimate aim(s) or goal(s) of the treaty, sometimes called the *telos* of the treaty. As described by Linderfalk,

> When two or more states enter into a treaty relation with each other, concluding the treaty usually is not seen as an end in itself. Of course, ensuring respect for the various provisions laid down in the treaty text is considered important. But above and beyond that it is most often a wish of the parties that some further state-of-affairs (or states-of-affairs) be attained – the telos (or teloi) of the treaty. From an extremist viewpoint it could be argued that fulfilling this wish is what the treaty is all about; if a treaty is applied without its telos (or teloi) being attained, then the conclusion of the treaty may indeed be considered in vain.[26]

Although separate concepts, they are in fact integrally related, in the sense that it is through the implementation of the obligations created by the treaty that States seek to fulfil or achieve its broader aim(s) or goal(s). Article 31 of the Vienna Convention allows for such an approach. According to Villiger, 'Article 31 . . . entrenches the teleological or functional approach. It enables consideration of the different aims of particular types of treaties'.[27] Some scholars draw from the French origins of the concept of object and purpose, '*objet et but*', and elaborate 'a distinction between "*l'objet*" of a legal act or instrument, that is what it does in the sense of creating a particular set of rights and obligations, and "*le but*" as

[22] *Golder v United Kingdom* (n 6) para 34. [23] See Klabbers (n 10) 148.

[24] *Witold Litwa v Poland* (n 6) para 58. See also *Golder v United Kingdom* (n 6) para 30.

[25] Ulf Linderfalk, On the Meaning of the 'Object and Purpose' Criterion, in the Context of the Vienna Convention on the Law of Treaties, Article 19' (2003) 72 Nordic Journal of International Law 429, 433–434.

[26] Ibid 443. See also Ulf Linderfalk, *On the Interpretation of Treaties: The Modern International Law as Expressed in the 1969 Vienna Convention on the Law of Treaties* (Springer 2007) 209.

[27] Mark E. Villiger, *Commentary on the 1969 Vienna Convention on the Law of Treaties* (Martinus Nijhoff 2009) 427.

the reason for establishing *"l'objet"*'.[28] Buffard and Zemanek, for example, note that it is 'a stream of French doctrine which gives special attention to the distinction between object and purpose of a treaty', while 'most scholars in the German, Austrian and English tradition treat "object and purpose" of a treaty as a joint notion'.[29]

> According to this French doctrine the term 'object' indicates thus the substantial content of the norm, the provisions, rights and obligations created by the norm. The object of a treaty is the instrument for the achievement of the treaty's purpose, and this purpose is, in turn, the general result which the parties want to achieve by the treaty. While the object can be found in the provisions of the treaty, the purpose may not always be explicit and be prone to a more subjective understanding.[30]

Similarly, Zoller suggests that the object and purpose describe separate concepts, the first being related to a treaty's more immediate goal(s) and the second reflecting the treaty's long term goal(s).[31]

An interesting example of this approach is found in the text of the 2013 Arms Trade Treaty.[32] Article 1 of the Treaty, which is entitled 'Object and Purpose', separates this concept into two distinct components. The first part of Article 1 defines the treaty's functional 'object' of establishing high international standards for regulating trade in conventional arms while preventing their diversion into illicit trade markets. This 'object' is described as intended to achieve the treaty's more aspirational 'purpose', defined in the second part of Article 1 as 'contributing to international and regional peace, security and stability' and to 'reducing human suffering'.[33] As will be explored below, the approach reflected in the Arms Trade Treaty has particular resonance when considering the object and purpose of the drug control regime.

5.3 The Object and Purpose of the International Drug Control Regime

As mentioned above, given the strongly prohibitionist legal regime established under the international drug control treaties, many would likely consider the question of the object and purpose of the conventions to be

[28] Gardiner, *Treaty Interpretation* (see chapter 1 n 55) 192.
[29] Isabelle Buffard and Karl Zemanek, 'The "Object and Purpose" of a Treaty: An Enigma?' (1998) 3 Austrian Review of International and European Law 311, 325.
[30] Ibid 326. Also cited in Gardiner, *Treaty Interpretation* (see chapter 1 n 55) 192.
[31] Elizabeth Zoller, *La bonnefoi en droit international public* (1977) 74. Cited in Klabbers (n 10) 144–145.
[32] Arms Trade Treaty (2 April 2013) UN Doc No A/RES/67/234B.
[33] Ibid art 1.

a simple one: the prohibition of illicit drugs (cultivation, manufacture, trafficking, sale, use). However, the development of the regime suggests otherwise, or at least something broader. Although the legal framework established by the drug treaties is clearly prohibitionist in both design and effect, this is a separate question to what that particular system of control is actually *intended to achieve.* Indeed, establishing the *intended outcome* of the drug control regime is critical to determining its object and purpose. A mere scrutiny of the structures and mechanisms of control is insufficient. As stated in 1943 by the Chief of the Drug Control Service of the Secretariat of the League of Nations, Bertil Renborg, activities to limit, supervise and regulate the availability of drugs were not the 'main object' of the regime, but rather the 'principal methods used' towards achieving its goal.[34] This in many ways reflects the approach enshrined in the Arms Trade Treaty, where the structures of weapons regulation and control it establishes do not define the broader aspirations of the treaty, but rather are intended to contribute to achieving them. If the structures of control established in the drug control treaties are simply the methods to be used to achieve the goal of the regime, this suggests that testing the object and purpose must move beyond a focus on these control structures and mechanisms alone, and explore both the immediate or utilitarian object and purpose of the regime, as well as the *telos*, to identify what these structures are intended to achieve.

Following this approach, the object and purpose of the drug conventions will be considered to be a single term embodying two separate concepts, the first being immediate or utilitarian object and purpose of the treaty, and second being the ultimate goals or *telos* of the treaty, the state of affairs the treaty hopes to achieve. Three primary sources will be used to explore these concepts in the context of drug control, in order to construct what Thirlway calls the 'scaffolding for the reasoning on questions of treaty interpretation'.[35] The first two elements of this scaffolding are the text and preambles of the three United Nations drug treaties, and the preparatory work and drafting histories of those conventions. However, this analysis will augment those two sources with a third historical

[34] Renborg, 'Principles of International Control of Narcotics' (see chapter 2 n 39) 436; Writing in 1957, Renborg reiterated this point. 'To achieve [its] objectives, the international narcotic drug instruments not only prescribe rules in the international field, but also define the measures of control to be maintained within each country.' Renborg, 'International Control of Narcotics' (chapter 2 n 3) 87.

[35] Hugh Thirlway, 'The Law and Procedure of the International Court of Justice 1960–1989, Supplement 2006: Part Three' (2006) 77 British Yearbook of International Law 1, 19.

legal source: the multilateral instruments on drug control that existed before the foundation of the United Nations in 1946. Given that the original intention of the 1961 Single Convention on Narcotic Drugs was to bring together the normative content of the preceding fifty years of international treaty law into one 'single' treaty,[36] the text and preambles of these earlier instruments will also be examined as an important historical legal source contributing to an understanding of the object and purpose of the modern international drug control regime.

5.3.1 *Utilitarian Object and Purpose: 'Medical and Scientific Purposes'*

Perhaps the most immediate entry point for consideration of object and purpose of any treaty is its title. As described by Klabbers, in some cases consideration of a treaty's name can in fact be a very valuable element in this determination.

> [W]hile one of the objectives of the Chemical Weapons Convention, as listed in its preamble, is the desire to 'promote free trade in chemicals as well as international cooperation and exchange of scientific and technical information... in order to enhance the economic and technological development of all States parties', it can hardly be maintained that this particular objective should qualify as the object and purpose of a treaty bearing the title Convention on the Prohibition of the Development, Production, Stockpiling and Use of Chemical Weapons and on their Destruction. Of course, the title of a treaty will only offer a presumption regarding the treaty's object and purpose, which will have to be substantiated by closer analysis of other factors, but it does not appear to be a presumption which will often be rebutted in practice. And where it will be rebutted, the treaty has been seriously misnamed.[37]

However, as an interpretive source, there is little obvious direction provided in this regard from the drug conventions. While the drafters' intent can be presumed from the titles of such instruments as the Convention on

[36] The Single Convention was intended to replace the following agreements: International Opium Convention 23 Jan 1912 and subsequent protocols; Opium Agreement and Protocol and Final 11 Feb 1925; Convention, Protocol and Final Act 19 Feb 1925 and later protocol; Convention for Limiting the Manufacture and Regulating the Distribution of Narcotic Drugs 13 July 1931; Opium Agreement and Final Act 27 Nov 1931; Convention for the Suppression of Illicit Traffic in Dangerous Drugs 26 June 1936; Protocol to bring under international control drugs outside the scope of the 1932 convention.

[37] Klabbers (n 10) 158.

the Prevention and Punishment of the Crime of Genocide or the Convention on the Prohibition of the Development, Production, Stockpiling and Use of Chemical Weapons and their Destruction, the relatively innocuous titles of Single Convention on Narcotic Drugs and the Convention on Psychotropic Substances offer little in the way of interpretive guidance, other than identifying the subject matter they address. This is less so in the case of the 1988 Convention Against Illicit Traffic in Narcotic Drugs and Psychotropic Substances, where working to prevent or suppress illicit traffic is clearly suggested in the title. However, given the title of the 1988 Convention, it is of note that the titles of the previous two treaties are not the Convention *Against* Narcotic Drugs or the Convention *Against* Psychotropic Substances. This would suggest that while the object and purpose of the 1988 treaty may well involve preventing or prohibiting an activity, that of the 1961 and 1971 Conventions are broader, different or at least more nuanced and open to interpretation. While the treaty titles themselves provide little guidance, a review of the other sources of interpretation lead to a conclusion that the immediate or utilitarian object and purpose of regime is to limit the production and use of controlled substances solely to 'medical and scientific purposes'.

Within the United Nations instruments on drug control, the concept of restricting drugs to medical and scientific purposes enters into use from a very early date, well before the adoption of the 1961 Single Convention. It first appears in the preamble to the 1948 Protocol Bringing under International Control Drugs Outside the Scope of the Convention of 13 July 1931 for Limiting the Manufacture and Regulating the Distribution of Narcotic Drugs,[38] the second ever instrument on drug control adopted by the UN General Assembly.[39] Paragraph two of the preamble states

> *Desiring* to supplement the provisions of the [1931] Convention and to place these drugs, including the preparations and compounds containing these drugs under control in order to limit by international agreement their manufacture to the world's legitimate requirements for medical and scientific purposes and to regulate their distribution.[40]

[38] 'Protocol Bringing under International Control Drugs Outside the Scope of the Convention of 13 July 1931 for Limiting the Manufacture and Regulating the Distribution of Narcotic Drugs, as amended by the Protocol signed at Lake Success, New York, on 11 December 1946' (19 November 1948, entry into force 1 December 1949) UNTS vol. 44, 277 (1948 Protocol).

[39] UN General Assembly, 'International provision for the control of certain drugs' (8 October 1948) UN Doc No A/RES/211(III).

[40] 1948 Protocol (n 38) preamble.

Here the protocol clearly indicates that the object is to control drugs only for 'legitimate' purposes, with those purposes being defined as 'medical and scientific'. Article 1 of the protocol also uses the term medical and scientific purposes to describe the drugs of relevance to the instrument.[41] The protocol itself is updating the obligations found within the 1931 Convention for Limiting the Manufacture and Regulating the Distribution of Narcotic Drugs, a treaty that is clearly intended to limit drugs to medical and scientific uses, an objective repeated throughout the instrument. Various provisions in the treaty refer to 'medical and scientific requirements' (Article 4), 'medical and scientific needs' (Articles 5, 6, 10, 11), 'medical or scientific purposes' (Article 11), 'medical or scientific value' (Article 11) and 'medical or scientific use' (Article 18). Therefore, both the protocol and its link to the 1931 Convention clearly bring this concept of controlling drugs for medical and scientific purposes firmly within the UN regime.

The concept of limiting drugs to medical and scientific purposes becomes increasingly visible as the UN drug treaty regime evolves. For example, the preamble of the 1961 Convention expresses the '[d]esir[e] to conclude a generally acceptable international convention replacing existing treaties on narcotic drugs, limiting such drugs to medical and scientific use, and providing for continuous international co-operation and control for the achievement of such aims and objectives'.[42] Significantly, this preambular statement explicitly characterises 'limiting such drugs to medical and scientific use' among the 'aims and objectives' of the treaty provisions. The treaty's General Obligations articulated at Article 4 state that '[t]he parties shall take such legislative and administrative measures as may be necessary . . . to the provisions of this Convention, to limit exclusively to medical and scientific purposes the production, manufacture, export, import, distribution of, trade in, use and possession of drugs'.[43] Similarly, the 1971 Convention notes in its preambular section 'that rigorous measures are necessary to restrict the use of such substances to legitimate purposes' and further '[r]ecogniz[es] that the use of psychotropic substances for medical and scientific purposes is indispensable and that their availability for such purposes should not be unduly restricted'.[44] The convention also includes a specific provision (Article 5) entitled 'Limitation of Use to Medical and Scientific Purposes', which applies varying degrees of control to all substances scheduled under the

[41] Ibid art 1. [42] 1961 Convention amended (see chapter 2 n 171) preamble.
[43] Ibid art 4(c). [44] 1971 Convention (chapter 2 n 154) preamble.

treaty.[45] In addition to the use of the specific phrase within the texts of the 1961 and 1971 Conventions, the centrality of the desire to limit the use of drugs to medical and scientific purposes is evident in the mechanisms of control the treaties establish. Of particular significance is the scheduling system established under the conventions, essentially the lists of substances placed under international control, and therefore the subjects of the controls created in international drug control law. In both the 1961 and 1971 treaties, the drugs listed in the schedules, and the level of control placed upon each, is explicitly linked to health risks,[46] in particular the likelihood of 'abuse' or of producing 'ill effects'.[47] In both treaties, changes to the substances included in the scheduling list are made with reference to recommendations of the World Health Organization, based upon its assessment of the relative health risks of the drug in question.[48] This background is significant when considering the text of the 1988 Convention, which does not refer to medical and scientific purposes but rather to 'licit' and 'illicit' traffic and use. However, the 1988 Convention defers to the two previous treaties for its definitions of both 'narcotic drugs'[49] and 'psychotropic substances'.[50] Similarly, the 1988 Convention's primary operative provision, Article 3, which sets out the scope of 'Offences and Sanctions' required of States Parties for various offences, also cites the 1961 and 1971 Conventions as the sources of law for interpreting these provisions.[51] Therefore, despite the lack of specific language on medical and scientific purposes within the 1988 treaty, its references to the previous two conventions clearly suggest such an approach also encompass consideration of its provisions.

The overriding objective of States to limit drugs to medical and scientific purposes is evident in the drafting histories of the three conventions. During the plenipotentiary conference that concluded the text of the 1961 Convention, for example, numerous delegations made reference to this objective. China commented that '[s]teady progress had been made towards the goal of limiting the use of narcotic drugs to medical and scientific purposes'.[52] The USSR described that '[c]areful supervision

45 Ibid art 5.
46 See generally, 1961 Convention amended (see chapter 2 n 171) arts 2, 3; 1971 Convention (see chapter 2 n 154) art 2.
47 1961 Convention amended (see chapter 2 n 171) arts 2(9)(a), 3(3)(iii); 1971 Convention (see chapter 2 n 154) art 2(4)(a)(ii).
48 1961 Convention amended (see chapter 2 n 171) art 3; 1971 Convention (see chapter 2 n 154) art 2.
49 1988 Convention (see chapter 2 n 162) art 1(n).
50 Ibid art 1(r).
51 Ibid art 3(1)(a).
52 1961 Official Records vol. I (see chapter 2 n 206) 13.

was also necessary to ensure that the drugs were used for medical and scientific purposes only', and that '[t]he success of international narcotics control depended entirely upon strict national control measures' to achieve this aim.[53] However, in using the *travaux preparatoires* as an interpretative source, statements made by individual parties are of little value on their own. What is much more significant is where the *travaux* document a 'common understanding' among States of the significance of a particular term.[54] One example of this is apparent when the plenipotentiary conference, in finalising the treaty text, took the step to move the commitment 'to limit exclusively to medical and scientific purposes the production, manufacture, export, import, distribution of, trade in, use and possession of drugs' from its original place as a basic treaty provision in draft Article 30 to a General Obligation of all States Parties in Article 4 of the final convention.[55] Even during the drafting conference of the 1988 Convention, the only UN drug treaty not to explicitly reference medical and scientific purposes in the text, the delegates discussed that the objective of 'the international drug control regime based on existing Conventions . . . was to limit the use of narcotic drugs and psychotropic substances to medical and scientific purposes'.[56]

The objective of limiting the availability of controlled drugs to medical and scientific uses is not a modern concept. It dates back to the very dawn of the international regime and has been central to the regime for a hundred years,[57] providing further support for this concept as the object and purpose of the UN regime that emerged from the League of Nations system. The term is found in Article 9 of the 1912 Opium Convention, which not only created controls to suppress opium use but also speaks of the need 'to confine to medical and legitimate purposes the manufacture, sale, and use of morphine, cocaine and their respective salts'.[58] It is

[53] 1961 Official Records vol. II (see chapter 3 n 40) 9.

[54] Humphrey Waldcock, 'Third Report on the Law of Treaties' (1964) Yearbook of the International Law Commission, vol. II, 58, Gardiner, 'Vienna Convention Rules' (n 3) 488.

[55] 1961 Official Records vol. II (see chapter 3 n 40) 11.

[56] United Nations Conference for the Adoption of a Convention against Illicit Traffic in Narcotic Drugs and Psychotropic Substances, Official Records: Vol. I (25 November–20 December 1988) UN Doc. No. E/CONF.82/16/Add.l, p 60, para 40.

[57] Collins explores in some detail the diplomatic context of the debates behind the enshrining of 'medical and scientific' purposes into the League of Nations drug treaties, and subsequently the 1961 Single Convention on Narcotic Drugs. See generally, Collins (see chapter 1 n 5).

[58] 1912 Convention (see chapter 1 n 51) art 9. For a review of early debates in the League of Nations regarding the interpretation of 'medical and scientific' uses in the 1912 Hague Convention, see Wright, 'The Opium Question' (see chapter 1 n 1).

also found under Article 5 of the1925 International Opium Convention, which obligates States Parties to 'enact effective laws or regulations to limit exclusively to medical and scientific purposes the manufacture, import, sale, distribution, export and use of the substances to which this Chapter applies'.[59] Significantly, in the 1931 Convention for Limiting the Manufacture and Regulating the Distribution of Narcotic Drugs, this concept is found in the preamble, and notes the 'desir[e] to . . . rende[r] by effective international agreement the limitation of the manufacture of narcotic drugs to the world's legitimate requirements for medical and scientific purposes'.[60] This treaty was drafted at the Conference on the Limitation of the Manufacture of Narcotic Drugs, the official proceedings of which state that '[t]he object of the Conference is to embody in an international Convention a practicable scheme whereby the manufacture of narcotic drugs may be limited to the medical and scientific needs of the world'.[61]

An unusual source providing further support for this conclusion is a 1933 memorandum prepared by the Secretary-General of the League of Nations for consideration during the Conference on the Reduction and Limitation of Armaments. Entitled 'Analogies between the Problem of the Traffic in Narcotic Drugs and that of the Trade in and Manufacture of Arms',[62] the document was prepared at the request of the Spanish delegation to determine what 'results obtained in the supervision of the manufacture of and traffic in opium . . . might be material for the supervision of the manufacture of and trade in arms'.[63] The memorandum begins by comparing and contrasting the aims of the two international regimes, so that similarities and differences in the international control regimes might be discerned. In the case of the international drug control system, the memorandum states that:

> As regards narcotics, the aim pursued by regulation is always the same – namely, to prohibit substances not required for medical or scientific purposes and which would only serve to foster drug addiction, and, above all, to prevent certain substances capable of being used both for medical and scientific purposes and for addiction from being employed for the latter purpose.[64]

[59] 1925 Convention (see chapter 1 n 19). art 5.

[60] 1931 Convention (see chapter 1 n 19) preamble.

[61] League of Nations, 'Conference on the Limitation of the Manufacture of Narcotic Drugs', Information Secretariat, League of Nations, 1932, 3.

[62] League of Nations, 'Conference on the Reduction and Limitation of Armaments: Analogies between the Problem of the Traffic in Narcotic Drugs and that of the Trade in and Manufacture of Arms' (4 May 1933) Official No Conf D, 1959.

[63] Ibid 2. [64] Ibid.

This clearly indicates that the systems and structures of narcotics control created in the treaty, and codified in its articles, are merely the functional machinery put in place to achieve greater goals. It also raises the question of whether this same case can be made for subsequent League of Nations, and even United Nations, drug treaties.

This conclusion also finds support among more modern sources. For example, the governments of Italy,[65] the Netherlands[66] and Ireland[67] have all expressed the position that the object and purpose of the 1961 Convention is to limit the use of drugs to medical and scientific purposes. Neil Boister, one of the few international legal scholars who has done detailed critical analysis of the drug conventions, states that 'the international multilateral conventions were established by the international community with the aim of preventing the non-scientific and non-medical production, supply and use of drugs while at the same time making them available for medical and scientific purposes'.[68] Renborg also states his opinion that

> The objectives of international control can be stated very simply: to prevent the abuse of narcotic drugs, while assuring their continued availability for medical and scientific purposes. To achieve these objectives, the international narcotic drug instruments not only prescribe rules in the international field, but also define the measures of control to be maintained within each country.[69]

Clearly in Renborg's estimation, the mechanisms of control are tools to advance the broader objectives of the regime. Therefore, the relevant legal and historical sources support a conclusion that the utilitarian object and purpose of the drug control regime is to limit controlled substances to medical and scientific purposes. The next question then becomes what broader purpose does this aspire to achieve?

[65] Permanent Mission of Italy to the United Nations, 'Italy: Objection to the Reservation contained in the communication by the Plurinational State of Bolivia' (28 December 2012) UN Doc No C.N.101.2013.TREATIES-VI.18 (Depository Notifications), 1.

[66] Permanent Mission of the Kingdom of the Netherlands to the United Nations, 'Netherlands: Objection to the Reservation contained in the communication by the Plurinational State of Bolivia' (8 January 2013) UN Doc No C.N.101.2013.TREATIES-VI.18 (Depository Notifications), 1.

[67] Permanent Mission of Ireland to the United Nations, 'Ireland: Objection to the Reservation contained in the in the communication by the Plurinational State of Bolivia' (9 January 2013) UN Doc No C.N.101.2013.TREATIES-VI.18 (Depository Notifications), 1.

[68] Boister, *Penal Aspects* (see chapter 1 n 57) 1.

[69] Renborg, 'International Control of Narcotics' (see chapter 2 n 3) 88.

5.3.2 Telos – *To Promote the Health and Welfare of Mankind*

If the immediate object and purpose of the international drug control regime is to limit the production and use of controlled substances solely to medical and scientific purposes, this objective is pursued in order to achieve a broader goal, which is to promote 'the health and welfare of mankind'. This represents the *telos* of the regime, the state of affairs that is hoped to be achieved by the treaty, and is one explicitly expressed in the preambles of all three UN drug control treaties. It is also a concept that finds its roots in the pre-United Nations instruments.

As detailed in Chapter 3, international legal instruments on drug control have articulated a core humanitarian mission since the foundation of the regime in the early 1900s, contextualising mechanisms and activities to control and suppress drugs as part of a campaign to achieve a grander goal. Under the League of Nations regime, this mission was not simply rhetorical but was also reflected in the law itself. An interesting provision of the 1931 Convention Limiting the Manufacture and Regulating the Distribution of Narcotic Drugs enshrined a legitimate humanitarian limitation on the treaty's otherwise strict controls over the export of controlled drugs from one country to another. The provisions of the 1931 Convention establish mechanisms through which States could estimate their legitimate need for controlled substances, as well as guidelines for monitoring imports and exports to ensure they did not exceed those approved levels. Article 14 established a notification system and consequences for States whose exports 'to any country or territory exceeds the total of the estimates for that country or territory'.[70] However, a subclause within Article 14 suspended these punitive consequences '[i]n exceptional cases where the export in the opinion of the Government of the exporting country is essential in the interests of humanity or for the treatment of the sick'.[71] This provision had the effect of establishing a derogation from other treaty obligations.

The concept of derogation clauses that 'provide legal avenues for states to break free of obligations that would normally constrain their actions' is one common in international human rights treaties.[72] In effect, the subclause in the 1931 Convention allowed a derogation to other provisions of the treaties, providing States the legal basis to avoid the punitive sanctions the convention otherwise imposed. What makes this particular derogation significant is that it is a human rights-based derogation,

70 1931 Convention (see chapter 1 n 19) art 14(2). 71 Ibid art 14(2)(ii).

72 Henry J. Steiner, Philip Alston and Ryan Goodman, *International Human Rights in Context: Law, Politics, Morals* (3rd ed, Oxford University Press 2008) 385.

allowing the State to opt out of other drug control obligations on the basis of humanitarian or medical reasons.

Interestingly, it enshrined a perspective almost exactly the *opposite* of that found in the modern human rights regime. Within many international rights treaties, States may derogate from particular human rights obligations on the basis of public emergencies, most typically being linked to public security.[73] Unusually, the 1931 drug treaty, the provisions of which might arguably fall within the realm of public security, allowed a derogation in order to respond to human rights or humanitarian emergencies. This derogation also links to Article 5, the main operative provision in the treaty. In this specific case, the operational aspects of drug control are made secondary to broader human rights demands.

A similar provision is included in the 1961 Convention in Article 21 on 'Limitation on Export and Manufacture'.[74] Under subclause 4, the national limitations on both domestic manufacture or import/export, as set by the International Narcotics Control Board under the estimates system, may be ignored without penalty '[i]n exceptional cases where the export, in the opinion of the Government of the exporting country, is essential for the treatment of the sick'.[75] According to the Official Commentary, this principle was incorporated into the Single Convention directly from Article 14 of the 1931 Convention, and under its provision a State Party

> is authorized not to carry out the Board's decision to discontinue exports of drugs to the country or territory in question in exceptional cases where the export is, in its opinion, essential for the treatment of the sick. As long as a Party makes use of this authority in good faith its opinion about the need of the drugs for the treatment of the sick cannot be questioned.[76]

These derogation clauses in effect allows States to evade a central operative function of the treaty – to establish a system of estimates to regulate imports and exports – in circumstances where obeying those provisions would undermine humanitarian or medical responses. These clauses in the 1931 and 1961 treaties provide additional normative support for the proposal that humanitarian objectives form the core aims of the regime, rather than strictly drug control, as in this instance humanitarian and

[73] See, for example, International Covenant on Civil and Political Rights (see chapter 4 n 67) art 4(1); Convention for the Protection of Human Rights and Fundamental Freedoms (European Convention on Human Rights, as amended) (ECHR) art 15(1).

[74] 1961 Convention amended (see chapter 2 n 171) art 21.

[75] Ibid art 21(4)(b)(ii).

[76] *Commentary on the Single Convention on Narcotic Drugs, 1961* (see chapter 4 n 174) 273, para 13.

medical needs legally trump key measures of drug control established by the treaties.

The humanitarian ethos expressed in the League of Nations treaties also finds its way into the core United Nations drug control instruments, and is conceptualised in both the 1961 and 1971 Conventions as a mission to promote 'the health and welfare of mankind'. As described earlier, the preambular section of the Single Convention on Narcotic Drugs begins

> *The Parties,*
>
> *Concerned with the health and welfare of mankind,*
>
> *Recognizing that the medical use of narcotic drugs continues to be indispensable for the relief of pain and suffering and that adequate provision must be made to ensure the availability of narcotic drugs for such purposes,*[77]

This opening statement on 'the health and welfare of mankind' is significant, suggesting that the treaty and its provisions are intended to advance broader health and humanitarian objectives. Furthermore, the preamble appears to link the utilitarian object and purpose of limiting the use of drugs for medical and scientific purposes with the achievement of this broader humanitarian aim. Indeed, the '[d]esir[e] to conclude a generally acceptable international convention replacing existing treaties on narcotic drugs, limiting such drugs to medical and scientific use' expressed in the preamble comes only at the end of the section, also suggesting that this is an operational objective intended as a mechanism to realise the larger goals of drug control.[78]

It is useful in this regard to consider the contributions of various Member States to the drafting of the 1961 Convention, during which the humanitarian objectives of the treaty were regularly cited. Iran, for example, stated that 'drug addiction was like a contagious disease: no country could be certain that it would be spared'. However, the delegate continued with 'when a country like Iran at great cost prohibited the cultivation of the poppy to abolish that evil, it was in fact eliminating a source of danger to the health of the whole world and benefiting all mankind'.[79] Iran is therefore stating that the purpose of prohibiting poppy cultivation is to promote health and 'benefit all mankind'. In other words, the prohibition itself is not an end, but a means. Similarly, the United Arab Republic stated that '[e]very country was under a moral obligation to make the Convention an effective instrument serving the interests of

[77] 1961 Convention amended (see chapter 2 n 171) preamble.
[78] Ibid. [79] 1961 Official Records vol. I (see chapter 2 n 206) 6.

the entire world. On behalf of mankind, therefore, his delegation urged all States to give it their full and whole-hearted support'.[80] A particularly detailed exposition of this overarching humanitarian vision was evident in comments made by the Holy See.

> [T]he Conference was to be congratulated on having drafted a convention which represented a substantial step forward in the moral and social welfare of mankind. His delegation attached great importance to the Convention, which would have a direct influence on the preservation of human dignity and contribute to the full development of the human personality. At the same time, the Convention recognized the fundamental necessity of providing for the rational use of drugs for medical and scientific purposes. In addition to its social, economic and legal content, the Convention had a moral aspect. The Holy See, which had always been concerned with the welfare of mankind and of civilization, was therefore happy to lend its moral support to the humanitarian aims of the Conference.[81]

Just as this broader concern for the well-being of humanity did not start with the Single Convention, it also did not end there. The preamble to the 1971 Convention reaffirms the concern for the health and welfare of mankind, while also linking the *telos* to the more immediate object and purpose by '[n]oting with concern the public health and social problems resulting from the abuse of certain psychotropic substances'.[82] The preamble of 1988 Convention modifies this common language to some extent, but still notes that the States are '[d]eeply concerned' at the 'serious threat to the health and welfare of human beings' posed by drugs.[83]

5.4 Conclusion

Based on the textual and historical analysis above, it is evident that an object and purpose test is not only possible in the context of the international drug control regime, but that such a test clearly reveals both a utilitarian object and purpose, and a larger more aspirational goal of the treaties. Having identified these two layers, the next question becomes what is the significance of this object and purpose test for the broader question of interpretation, and in particular interpretation of the drug conventions in a human rights context? These questions will be explored in Chapter 6.

80 Ibid. 81 Ibid 216.
82 1971 Convention (see chapter 2 n 154) preamble.
83 1988 Convention (see chapter 2 n 162) preamble.

6

The Case for Dynamic Interpretation of the International Drug Control Conventions

> All treaty provisions receive their force and validity from general law, and set up rights and obligations that exist alongside rights and obligations established by other treaty provisions and rules of customary international law. None of such rights or obligations has any intrinsic priority against the others. The question of their relationship can only be approached through a process of reasoning that makes them appear as parts of some coherent and meaningful whole.[1]
>
> Report of the Study Group of the International Law Commission

6.1 Introduction

As explored in Chapter 5, the utilitarian or immediate object and purpose of international drug control law is to limit controlled substances to medical and scientific purposes. This, in turn, is intended to pursue the larger overarching goal, or *telos*, of the regime, to promote the health and welfare of mankind. The systems of administrative and penal control that characterise the international drug control regime are therefore designed to pursue the object and purpose, or, as described by Renborg, are the 'principal methods used' to achieve the goal of the regime.[2] What then are the implications for treaty interpretation when these administrative or penal mechanisms of drug control engage, or even violate, obligations under international human rights law? How are the competing yet concurrent obligations under the two regimes to be balanced, and potential conflicts interpreted and resolved, in a manner that maintains the integrity of both legal systems, while not violating human rights protections? This chapter will begin to explore this question by examining the application of a human rights-based interpretation of international drug control law.

There are generally considered to be three main approaches to treaty interpretation: an 'objective' approach, which focusses on the treaty text

[1] Fragmentation Report (see chapter 1 n 54) p 208, para 414.

[2] Renborg, 'Principles of International Control of Narcotics' (see chapter 2 n 39) 436.

as an 'authentic expression' of the drafters' intentions; a 'subjective' approach, which focusses on an assessment of the original intentions of the drafters, as a separate element from the text; and a 'teleological' approach, which interprets a treaty's obligations in light of its object and purpose.[3] A teleological approach, which is often described as 'dynamic' or 'evolutive' interpretation,[4] is well established in international human rights law.[5] However, as described by the International Law Commission in 2006, it is an approach 'much more deeply embedded in human rights law than in general international law',[6] suggesting that its application in the context of international drug control law must be considered cautiously, not least because dynamic interpretation remains '[o]ne of the most contentious, disputed and discussed issues in treaty interpretation'.[7] Drawing on the object and purpose of the drug control regime identified in Chapter 5, this chapter will argue that a teleological approach is most appropriate to apply in this context, and that the international drug conventions must be interpreted dynamically in instances where drug control activities engage human rights obligations. Furthermore, it will make the case that this evolutive interpretation must be driven by human rights considerations, and at minimum be consistent with, and at best advance, core human rights principles and obligations.

6.2 Dynamic Interpretation and International Human Rights Law

A teleological approach, or the process of 'dynamic' or 'evolutive' interpretation, 'seek[s] the interpretation [of a treaty provision] that is most appropriate in order to realise the aim and achieve the object of the treaty, not that which would restrict to the greatest possible degree the obligations undertaken by the Parties'.[8] In other words, the provisions of a treaty are interpreted in a manner consistent with, and so as to achieve, the overarching goals of the instrument itself, and not limited to a narrow textual assessment. In doing so, a dynamic interpretation may 'go beyond, or even diverge from, the original intentions of the parties as

[3] Malgosia Fitzmaurice, 'The Practical Working of the Law of Treaties' in M. Evans (ed) *International Law* (3rd ed, Oxford University Press 2010) 184, International Law Commission, 'Yearbook vol II' (see chapter 5 n 13) p 218, para 2.

[4] Fragmentation Report (see chapter 1 n 54) p 69, para 130.

[5] Gardiner, 'Vienna Convention Rules' (see chapter 5 n 3) 499, Malcolm N. Shaw, *International Law* (6th ed, Cambridge University Press 2008) 937.

[6] Fragmentation Report (see chapter 1 n 54) para 130.

[7] Fitzmaurice (n 3) 184.

[8] *Wemhoff v FRG* (1968) Series A no 7, para A(8).

expressed in the text'.[9] Dynamic or evolutive interpretation is perhaps most closely associated with international human rights law,[10] in particular the jurisprudence of the European Court of Human Rights, which places a particular emphasis on interpreting the provisions of the European Convention on Human Rights in light of its object and purpose.[11] As first established in the case of *Tyrer v UK*, the Court views the Convention as 'a living instrument which . . . must be interpreted in light of present day conditions'.[12] Following this approach, the European Court interprets treaty provisions in the context of contemporary social standards and norms, rather than those existing at the time of the treaty's conclusion.[13] As described in the 1995 case of *Loizidou v Turkey*, the Convention's 'provisions cannot be interpreted solely in accordance with the intentions of their authors as expressed more than forty years ago'.[14]

Although most closely associated with the European Court, other human rights bodies have also adopted an evolutive approach to treaty interpretation. The Inter-American Court of Human Rights, for example, takes the approach that 'human rights treaties are living instruments whose interpreters must consider changes over time and present-day conditions', and '[t]hat evolutive interpretation is consistent with the general rules of treaty interpretation established in the 1969 Vienna Convention'.[15] According to the Inter-American Court,

> [D]ynamic evolution has had a positive impact on international law in affirming and building up the latter's faculty for regulating relations between States and the human beings within their respective jurisdictions. This Court, therefore, must adopt the proper approach to consider this question in the context of the evolution of the fundamental rights of the human person in contemporary international law.[16]

The UN Human Rights Committee also 'considers that the Covenant [on Civil and Political Rights] should be interpreted as a living instrument and the rights protected under it should be applied in context and in

[9] International Law Commission, 'Yearbook vol II' (see chapter 5 n 13) p 218, para 2.

[10] Fragmentation Report (see chapter 1 n 54) p 69, para 130.

[11] David J. Harris, Michael O'Boyle, Edward Bates and Carla Buckley, *Law of the European Convention on Human Rights* (2nd ed, Oxford University Press 2009) 5–7.

[12] *Tyrer v United Kingdom*, App no 5856/72 (ECtHR, 25 April 1978) para 31.

[13] Harris, et al. (n 11) 7.

[14] *Loizidou v Turkey (Preliminary Objections)* (1995) Series A no 310, p 26, para 71.

[15] *The Right to Information on Consular Assistance in the Framework of the Guarantees of the Due Process of Law*, Advisory Opinion OC-16/99, Inter-American Court of Human Rights Series A No 16 (1 October 1999).

[16] Ibid para 115.

the light of present day conditions'.[17] For example, in the case of *Roger Judge v Canada*, the Committee found that 'a broadening international consensus in favour of abolition of the death penalty' was a sufficient basis to 'review... the scope of the application of the rights protected' under Article 6 of the International Covenant on Civil and Political Rights.[18] In finding Canada in violation of its obligations under Article 6 for deporting a prisoner to the United States without seeking assurances he would not be subjected to the death penalty, the Committee noted,

> As to the State party's claim that its conduct must be assessed in the light of the law applicable at the time when the alleged treaty violation took place, the Committee considers that the protection of human rights evolves and that the meaning of Covenant rights should in principle be interpreted by reference to the time of examination and not, as the State party has submitted, by reference to the time the alleged violation took place.[19]

However, the dynamic or evolutive approach is not without its detractors. As described by Fitzmaurice, 'such an interpretative method was subject to much criticism... as overriding intention and the consent to be bound of Parties to the Convention and introducing the element of uncertainty to the Parties due to much more extensive interpretation of the provisions'.[20] For its part, the International Narcotics Control Board, the treaty body established under the drug conventions, has traditionally adopted a static approach to interpreting treaty provisions. As described by Bewley-Taylor, the Board's approach 'is shaped more by fears for the defence of the status quo regarding global prohibition than any broader concerns for the "health and welfare of humankind" as laid out in the conventions'.[21] Indeed, the Board's often repeated description of itself as being the 'guardian of the international drug control conventions' suggests a static, preservationist conception of its mandate, rather than a dynamic one that sees the conventions as in any way 'living instruments'.[22] These concerns, combined with the general association of the evolutive

[17] *Roger Judge v Canada* (2003) Communication No 829/1998 UN Doc CCPR/C/78/D/829/1998, para 10.3.

[18] Ibid. [19] Ibid para 10.7. [20] Fitzmaurice (see chapter 5 n 3) 188.

[21] Bewley-Taylor, *International Drug Control* (see chapter 2 n 2) 230.

[22] See, for example, United Nations Information Service, 'International Narcotics Control Board Elects New President' (16 May 2000) UN Doc No UNIS/NAR/688; 'Statement by Professor Hamid Ghodse, President of the International Narcotics Control Board', 2001 substantive session of the Economic and Social Council, July 2001, 1; International Narcotics Control Board, 'INCB Welcomes Bosnia and Herzegovina's Adoption of National Drug Control Legislation', Press Release No 5, 1 March 2006; 'Improving the implementation of the international drug control conventions through enhanced capacity of national

approach to the human rights context, urge a cautious approach when applying the principle of dynamic interpretation to the international drug control regime.

6.3 Dynamic Interpretation and other Legal Regimes

The first consideration when seeking to apply an evolutive interpretation to the international drug conventions is to examine whether, and in what context(s), the principle has been applied to treaty regimes other than international human rights law. In doing so, it is clear that a dynamic approach is not unique to human rights law and has been adopted by courts and tribunals outside of the human rights context to inform their interpretive approaches, and to advance the development of the relevant areas of law. The fact that a dynamic approach has been considered appropriate within other treaty regimes supports the legitimacy of applying it to the drug conventions.

For example, in the case of *Srl CILFIT and Lanificio di Gavardo SpA v Ministry of Health*, the European Court of Justice adopted an evolutive approach in order to resolve a dispute between Italian wool importers and the Ministry of Health on a dispute over inspection levies imposed on wool imported from outside the then European Economic Community. According to the Court, 'every provision of [European Economic] Community law must be placed in its context and interpreted in the light of the provisions of Community law as a whole, regard being had to the objectives thereof and to its state of evolution at the date on which the provision in question is to be applied'.[23] In this case, the European Court of Justice considered not only that the relevant treaty must be interpreted evolutively, but also that the relevant provision could not be considered in isolation, but must be assessed within the broader context of relevant law. Both of these conclusions are significant in the question of a human rights-based interpretation of the drug conventions.

The Appellate Body of the World Trade Organization has also adopted an evolutive approach in its jurisprudence. A particularly useful case in this regard is *Import Prohibition of Certain Shrimp and Shrimp Products*,[24]

drug control administrations: Statement by Raymond Yans, President, International Narcotics Control Board', Rome, 10 October 2012.

[23] Case 283/81 *Srl CILFIT and Lanificio di Gavardo SpA v Ministry of Health* [1982] ECR 3415, para 20.

[24] World Trade Organization, *United States – Import Prohibition of Certain Shrimp and Shrimp Products – Report of the Appellate Body* (22 October 2001) WT/DS58/AB/R (US-Shrimp).

sometimes known as 'US-Shrimp', which considered a challenge by four Asian States to a US prohibition on the import of shrimp harvested by countries whose fleets did not take precautions to minimise the inadvertent killing of sea turtles, a protected species in US environmental legislation. The Appellate Body took a dynamic interpretive approach to address the question, noting that the disputed treaty provision under the General Agreement on Tariffs and Trade, drafted fifty years earlier, 'must be read by a treaty interpreter in the light of contemporary concerns of the community of nations about the protection and conservation of the environment'.[25] In making this evolutive determination, the Appellate Body referred to the preambular section of the 1995 Agreement Establishing the World Trade Organization to inform its approach to reading the General Agreement on Tariffs and Trade, 'not[ing] that the generic term "natural resources" in Article XX(g) is not "static" in its content or reference but is rather "by definition, evolutionary"'.[26] Also of interest is the fact that, as part of the process of interpretation, the Appellate Body reached outside of world trade law into other international legal regimes – including the United Nations Convention on the Law of the Sea,[27] the Convention on Biological Diversity[28] and the Convention on the Conservation of Migratory Species of Wild Animals[29] – to assist in its interpretation and inform its conclusions. Gardiner cites environmental law as an example showing there is 'scope for evolutionary interpretation by reference to developments in the law outside the immediate confines of a particular treaty'.[30] In a conclusion of interest to the matter of international drug control law and human rights, Gardiner states that '[s]uch [environmental] rules may need to be taken into account when interpreting treaties pre-dating these developments'.[31]

A subsequent 2006 decision of a WTO panel in the case of *EC – Measures Affecting the Approval and Marketing of Biotech Products*,[32] generally known as 'EC-Biotech', took a more limited view on the application

[25] Ibid para 129. [26] Ibid paras 129–130.

[27] United Nations Convention on the Law of the Sea (adopted 10 December 1982, entered into force 16 November 1994) UN Doc No A/CONF.62/122.

[28] Convention on Biological Diversity (adopted 5 June 1992, entered into force 29 December 1993) 1760 UNTS 79.

[29] Final Act of the Conference to Conclude a Convention on the Conservation of Migratory Species of Wild Animals (23 June 1979) 19 International Legal Materials 11.

[30] Gardiner, *Treaty Interpretation* (see chapter 1 n 55) 252. [31] Ibid.

[32] *EC - Measures Affecting the Approval and Marketing of Biotech Products* (7 February 2006) WT/DS291–293/INTERIM.

of Article 31(3)(c) for treaty interpretation than was the case in US-Shrimp. In EC-Biotec, the panel found that the only treaties which could be brought to bear when interpreting WTO treaties were those to which *all* WTO members were States Parties, not simply those treaties ratified by the parties to the dispute in question.[33] However, this contention was strongly critiqued in the Fragmentation Report as making it 'practically impossible ever to find a multilateral context where reference to other multilateral treaties as aids to interpretation under article 31 (3) (c) would be allowed'.[34]

> Bearing in mind the unlikeliness of a precise congruence in the membership of most important multilateral conventions, it would become unlikely that *any* use of conventional international law could be made in the interpretation of such conventions. This would have the ironic effect that the more the membership of a multilateral treaty such as the WTO covered agreements expanded, the more those treaties would be cut off from the rest of international law. In practice, the result would be the isolation of multilateral agreements as "islands" permitting no references *inter se* in their application. It would also prohibit any use of regional or other particular implementation agreements – including *inter se* agreements – that may have been concluded under a framework treaty, as interpretative aids to the latter. This would seem contrary to the legislative ethos behind most of multilateral treaty-making and, presumably, with the intent of most treaty-makers.[35]

The Fragmentation Report criticises the panel's limitations on engaging Article 31(3)(c) for treaty interpretation, proposing instead '[a] better solution . . . to permit reference to another treaty provided that the *parties in dispute* are also parties to that other treaty'.[36]

It is clear from above that the application of dynamic interpretation is not limited to international human rights law, and has indeed influenced the approaches of adjudication bodies in other legal regimes. Therefore, the use of an evolutive approach to the interpretation of obligations of other treaty regimes, such as international drug control law, is not in and of itself unique or without precedent. However, this is not sufficient evidence alone to support a case that the drug conventions can and should be interpreted in such a fashion. Reaching this conclusion requires a secondary test to determine the conditions necessary for the application of dynamic interpretation to a treaty outside of the human rights regime, and then whether those conditions exist in the context of international drug

[33] Ibid para 7.68. [34] Fragmentation Report (see chapter 1 n 54) para 450.
[35] Ibid para 471. [36] Ibid para 472.

control law. Guidance in forming such a test is found in the jurisprudence of the International Court of Justice.

6.4 Dynamic Interpretation and the International Court of Justice

When examining the application of evolutive interpretation outside of the human rights system, the approach of the International Court of Justice is of particular interest, both because of the Court's authoritative role in dispute settlement between States, and because the Court is the body empowered within the drug conventions to arbitrate treaty disputes between States Parties.[37] As will be explored, the International Court of Justice has taken an evolutive approach to treaty interpretation in several cases, which has clear significance to the question of dynamic interpretation of international drug control law.[38]

The Court has adopted two separate approaches to determining when an evolutive approach to treaty interpretation should be engaged. These approaches are described by Helmersen as being 'value driven' and 'non-value driven' in nature,[39] and both are of relevance to the question of international drug control law. The 'value driven' approach is based on a consideration of the original intention of the parties, and is drawn from the Court's 1970 *Advisory Opinion on Namibia*.[40] In considering language within Article 22(1) of the Covenant of the League of Nations,[41] which was central to the case, the Court found that terms such as 'the well-being and development' of peoples, 'sacred trust' and 'the strenuous conditions of the modern world' were intended by the drafters to be read in evolutive manner. According to the Court, the concepts 'were by definition evolutionary... [and] [t]he parties to the Covenant must consequently be deemed to have accepted them as such'.[42] In this circumstance, where the terms in question were 'value driven' and therefore 'by definition evolutionary', the Court concluded that the intent of the drafters was that

37 1961 Convention amended (see chapter 2 n 171) art 48; 1971 Convention (see chapter 2 n 154) art 31; 1988 Convention (see chapter 2 n 162) art 32.

38 Sondre Torp Helmersen, 'Evolutive Treaty Interpretation: Legality, Semantics and Distinctions' (2013) 6/1 European Journal of Legal Studies 127, 132.

39 Ibid 139.

40 *Legal Consequences for States of the Continued Presence of South Africa in Namibia (South West Africa) notwithstanding Security Council Resolution 276 (1970)* [1971] ICJ Reports 16 (Namibia Case); *Dispute Regarding Navigational and Related Rights (Costa Rica v Nicaragua)* (judgement of 13 July 2009) (Costa Rica v Nicaragua).

41 Covenant of the League of Nations (see chapter 1 n 17) art 22(1).

42 *Namibia Case* (n 40) para 53.

the language should be interpreted dynamically, 'presumably because values inevitably change over time, as new generations will have their own views on what is (for example) "inhuman" or "fair"'.[43]

However, the absence of such 'value driven' language does not necessarily mean the Court will not find it appropriate to adopt a dynamic approach to interpreting a treaty. Where a dynamic, 'value driven' intent of the drafters cannot be reasonably inferred from the language in question, the Court has developed a test or 'general rule' to consider the question of interpretation. This 'general rule' originates in the 2009 judgement in the *Dispute Regarding Navigational and Related Rights*, in which the Court was required to apply the terms of an 1858 treaty between Costa Rica and Nicaragua. In doing so, the Court decided that,

> [W]here the parties have used generic terms in a treaty, the parties necessarily having been aware that the meaning of the terms was likely to evolve over time, and where the treaty has been entered into force for a very long period or is "of continuing duration", the parties must be presumed, as a general rule, to have intended those terms to have an evolving meaning.[44]

In the *Costa Rica v Nicaragua* case, the Court decided that the key treaty terminology at the heart of the dispute was intended by the drafters to evolve, and that therefore the Court should adjudicate the dispute in the context of the modern understanding of the terms.[45] This 'non-value driven' approach, then, is utilised by the Court where clear intent of the drafters is not evident, yet where the language is also non-specific. As described in the judgement above, the 'general rule' has two components. The first element is the use of 'generic terms', which the Court characterises as a 'referring to a class of activity'.[46] In addition, these 'generic terms' must be ones that the parties would be 'aware that the meaning of the terms was likely to evolve over time'.[47] The second element of the Court's general rule is 'where the treaty has been entered into force for a very long period or is "of continuing duration"'.[48] Both of these conditions are relevant to the question of the international drug control treaties.

6.5 Dynamic Interpretation and International Drug Control Law

The International Court of Justice's approach to dynamic interpretation is instructive in considering the question of whether the international drug

[43] Helmersen (n 38) 139. [44] *Costa Rica v Nicaragua* (n 40) para 66.
[45] Helmersen (n 38) 136. [46] *Costa Rica v Nicaragua* (n 40) para 67.
[47] Ibid para 66. [48] Ibid.

control treaties should be considered in an evolutive or a static manner. The two approaches to this question reflected in the Court's jurisprudence, 'value driven' and 'non-value driven',[49] sit neatly alongside the teleological analysis of the drug conventions explored in Chapter 5, and in both cases support the case for a dynamic approach.

In the first instance, as seen in the *Namibia* case, the Court opted for an evolutive interpretation based on its determination that the language embodied in Article 22 of the Covenant of the League of Nations expressed values that were intended to be evolutive. The Court considered that the use of concepts such as 'well-being and development' and 'sacred trust' were intended to be read in a dynamic manner, as they 'were by definition evolutionary'.[50] This 'value driven' approach supports an evolutive reading of the drug conventions, where the *telos* – to promote 'the health and welfare of mankind' – is nearly identical in meaning, and indeed in actual textual formulation, to the obligation to promote 'the well-being and development of . . . peoples' enshrined in Article 22 of the Covenant. 'Health and welfare' in this context clearly describe societal values, the content and meaning of which necessarily change and evolve with each generation and therefore meet the Court's criteria for applying dynamic interpretation to the drug conventions.

The Court's second, 'non-value driven' approach, which is engaged where clear intent of the drafters is not evident, also supports the case of an evolutive interpretation of the drug conventions when applied to the utilitarian object and purpose of the regime. The first element of the two part 'general rule' developed by the Court is use of 'generic terms' in the treaty, which the Court characterises as a one 'referring to a class of activity'.[51] In addition, these 'generic terms' must be ones that the parties would be 'aware that the meaning of the terms was likely to evolve over time'.[52] As an example, in discussing the use of generic terms in world trade law, Pauwelwn suggests

> [I]t could be submitted that the use of broad, unspecified terms – such as 'exhaustible natural resources', 'public morals' or 'essential security interests' . . . is an indication that the drafters intended these terms to be interpreted in an 'evolutionary' manner. It may, indeed, be an indication that WTO members *wanted* these terms to evolve with society and international law or, at least, *should have realised* that the vagueness of these

[49] Helmersen (n 38) 139. [50] *Namibia Case* (n 40) para 53.
[51] *Costa Rica v Nicaragua* (n 40) para 67. [52] Ibid para 66.

> terms would result in their meaning being open to discussion and variation depending on the context and times.[53]

This first element of the Court's test is clearly met by the term 'medical and scientific purposes' used to describe the utilitarian object and purpose of the drug control regime. In a similar manner to that described by Pauwelyn, 'medical and scientific purposes' is a generic, blanket term, that refers to broad classes of activities. Furthermore, it is one clearly intended to evolve over time, in keeping with global medical and scientific progress. Medical and scientific knowledge is by its very nature constantly evolving, changing and expanding. What was known about legitimate medical and scientific purposes in 1912 is different than in 1961, and different again in the present day. Indeed, evidence can be found of the evolutive nature of the term 'medical and scientific' in the drafting history of the 1961 Convention, and a reluctance of States as a consequence to be locked into a static interpretation of treaty language.

During the drafting of Article 38 on the 'Treatment of Drug Addicts',[54] the delegation of the United States proposed that the provision include specific language mandating 'compulsory drug treatment in closed institutions'.[55] However, this proposal was opposed, and eventually rejected, in large part because it undermined the ability of States to interpret the language in a manner that evolved in keeping with modern medical knowledge. In arguing against the US proposal, The Netherlands opposed this language as 'better methods of treatment might be devised in the future', while the delegate from Uruguay noted that 'modern techniques [of treatment] were being improved every day'.[56] The delegate from Canada stated that 'since the treatment of drug addicts involved medical responsibilities, it might unduly impede or hamper the development of improved treatment facilities or procedures in the future if the Convention limited treatment to that provided in closed institutions only'.[57] The United Kingdom expressed concern that as '[t]he Single Convention was intended to be a lasting instrument; it could hardly recommend methods which, even if they were the best at the moment, might not continue to be the best in the more or less distant future'.[58] Making an even more

53 Pauwelyn (see chapter 1 n 55) 267.

54 This article was draft Article 47 in the drafting history. It was renamed 'Measures against the Abuse of Drugs' when the Single Convention was amended by the 1972 Protocol.

55 1961 Official Records vol. I (see chapter 2 n 206) 110.

56 Ibid 113.

57 1961 Official Records vol. II (see chapter 3 n 40) 18, fn 47.

58 1961 Official Records vol. I (see chapter 2 n 206) 111.

specific case for the need for evolutive interpretation of the obligation, the delegation from Israel called for flexibility 'to allow for . . . eventual scientific progress' while Peru stated 'it would be better to adopt a wording which was not as likely to become outdated by scientific progress'.[59] Similar concerns were voiced by the delegation of Yugoslavia, who stated that '[j]ust as some diseases which had formerly required long treatment were now quickly cured by a few injections, it might be hoped that, before the Single Convention ceased to be operative, new and more rapid means of treatment would have been discovered which would make the measures provided for in paragraph 2 obsolete'.[60] In the end, the final agreed wording was 'desirable' that States 'establish adequate facilities for the effective treatment of drug addicts'.[61] There are clearly limitations to extrapolating the significance of the drafting debate of a single article to apply to the regime as a whole. However, this record is notable in this context as it demonstrates that the drafters recognised that the concept of 'medical and scientific' knowledge within the drug conventions was one that would necessarily evolve over time. It also shows reluctance to enshrine language that would have the effect of limiting the ability of States Parties to apply evolving medical standards to the question of drug treatment. In this sense, it supports the application of the International Court of Justice's general rule in this case, and that 'medical and scientific' is a generic term whose nature was seen as evolving over time.

The second element of the Court's general rule is that evolutive interpretation may be appropriate 'where the treaty has been entered into force for a very long period or is "of continuing duration"'.[62] Both of these conditions are applicable to the international drug control regime. Although not as old as the 1858 treaty at the heart of the *Costa Rica v Nicaragua* dispute in which the Court's test was established, the Single Convention on Narcotic Drugs was adopted in the early 1960s, and as described in Chapter 2, is based upon treaty law developed over the fifty years preceding it. In this sense, the core tenets of international drug control law have been in force for a century. In addition, the obligations enshrined in the drug control treaties are of a continuing character, in that they describe what is intended to be a framework of ongoing international control and cooperation in the area of drugs. Pauwelyn characterises 'continuing' treaties as instruments in which the 'regulatory framework or legal

[59] Ibid 113. [60] Ibid 111. [61] 1961 Convention (see chapter 2 n 134) art 38(2).
[62] *Costa Rica v Nicaragua* (n 40) para 66.

system . . . was created at one point in time but continues to exist and evolve over a mostly indefinite period'.[63] He continues,

> Most rules of modern multilateral conventions are of this nature . . . They are rules part of a framework or system which is continuously confirmed, implemented, adapted and expanded, for example, by means of judicial decisions, interpretations, new norms or the accession of new state parties . . . Such treaty norms were not only consented to when they originally emerged, but continue to be confirmed, either directly or indirectly, throughout their existence, in particular when monitored and evolving within the context of an international organisation.[64]

This again is applicable to the international drug control conventions. Therefore, following the approach of the International Court of Justice to the question of evolutive interpretation of treaties, it is clear that the drug conventions meet both of the Court's tests for where dynamic interpretation is warranted.

6.6 The Case for a Dynamic, Human Rights-based Interpretation of International Drug Control Law

Taking these conclusions a step further, and considering the utilitarian object and purpose alongside the *telos* of the regime, not only should the interpretation of drug treaty obligations evolve, but it should evolve in a dynamic manner consistent with, and in some cases directed by, obligations in international human rights law. The necessity of engaging other concurrent international legal regimes in interpreting the drug conventions is supported by the Vienna Convention on the Law of Treaties. Returning to the Article 31, which defines the 'General rule of interpretation' under the treaty, subsection (3)(c) identifies that 'any relevant rules of international law applicable in the relations between the parties' is one of the elements to 'be thrown into a crucible, and their interaction would give the legally relevant interpretation', using the description of the International Law Commission.[65] Article 31(3)(c) allows for consideration not only of laws of custom, but also of other treaty obligations, in the process of interpretation.[66] As explained by Villiger, '[i]t is assumed that

[63] Pauwelyn (see chapter 1 n 55) 378. [64] Ibid.

[65] International Law Commission, 'Yearbook vol II' (see chapter 5 n 13) 218–219, para 8; Gardiner, 'Vienna Convention Rules' (see chapter 5 n 3) 480.

[66] Gardiner, 'Vienna Convention Rules' (see chapter 5 n 3) 485–487; Fragmentation Report (see chapter 1 n 54) p 215; Villiger, *Commentary* (see chapter 5 n 17) 433; Gardiner, *Treaty Interpretation* (see chapter 1 n 55) 260–263.

in entering treaty obligations, the parties did not intend to act inconsistently with other previous obligations'.[67] Indeed, according to Sorel and Eveno, the 'context [of interpretation] also includes agreements with a bearing on the treaty [in question] as well as similar agreements between certain parties to the treaty which have been approved by other parties'.[68] McLachlan describes this as reflecting the principle of 'systemic integration', arguing that 'treaties are themselves creatures of international law. However wide their subject matter, they are all nevertheless limited in scope and are predicated for their existence and operation on being part of the international law system'.[69]

Article 31(3)(c) has been engaged by several international courts and tribunals to inform their interpretation of treaty provisions. The European Court of Human Rights, for example, has a long history of citing the Article 31 in its jurisprudence,[70] characterising it as a 'generally accepted principle of international law'.[71] For example, in the 1975 case of *Golder v United Kingdom*, the Court explicitly cited Article 31(3)(c) in finding that 'for the interpretation of the European Convention account is to be taken of those Articles subject, where appropriate, to "any relevant rules of the organization" – the Council of Europe – within which it has been adopted'.[72] It has subsequently reaffirmed its embrace of Article 31 in a number of cases, noting in *Saadi v United Kingdom*, for example, that 'the Court must also take into account any relevant rules and principles of international law applicable in relations between the Contracting Parties'.[73] In the case of *Al-Adsani v United Kingdom*, the Court again cited Article 31(3)(c), noting that the European 'Convention should so far as possible be interpreted in harmony with other rules of international law of which it forms part'.[74] The International Court of Justice has also cited Article 31(3)(c) in its jurisprudence, noting in the *Oil Platforms Case* that, when interpreting a provision of the Friendship Treaty between the United States and Iran, '[t]he Court cannot accept that Article XX, paragraph 1 (d), of the 1955 Treaty was intended to operate wholly independently of the relevant rules of international law'.[75] Similarly, the Appellate Body

[67] Villiger, *Commentary* (see chapter 5 n 17) 433.
[68] Sorel and Eveno (see chapter 5 n 4) 808.
[69] McLachlan (see chapter 1 n 53) 280.
[70] Sorel and Eveno (see chapter 5 n 4) 821, 828.
[71] *Golder v United Kingdom* (see chapter 5 n 6) para 29.
[72] Ibid.
[73] *Saadi v United Kingdom* App no 13229/03 (ECtHR, 29 January 2008) para 62.
[74] *Al-Adsani v United Kingdom* App no 35763/97 (ECtHR, 21 November 2001) para 55.
[75] *Case Concerning Oil Platforms (Islamic Republic of Iran v United States of America*, judgement of 6 November 2003, para 41; Sorel and Eveno (see chapter 5 n 4) 828.

of the World Trade Organization has invoked the principle, if not the actual provision, in its work, noting that the General Agreement on Tariffs and Trade should not be interpreted 'in clinical isolation from public international law'.[76]

As the Vienna Convention rule allows for the consideration of other treaty regimes within the interpretive process, and given the explicit invocation of this provision within the interpretative approaches of major international courts and adjudicatory bodies, it is reasonable to conclude that the application of this principle to international drug control is a legitimate exercise. The question then becomes one of how should the obligations within the drug control treaties be interpreted in the context of concurrent commitments within international human rights law? Consideration of the object and purpose of the drug control regime explored in Chapter 5, in the context of the interpretive rules explored above, suggests not only that the principle of dynamic interpretation should be applied when interpreting international drug control law, but also that this interpretation should be done in a manner that is consistent with principles and parallel obligations under international human rights law. As described in the 2006 Report of the Study Group on Fragmentation of International Law,

> [A]ll international law exists in systemic relationship with other law, no such application [of interpretation] can take place without situating the relevant jurisdiction-endowing instrument in its normative environment. This means that although a tribunal may only have jurisdiction in regard to a particular instrument, it must always *interpret* and *apply* that instrument in its relationship to its normative environment – that is to say "other" international law.[77]
>
> [emphasis in original]

This question of situating a treaty within its 'normative environment' for the purposes of interpretation is key, as the object and purpose test applied to the international drug control regime illustrates that, in core areas, the normative environment of the drug control regime is also one shared by international human rights law. This is important to the interpretive process as, in order for Article 31(3)(c) to be engaged, the other rules in question 'have to be relevant, i.e., concern the subject-matter of the treaty term at issue'.[78]

[76] World Trade Organization, *Standards for Reformulated and Conventional Gasoline* (29 April 1996) WT/DS2/AB/R, 19; Sorel and Eveno (see chapter 5 n 4) 828–829.

[77] Fragmentation Report (see chapter 1 n 54) p 212–213, para 423.

[78] Villiger, *Commentary* (see chapter 5 n 17) 433.

In this case, both the concepts of 'medical and scientific purposes' and 'concern for the health and welfare of mankind' are integrally linked, if not inextricable, from international human rights norms. For example, the 1948 Universal Declaration of Human Rights, under Article 25, enshrines the 'right to a standard of living adequate for the health and well-being of himself and of his family',[79] language very similar in both construction and content to 'the health and welfare of mankind' found in the preambles of the 1961 and 1971 drug treaties. Similarly, the 1946 Constitution of the World Health Organization describes 'the enjoyment of the highest attainable standard of health' as being 'one of the fundamental rights of every human being'.[80] The consideration of health and well-being within a human rights framework was therefore enshrined in important early United Nations instruments, suggesting that concepts of health, welfare and medical purposes as described in the drug treaties engaged human rights norms even at the time of their drafting. In a present day context, where the right to the highest attainable standard of physical and mental health has been enshrined within both the International Covenant on Economic, Social and Cultural Rights[81] and the Convention on the Rights of the Child,[82] the argument that the normative environment for international drug control law is one shared by international human rights law is compelling. Indeed, in addition to the right to health, the specific concept of medical and scientific purposes relates to, and must be considered alongside, the right to enjoy the benefit of scientific progress, originally enshrined under Article 27 of Universal Declaration of Human Rights[83] and later expressed under Article 15 of the Covenant on Economic, Social and Cultural Rights.[84]

Examples of this common normative environment in practice, and the engagement between the two regimes, can be found in both the human rights and drug control systems. For example, the Committee on the Rights of the Child, in its General Comment on the right to health, 'encourages States . . . to ratify the international drug conventions', in this context viewing the obligations the drug treaties create within the context

[79] Universal Declaration of Human Rights (see chapter 3 n 86) art 25(1).

[80] Constitution of the World Health Organization (adopted 22 July 1946, entered into force on 7 April 1948), Official Records of the World Health Organization no 2, p 100, preamble.

[81] International Covenant on Economic, Social and Cultural Rights (see chapter 4 n 45) art 12.

[82] Convention on the Rights of the Child (adopted 20 November 1989, entered into force 2 September 1990) 1577 UNTS 3, art 24.

[83] Universal Declaration of Human Rights (see chapter 3 n 86) art 27.

[84] International Covenant on Economic, Social and Cultural Rights (see chapter 4 n 45) art 15.

of Article 24 of the Convention on the Rights of the Child.[85] In doing so, the Committee conceptualises drug control efforts as measures towards fulfilment of the right to health. This suggests that the drug control regime's overarching goal of promoting the health and welfare of mankind is not one that can be measured in drug control terms, as the presence of effective drug control does not in itself mean the presence of health and welfare. Realising this overarching purpose is one that can only be measured and achieved in human rights terms, where the success of drug control efforts is a single component. In that same General Comment, the Committee also 'underscores the importance of adopting a rights-based approach to substance use', again demonstrating its perspective that drug control obligations engage, and must be interpreted in a manner consistent with, human rights norms.[86]

Another example is found in the Single Convention's preambular statement on the importance of the 'adequate provision' of medicines, and the need for States to 'ensure the availability of narcotic drugs' for the purpose of 'the relief of pain and suffering'.[87] This preambular section specifically engages State obligations under Article 12 of the International Covenant on Economic, Social and Cultural Rights,[88] as the Committee on Economic, Social and Cultural Rights considers that the fulfilment of the right to health includes proper access to essential drugs.[89] In its General Comment on the right to health, the Committee includes such access among the Core Obligations of States.[90] The Single Convention's language on the importance of 'ensur[ing] availability' of controlled medicines also engages State obligations 'to take positive measures that enable and assist individuals and communities to enjoy the right to health', as described in the Committee's General Comment.[91] The failure of States to provide access to medicines to alleviate pain and suffering has also prompted critical comment from the UN Special Rapporteur on torture and other

[85] Committee on the Rights of the Child, 'General comment No. 15 (2013) on the right of the child to the enjoyment of the highest attainable standard of health' (17 April 2013) UN Doc No CRC/C/GC/15, para 66.

[86] Ibid. [87] 1961 Convention amended (see chapter 2 n 171) preamble.

[88] International Covenant on Economic, Social and Cultural Rights (see chapter 4 n 45) art 12.

[89] UN Committee of Economic, Social and Cultural Rights, 'General Comment No. 14' (chapter 4 n 46) paras 12(a), 17.

[90] Ibid para 43(c).

[91] UN Committee of Economic, Social and Cultural Rights, 'General Comment No. 14' (see chapter 4 n 46) para 37.

cruel, inhuman or degrading treatment or punishment,[92] evidence that the shared normative environment of the drug treaties extends beyond the right to health and also engages other human rights regimes.

The example of access to controlled medicines also offers an illustration of the limitations of drug control alone as a tool in measuring progress towards achieving the regime's object and purpose. While the system of estimates and import/export controls established by the drug treaties can, in theory, measure the supplies of controlled medicines reaching an individual State, it does nothing to measure the impact of those medicines. It does not measure, for example, whether medicines are being appropriately distributed within a State, or if they are having the desired impact of promoting health and welfare of the populace. This requires human rights-based indicators and measurements, as illustrated by the comments of both the Committee on Economic, Social and Cultural Rights and the Special Rapporteur on torture on this issue, again demonstrating the interconnectedness of the regimes and the common normative environment in which they exist.

Although significant, the right to the highest attainable standard of health is only one example where human rights law and drug control law intersect, and where an interpretation of drug control obligations must incorporate concurrent human rights obligations. According to the Committee on Economic, Social and Cultural Rights, the right to health itself incorporates a broad range of other rights.

> The right to health is closely related to and dependent upon the realization of other human rights, as contained in the International Bill of Rights, including the rights to food, housing, work, education, human dignity, life, non-discrimination, equality, the prohibition against torture, privacy, access to information, and the freedoms of association, assembly and movement. These and other rights and freedoms address integral components of the right to health.[93]

Based upon the Committee's approach, the normative environment in which the drug conventions operate and must be interpreted is extremely broad. As a result, according to the Barrett and Nowak, '[t]here are inevitable crossovers [between the two legal regimes], and upon analysis, there is a strong case that the drug conventions are insufficient, alone,

[92] UN Human Rights Council, 'Nowak Report' (see chapter 1 n 41) paras 68–70.

[93] UN Committee of Economic, Social and Cultural Rights, 'General Comment No. 14' (see chapter 4 n 46) para 3.

as a legal framework for the range and complexity of issues involved'.[94] They argue that in many cases, human rights law must be the guide for what constitutes appropriate measures in drug control. They argue that '[w]here the drug conventions fail to legislate or are unclear, human rights law must fill the gaps'.[95]

Explicit examples illustrating this point can be found within the core instruments of the two regimes. For example, Article 14(2) of the 1988 drug convention, which creates obligations for States to 'Eradicate Illicit Cultivation of Narcotic Plants',[96] states that

> Each Party shall take appropriate measures to prevent illicit cultivation of and to eradicate plants containing narcotic or psychotropic substances, such as opium poppy, coca bush and cannabis plants, cultivated illicitly in its territory. The measures adopted shall respect fundamental human rights and shall take due account of traditional licit uses, where there is historic evidence of such use, as well as the protection of the environment.[97]

In this instance, engagement between the two regimes is not inferred but is specifically prescribed. Article 14(2) is in fact the only provision within the three UN drug treaties that explicitly mentions human rights. While this is itself significant and worthy of attention, the context is of particular relevance to the question of evolutive treaty interpretation. In directing that States take 'appropriate measures' to prevent cultivation and to eradicate illicit crops, it necessitates that a determination of what measures are, or are not, 'appropriate' must include an assessment of the human rights impacts of the measure in question. In essence, a process of interpretation must be undertaken, and this process must include consideration of human rights norms, which are generally agreed to be evolutive. Therefore, any interpretation of the obligation created under Article 14(2) must *by definition* not only be dynamic, but dynamic *and* human rights-based. It is also notable that Article 14(2) includes environmental protection as an element that must be considered in determining whether a measure is 'appropriate'. As described above, the Appellate Body of the World Trade Organization considers that concepts of environmental protection are also evolutive in nature, again suggesting that this specific provision of the drug treaties must be subject to dynamic interpretation, and an interpretation be consistent with international environmental treaties.

[94] Barrett and Nowak (see chapter 1 n 24) 462.
[95] Ibid 465. [96] 1988 Convention (see chapter 2 n 162) art 14. [97] Ibid art 14(2).

Barrett and Veerman make a similar point in their work on Article 33 of the Convention on the Rights of the Child,[98] the only provision within the United Nations human rights treaty regime to explicitly mention drugs.[99] Under Article 33,

> States parties shall take all appropriate measures, including legislative, administrative, social and educational measures, to protect children from illicit use of narcotic drugs and psychotropic substances as defined in the relevant international treaties and to prevent the use of children in the illicit production and trafficking of such substances.[100]

In addressing the question of how drug control obligations should be interpreted in the context of children's rights, Barrett and Veerman argue that '[w]hen it comes to children, the drug treaties must be read in the light of the [Convention on the Rights of the Child] to ensure appropriate interpretation'.[101] Focusing on the language of 'appropriate measures' common to both Article 33 of the Convention on the Rights of the Child and Article 14(2) of the 1988 drug treaty, they argue that any assessment of what is or is not 'appropriate' in the context of drug control or enforcement measures where children are affected must be made with best interests of the child at the centre, and therefore be consistent with and supportive of children's rights norms, as '[t]he reverse would be anathema to the role of human rights as a check and balance against the impact of law and policy on individuals and groups'.[102] Using a number of case examples from the drug control regime, including crop eradication and drug treatment, the authors conclude that in order for these obligations 'to have relevance to children, and if their rights are to

[98] Damon Barrett and Philip E. Veerman, 'Article 33: Protection from Narcotic, Drugs and Psychotropic Substances' in A. Alen, J. Vande Lanotte, E. Verhellen, F. Ang, E. Berghmans, M. Verheyde and B. Abramson (eds) *A Commentary on the United Nations Convention on the Rights of the Child* (Martinus Nijoff 2012). See also Damon Barrett and John Tobin, 'Article 33: Protection from Narcotic Drugs and Psychotropic Substances' in J. Tobin and P. Alston (eds) *A Commentary to the United Nations Convention on the Rights of the Child* (Oxford University Press, in press).

[99] Within the regional systems, a further explicit reference to drugs is found in Article 5 of the European Convention on Human Rights, where Article 5(1)(e) lists 'drug addiction' as a legitimate limitation on the right to liberty and security. Convention for the Protection of Human Rights and Fundamental Freedoms (European Convention on Human Rights, as amended) art 5. For further analysis of this provision see Lines, 'Treatment in Liberty' (see chapter 4 n 108).

[100] Convention on the Rights of the Child (n 82) art 33.

[101] Barrett and Veerman (n 98) 79, para 180. [102] Ibid.

be respected, protected and fulfilled, [the obligations] must be read in the light of the [Convention on the Rights of the Child]'.[103]

Returning to the drug conventions, while the case for dynamic interpretation of Article 14(2) is clear, it would be nonsensical to suggest that evolutive interpretation of international drug control law be limited to this single provision. Given the multiple areas in which drug treaty obligations engage other human rights norms, and applying Barrett and Veerman's child rights approach to encompass the broader tapestry of rights protections, it is clear that a dynamic, human rights-based approach should also be applied when interpreting other areas of the drug control regime. For example, all three drug treaties include provisions on extradition[104] and on penal sanctions.[105] In both of these cases, international human rights law provide essential rules and safeguards regulating the behaviour of States that contribute to the normative environment occupied by the drug treaties. While international drug control law may define the content of State response, or the circumstances in which the response is triggered in the context of drugs, human rights law defines the limitations of those responses as they affect the rights of individuals. Without such balances and safeguards, 'appropriate' drug control and enforcement measures 'could be read to justify anything'.[106]

Therefore, rather than a limitation on where such a balancing process is warranted, Article 14(2) should instead be seen as a window into how drug control measures emerging from treaty obligations should be interpreted in light of the normative environment as a whole. If measures deemed 'appropriate' for controlling cultivation must include consideration of human rights, then surely those addressing penal laws and sanctions, extradition and health concerns must similarly undertake this same process, an interpretive process that is both *dynamic* and *human rights-based*. When interpreting drug control obligations within the broader normative environment in which the treaties exist, for example, it cannot be the case that an 'appropriate' measure in drug control terms is one fundamentally 'inappropriate' in human rights terms. As described by the Study Group on the Fragmentation of International Law, '[i]n international law, there is a strong presumption against normative conflict. Treaty interpretation is

[103] Ibid 84, para 187.

[104] 1961 Convention amended (see chapter 2 n 171) art 36(2)(b); 1971 Convention (see chapter 2 n 154) art 22(2); 1988 Convention (see chapter 2 n 162) art 6.

[105] 1961 Convention amended (see chapter 2 n 171) art 36; 1971 Convention (see chapter 2 n 154) art 22; 1988 Convention (see chapter 2 n 162) art 3.

[106] Barrett and Veerman (n 98) p 63, para 137.

diplomacy, and it is the business of diplomacy to avoid or mitigate conflict. This extends to adjudication as well'.[107] Similarly, Jenks states it is 'reasonable to presume, when the interpretation of an instrument is doubtful, that the parties intended it to be construed in a manner consistent with the obligations of some or all of them under other instruments'.[108] This is also the approach of the European Court of Human Rights.

> Where a number of apparently contradictory instruments are simultaneously applicable, international case-law and academic opinion endeavour to construe them in such a way as to coordinate their effects and avoid any opposition between them. Two diverging commitments must therefore be harmonised as far as possible so that they produce effects that are fully in accordance with existing law.[109]

Clearly, then, the 'correct', or at least most preferable, interpretation is one that strives for consistency between all concurrent obligations.

6.7 Conclusion

Chapter 6 has proposed a dynamic, human-rights based interpretive approach be applied to international drug control law. Despite the strong case supporting such an approach, and the need for such a process to resolve current or future conflicts, the question remains as to where such matters are to be adjudicated, and how the progressive development of international law will therefore take place. The areas of engagement between the two legal regimes is clear, as are some of the potential human rights impacts of State activities implemented to meet drug treaty obligations. However, unlike other legal regimes, such as world trade law, or even human rights law, international drug control law creates no judicial or adjudicatory body where such questions or disputes might be considered, and where such dynamic interpretation of drug control obligations might take place. Therefore, dynamic interpretation of international drug control law will largely take place outside of the structures of the drug control regime itself. The following chapter will explore the question of potential adjudicatory bodies, and examine existing jurisprudence where such conflicts have been addressed.

[107] Fragmentation Report (see chapter 1 n 54) p 25, para 37.
[108] Jenks (see chapter 4 n 34) 429.
[109] *Nada v Switzerland* App no 10593/08 (ECtHR, 12 September 2012) para 170.

7

Moving the 'thumb on the scales' – Towards a Dynamic Human Rights-based Interpretation of International Drug Control Law

Drug abuse and illicit trafficking are dynamic processes; consequently any effective response to them must also be dynamic.[1]

International Narcotics Control Board

For the purposes of balancing, some laws (or parts of laws) will of necessity be more equal than others.[2]

Justice Albie Sachs

7.1 Introduction

Previous chapters have explored the evolution of the international law of drug control. They have examined the historic tensions within the regime, and their impacts on human rights in the modern era; the object and purpose of the international drug conventions; and made the case that the drug treaties must be interpreted in a dynamic fashion, particularly where their provisions engage human rights. The final questions to be considered are where such a process of dynamic interpretation should take place, and how it might be applied. In short, what might a 'fifth stage' of international drug control law look like in practice? This chapter will explore these questions. It will review the key international and domestic fora through which a dynamic interpretation of drug control law might take place. It will also consider how a dynamic human rights-based interpretation of international drug control law might proceed, using the examples examined in Chapter 4, that resolve regime tensions and conflicts in a manner that promotes human rights. Through this process, the chapter will offer principles of how a 'fifth stage' of international drug control law should develop.

[1] International Narcotics Control Board, 'Report of the International Narcotics Control Board for 1994' (1995) para 33(d).

[2] Justice Albie Sachs (dissenting opinion), *Prince v President, Cape Law Society and Others* [2002] 2 SA 794 (SACC), para 154.

7.2 Key Interpretive Bodies

It has been observed that treaty 'interpretation occupies a prime position on the crossroads between law and politics'.[3] This assessment is certainly appropriate to describe the interpretive challenges in this context, where both international drug control law and international human rights law are regimes intertwined with domestic and international history and politics. Coupled with this existential challenge is the more immediate one of identifying in what venue(s) the dynamic human rights-based interpretation of international drug control law might take place. As explored in Chapter 2, international drug control law establishes a system of indirect control, in which the treaties define the laws and administrative practices that States are required to implement within their own territories, as well as creating a supervisory organ to monitor and assist States in fulfilling these obligations. Unlike some other areas of international law, international drug control law provides no formal adjudication mechanism or body through which tensions or conflicts might be examined, and dynamic interpretation might occur. Therefore, rather than taking place via the jurisprudence of a central court or other body, a 'fifth stage' of international drug control must necessarily emerge from the interaction between several key fora, each with its own role to play in, and mandate to influence, this process. The most influential actors in this context are the International Narcotics Control Board, domestic constitutional courts and international human rights courts and treaty bodies.

7.2.1 International Narcotics Control Board

As was described in Chapter 2, the International Narcotics Control Board is the treaty body established under the 1961 drug convention to monitor State compliance with the regime.[4] Although the Board's primary functions are technical in nature, over the years it has taken on what it describes itself as a 'quasi-judicial' role regarding the treaties[5] and is often characterised as being the 'guardian of the conventions'.[6] While it possesses no direct powers of sanction for treaty violation, the Board does wield

[3] Sorel and Eveno (see chapter 5 n 4) 807.

[4] 1961 Convention amended (see chapter 2 n 171) art 9.

[5] See, for example, International Narcotics Control Board, 'Report of the International Narcotics Control Board for 2013' (2014) UN Doc No E/INCB/2013/1, 107.

[6] See, for example, Raymond Yans, 'Improving the implementation of the international drug control conventions through enhanced capacity of national drug control administrations:

significant moral authority through its ability to 'name and shame' States via its high profile annual reports, as well as to influence the overall tone of the regime towards drug control and related issues.[7] Therefore, the Board has a potentially significant role in 'fifth stage' interpretive processes.

Numerous human rights criticisms have been legitimately levelled at the Board in the past, ranging from its failure to criticise abusive State policies and practices, to its praising of human rights violating governments for their supposed success in combatting drug trafficking.[8] In addition, the Board has historically resisted any suggestion that it has a human rights mandate, or that its deliberations should be informed by human rights concerns.[9] As a result, the response from some observers has been to argue that the Board's functions should be limited to narrow technical parameters, and therefore isolate it from engagement with broader policy and rights issues.[10] Others have suggested that the principle of State sovereignty means that the Board's ability to legitimately criticise individual governments on drug control should be curtailed.[11] Such proposals appear rooted in critiques of the Board's practice and public statements on key issues, which, it can be argued, are more reflective of the individual membership of the Board, rather than its mandate as an international treaty organ. On the other hand, Barrett and Nowak argue against the narrowing of the Board's mandate and functions, proposing instead an 'alternative view, that the INCB has an important role in ensuring not only that the drug conventions are applied, but applied in full conformity with human rights. This would mean expanding the Board's mandate, rather than limiting it, demanding an invigorated Board membership'.[12]

Statement by Raymond Yans, President, International Narcotics Control Board', Prevention Strategy and Policy Makers: A 'Solidarity Consortium' (10 October 2010) 4.

7 Bewley-Taylor, *International Drug Control* (see chapter 2 n 2) 224–229.

8 See, for example, Barrett and Nowak (see chapter 1 n 24) 474, Csete, 'Overhauling Oversight' (see chapter 4 n 96), Csete and Wolfe (see chapter 2 n 220).

9 Koli Kouame, Secretary of the International Narcotics Control Board, UN Press Conference, 7 March 2007, cited in Barrett and Nowak (see chapter 1 n 24) 457–458; Patrick Gallahue, 'Narcotics Watchdog Turns Blind Eye to Rights Abuses' *Inter Press Service* (28 March 2012) (Watchdog).

10 See, for example, Bewley-Taylor, *International Drug Control* (see chapter 2 n 2) 245–249; International Drug Policy Consortium (see chapter 4 n 141) 8.

11 See, for example, Bewley-Taylor, *International Drug Control* (see chapter 2 n 2) 246, 248; Transnational Institute, 'The Erratic Crusade of the INCB', TNI Drug Policy Briefing, Nr (Transnational Institute 2003) 3.

12 Barrett and Nowak (see chapter 1 n 24) 474.

If a 'fifth stage' drug control regime is to emerge, in which human rights become a central feature, the role of the International Narcotics Control Board is indeed a critical one, not least because the tone of the Board's work, and whether or not it chooses to embrace human rights norms, has an influence on State practice. For example, in a 2014 case before the Supreme Court of India on the death penalty for drug offences, the State's submission in defence of its capital drug laws cited the absence of Board criticism of such laws as evidence that the practice was supported under the international drug control treaties. According to the State,

> [T]here has never been any objection from the INCB regarding the provision of the death penalty in the NDPS [Narcotic Drugs and Psychotropic Substances] Act... It is therefore apparent that even the body which is mandated to ensure compliance of the UN Drug Conventions has no objection to the presence of capital punishment in the NDPS Act. It is, therefore, wrong to say that such provisions are contrary to the UN Conventions.[13]

Given its central role within the regime, and its influence on States' perceptions and practice, a 'fifth stage' of international drug control law cannot emerge without the active engagement and support of the International Narcotics Control Board. While the role of the Board is critical, playing such a constructive role would require a fundamental shift in the way the Board conceptualises its mandate, and carries out its activities. Csete details a number of needed areas of Board reform in this regard, in order for it to play a positive role in limiting 'the ready tendency of states to limit human rights in the name of drug control'.[14] While the challenges in moving the Board forward in this fashion should not be underestimated, they are less difficult than are the challenges of shaping a human-rights based approach to drug control in the face of an openly obstructionist treaty organ at the centre of the drug control regime.

7.2.2 Domestic Courts

As the Indian Supreme Court case above illustrates, a second critical forum for the dynamic human rights-based interpretation of international drug control law are domestic constitutional courts. The role of national high courts in this regard is crucial for a number of reasons. The first is that the system of indirect control established by the

[13] Supreme Court of India (see chapter 4 n 76) para 4(v).
[14] Csete, 'Overhauling Oversight' (see chapter 4 n 96) 68.

drug treaties means that drug administrative, control and enforcement practices are the responsibility of States to implement, therefore placing these activities and policies squarely within the realm of national legislation and domestic court oversight. The second is that all three drug treaties contain various caveats on key provisions, specifying that the relevant obligations are subject to domestic or constitutional law. These are generally described as 'safeguard clauses',[15] examples of which are found in Articles 35 ('Action Against the Illicit Traffic') and Article 36 ('Penal Provisions') of the 1961 Convention.[16] Article 36 specifies that its obligations are '[s]ubject to . . . constitutional limitations',[17] and that '[n]othing contained in this article shall affect the principle that the offences to which it refers shall be defined, prosecuted and punished in conformity with the domestic law of a Party'.[18] Similar safeguard clauses are present in the 1988 Convention, particularly in 'the more contentious penal provisions'[19] under several parts of Article 3, which are 'subject to [the State's] constitutional principles and the basic concepts of its legal system'.[20] Similar clauses within the 1988 treaty are found at Article 5 on confiscation of property[21] and Article 6 on extradition,[22] among others.[23] As mentioned in Chapter 6, one safeguard clause worthy of particular note is Article 14 on the eradication of illicit crops, the only provision within the three treaties with a specific provision specifying that the 'measures adopted shall respect fundamental human rights'.[24] Therefore, domestic courts have a clear role to play in the evolution of a 'fifth stage' of drug control, and in applying national constitutional rights to issues of drugs.[25] However, such balancing tests are not without their own risks and challenges. As described by Boister, 'limitation clauses provide no guarantee of constitutional limitation. A municipal court may . . . choose to limit the constitutional protection rather than the domestic law flowing from the

15 See, for example, *Commentary on the United Nations Convention Against Illicit Traffic in Narcotic Drugs and Psychotropic Substances 1988* (see chapter 2 n 167) 41, fn 93, Neil Boister, 'Human Rights Protections in the Suppression Conventions' (2002) 2 Human Rights Law Review 199, 210 (Suppression Conventions).

16 1961 Convention amended (see chapter 2 n 171) arts 35, 36.

17 Ibid arts 36(1), 36(2).

18 Ibid art 36(4).

19 Boister, 'Suppression Conventions' (n 15) 208.

20 1988 Convention (see chapter 2 n 162) arts 3(1), 3(2), 3(5), 3(10).

21 Ibid art 5(7).

22 Ibid arts 6(8), 6(10).

23 *Commentary on the United Nations Convention Against Illicit Traffic in Narcotic Drugs and Psychotropic Substances 1988* (see chapter 2 n 167) 41, fn 93.

24 1988 Convention (see chapter 2 n 162) art 14(2).

25 Indeed, South African Constitutional Court Justice Ngcobo cited the safeguard clauses in his dissent in the case of *Prince v President, Cape Law Society and Others*, discussed later in this chapter.

treaty provision and justify doing so by giving disproportionate weight to the international authority behind the domestic law'.[26] Alejandro Madrazo Lajous has specifically explored the undermining effect of drug laws on human rights protections in Mexico, Colombia and the United States, arguing that '[c]onstitutional texts, interpretations and practices have been transformed in order to, in theory, better tackle drugs'.[27] Therefore, in order for domestic courts to contribute to the development of the 'fifth stage' of international drug control, they would be required to adopt a dynamic human rights-based approach to considering tensions and conflicts taking place within national law, or between national law and international obligations, as will be explored below.

7.2.3 *United Nations and Regional Human Rights Mechanisms*

A third key forum for dynamic interpretation to emerge is within international human rights courts and treaty bodies themselves. Given the multiple areas in which drug control and enforcement activities have an impact on human rights protections, as explored in previous chapters, there is a clear role for human rights courts and treaty bodies to be active agents in shaping 'fifth stage' drug control. This could take place through specific challenges before courts, through periodic reporting functions, general comments or the consideration of individual complaints (where such a mechanism exists) of treaty bodies. Given that the principle of evolutive interpretation is well established within international human rights jurisprudence,[28] the potential to expand this approach in the context of drug control issues is significant. However, this will again require the human rights bodies to confidently embrace their role as a legitimate voice of oversight on drug control issues, which, as has been explored, has been far from common practice. Indeed, human rights bodies have traditionally been quite silent in commenting directly on drug control issues.

7.3 'Nullification' as an Obstacle to Dynamic Interpretation

Several different domestic and international legal fora have potentially significant roles to play in shaping a 'fifth stage' of international drug control law. Indeed, questions of drug control law and human rights law

[26] Boister, 'Suppression Conventions' (n 15) 208–209.

[27] Alejandro Madrazo Lajous, 'The Constitutional Costs of the "War on Drugs"' in J. Collins (ed) *Governing The Global Drug Wars LSE Ideas: Special Report* (LSE Ideas 2012).

[28] See Chapter 6.

have been considered before domestic constitutional courts, as well as international courts and treaty bodies in both the human rights and drug control regimes. However, in reviewing the approach of these bodies, a trend is often apparent that stands in the way of the development of a dynamic, human rights-based approach to treaty interpretation. This trend might be described as a process of 'nullification', which is exhibited in two divergent but equally problematic ways: 'passive nullification' and 'active nullification'.

As explored in previous chapters, the relevant drug control and human rights treaty bodies rarely consider the intersection between these two international legal regimes in their deliberations, or do not embrace a mandate to comment in an inter-disciplinary fashion on an area often seen as outside their mandates. As a result, the UN human rights treaty bodies rarely comment on drug control issues, and the International Narcotics Control Board rarely mentions human rights issues. The result is a process of passive nullification, in which a narrow focus solely on their own legal regimes creates institutional blinders, nullifying any consideration of the many important areas where those regimes intersect and mutually affect the realisation of both objectives. The proportionally tiny number of examples where the treaty bodies of one regime have commented robustly on the other is evidence that passive nullification represents a clear institutional barrier to the development of a 'fifth stage' of drug control. Indeed, a continuation of passive nullification in this manner will mean dynamic interpretation cannot develop, as the failure of each regime to engage with the legal obligations of the other means no interpretative process even takes place.

The second form, active nullification, is found where an interpretative process has taken place. In these cases, the court or other adjudicative body has decided that drug control law either supersedes the relevant human right protections, or that the objective of drug suppression is so pressing that the human rights questions need not be considered at all, or not considered in a robust manner. In effect, the objectives of drug control are allowed to trump human rights obligations. Examples of active nullification are evident at both domestic and international level, and within both legal regimes.

For example, the International Narcotics Control Board has traditionally maintained a position that it has no human rights mandate, an opinion expressed both by the Board's Secretariat[29] as well as by its past

[29] Kouame (n 9).

President.[30] As a consequence, the Board has, on numerous occasions, failed to express concerns about human rights abuses committed in the name of drug control. Going even further, the narrow focus on drug control in isolation from human rights considerations has led to instances where the Board's influential Annual Report has praised States for what are known to be fundamentally abusive policies. For example, in Thailand in 2003 more than 2,000 people were killed by police during a government-led 'war on drugs'. Despite wide criticism of the government by human rights monitors,[31] the Board failed to criticise the execution campaign, commenting only that it 'trusts that the Government will continue to provide information to it regarding the progress of those investigations'.[32] The Board's Annual Reports also have a history of commending governments for their 'success' in combatting drugs, in cases where the drug policies of the countries in question have been criticised as human rights violations.[33] On the other side, the Board has been openly hostile towards governments that have implemented harm reduction programmes to prevent HIV infections among people who inject drugs,[34] approaches that are widely supported by other United Nations agencies.[35] In effect, the Board's exclusive focus on drug control has actively nullified any consideration of the human rights impacts, both negative and positive, of the drug control policies and activities it is mandated to monitor, a result that

[30] Gallahue, 'Watchdog' (n 9); Audio recording of former INCB President Hamid Ghodse's remarks is available online www.ihra.net/contents/1196 accessed 11 June 2014.

[31] See, for example, Human Rights Watch, 'Not Enough Graves: The War on Drugs, HIV/AIDS, and Violations of Human Rights' (Human Rights Watch 2004), vol. 16, no 8 (C); 'UN Expert on Extrajudicial Executions Expresses Concern over Recent Killings in Thailand', United Nations Press Release HR/4645 (24 February 2003).

[32] International Narcotics Control Board, 'Report of the International Narcotics Control Board for 2004' (see chapter 4 n 134) para 388.

[33] For the example of Vietnam, see International Narcotics Control Board 2011 (see chapter 4 n 94) para 117. See, also for example, Human Rights Watch, 'Rehab Archipelago' (see chapter 4 n 85); World Health Organization Western Pacific Region (see chapter 4 n 85).

[34] See, for example, International Narcotics Control Board, 'Report of the International Narcotics Control Board for 2010' (2011) UN Doc No E/INCB/2010/1, para 123; 'Concerns Over Heroin Use for Addicts Remain After Swiss Project Evaluated, INCB Says', Press Statement, UN Doc No UNIS/NAR/663 (19 May 1999); International Narcotics Control Board, 'Report of the International Narcotics Control Board for 2008' (2009) UN Doc No E/INCB/2008/1, para 430.

[35] See, for example, World Health Organization, UN Office on Drugs and Crime and UNAIDS, 'Technical Guide for Countries to set targets for Universal Access to HIV Prevention, Treatment and Care for Injecting Drug Users' (World Health Organization 2009).

has been widely criticised by human rights advocates.[36] Indeed, the Board has in the past gone on record to affirm that commenting on domestic laws and policies, such as the death penalty for drug offences, 'lie beyond the mandate and powers which have been conferred upon the Board by the international community',[37] although this position has begun to shift.

While one might expect to find active nullification in the work of the International Narcotics Control Board, given its location within the drug control regime, this approach is also found in the work of UN and regional human rights treaty bodies. A particularly illustrative example is the case of *Prince v South Africa* of the UN Human Rights Committee in 2007. The case concerned a qualified attorney (Prince), who was Rastafarian. The use of cannabis is a central tenet of the Rastafarian faith, and Prince had two convictions for cannabis offences on his criminal record as a result. These drug charges, along with Prince's assertion that he would continue to use cannabis as part of his religious practice, led the Law Society to reject his application for registration as a lawyer. In effect, he was 'placed in a position where he must choose between his faith and his legal career'.[38] Prince unsuccessfully took his case as far as the South African Constitutional Court, where a narrowly divided Court ruled against him.[39] Before the Human Rights Committee, he argued that the decisions of the South African courts violated his rights under Article 18(1) of the International Covenant on Civil and Political Rights, which enshrines both the freedom of religion and the right 'to manifest his religion or belief in worship, observance, practice and teaching'.[40]

Whether or not one agrees with Prince on the merits, there are clearly legal questions to be balanced in coming to a reasoned judgement. Indeed, both the majority and minority opinions in the judgement from the South African Constitutional Court engaged in such tests, coming to a divided 5–4 decision against him.[41] However, the approach of the Human Rights Committee was that such a robust test was not necessary or warranted. In the key paragraph of the judgement,

[36] See, for example, Barrett and Nowak (see chapter 1 n 24) 457–458, Joanne Csete, 'Overhauling Oversight' (see chapter 4 n 96), Csete and Wolfe (see chapter 2 n 220).

[37] Secretariat, International Narcotics Control Board (see chapter 4 n 75).

[38] UN Human Rights Committee, '*Prince v South Africa*, Communication No 1474/2006' (14 November 2007) UN Doc No CCPR/C/91/D/1474/2006, para 2.4.

[39] *Prince v President, Cape Law Society and Others* (n 2).

[40] International Covenant on Civil and Political Rights (see chapter 4 n 67) art 18(1).

[41] *Prince v President, Cape Law Society and Others* (n 2).

> The Committee observes that the prohibition of the possession and use of cannabis, which constitutes the limitation on the author's freedom to manifest his religion, is prescribed by the law. . . . It further notes the State party's conclusion that the law in question was designed to protect public safety, order, health, morals or the fundamental rights and freedoms of others, based on the harmful effects of cannabis, and that an exemption allowing a system of importation, transportation and distribution to Rastafarians may constitute a threat to the public at large, were any of the cannabis enter into general circulation. ***Under these circumstances the Committee cannot conclude that the prohibition of the possession and use of drugs, without any exemption for specific religious groups, is not proportionate and necessary to achieve this purpose.*** The Committee finds that the failure of the State party to grant Rastafarians an exemption to its general prohibition of possession and use of cannabis is, in the circumstances of the present case, justified under article 18, paragraph 3, and accordingly finds that the facts of the case do not disclose a violation of article 18, paragraph 1.[42]
>
> (emphasis added)

In its judgement, the Committee cites Article 18(3) of the Covenant, which states that the freedom of religion 'may be subject only to such limitations as are prescribed by law and are necessary to protect public safety, order, health, or morals or the fundamental rights and freedoms of others'.[43] Article 18(3) demands a proportionality test. However, the Committee failed to conduct a thoughtful test in this instance.

In its opinion, the Committee notes that cannabis prohibition, which was the source of the limitation on Prince, was prescribed by law. However, this fact was not in dispute. Rather, the test should have focussed on whether that law was in fact a proper and proportionate response 'necessary to protect public safety, order, health, or morals or the fundamental rights and freedoms of others'. Yet rather than interrogate the merits of the law in this regard, the Committee instead deferred to the 'State party's conclusion' that the legislation met these thresholds. It can hardly be imagined that the State would argue its own law was anything other than appropriate. Therefore, the Committee's uncritical acceptance of the State's own assessment of the purpose and effect of its drug laws not only actively nullified consideration of the freedom of religion, it also nullified the need to properly weigh the merits of the case. Such an outcome was presciently described by Justice Albie Sachs in his dissent to

[42] UN Human Rights Committee, '*Prince v South Africa*' (n 38) para 7.3.

[43] International Covenant on Civil and Political Rights (see chapter 4 n 67) art 18(3).

the majority opinion in Prince before the South African Constitutional Court. Wrote Sachs,

> [T]here is the tendency somnambulistically to sustain the existing system of administration of justice and the mind-set that goes with it, simply because, like Everest, it is there; in the words of Burger CJ, it is necessary to be aware of "requirements of contemporary society exerting a hydraulic insistence on conformity to majoritarian standards."[44]

The African Commission on Human and People's Rights also adopted an active nullification approach in its hearing of the Prince case, finding that 'the respondent state's interest to do away with the use of cannabis and its abuse/trafficking . . . constitutes a legitimate limitation on the exercise of the right to freedom of religion within the spirit of article 27(2) cum article 8'.[45] Prince also argued before the African Commission that his right to occupational choice under Article 15 had also been violated in the decision of the Law Society. Again, the Commission took an active nullification approach, noting 'the legitimate interest the state has in restricting the use and possession of cannabis' and that his right to choose a profession was not violated 'as he himself chose . . . to disqualify himself from inclusion by choosing to confront the legitimate restrictions' of the Law Society.[46] In effect, the Commission found that in choosing to observe his religious practice and use cannabis, Price was also making the decision to be barred from registration as an attorney.

Examples of an active nullification approach are also evident in domestic jurisprudence. One example is the 2007 case of *Edith Yunita Sianturi and others*, before the Constitutional Court of Indonesia.[47] The case examined the question of the death penalty for drug offences, and whether such offences met the threshold of 'most serious crimes' necessary for capital punishment under Article 6(2) of the International Covenant on Civil and Political Rights.[48] Although recognising the evidence from the petitioners that the UN Human Rights Committee, the body that oversees the Covenant, had found that drug offences do not meet this threshold, the majority of the Constitutional Court justices ruled that Indonesia's status as a State Party to the 1988 drug convention superseded its international

[44] Sachs dissenting opinion, *Prince v President, Cape Law Society and Others* (n 2) para 154.

[45] African Commission on Human and People's Rights, *Prince v South Africa* (2004) AHRLR 105 (ACHPR 2004), para 43.

[46] Ibid para 46. [47] *Edith Yunita Sianturi and others* (see chapter 4 n 178).

[48] International Covenant on Civil and Political Rights (see chapter 4 n 67) art 6(2).

human rights obligations. Specifically, the judgement referred to Article 24 of the 1988 Convention, which states that, '[a] Party may adopt more strict or severe measures than those provided by this Convention if, in its opinion, such measures are desirable or necessary for the prevention or suppression of illicit traffic'.[49] Referring to Article 24, the Court stated,

> In other words . . . if according to Indonesia, more severe measures are needed to prevent and eradicate such crimes, such measures are not contradictory to but rather are justified and suggested instead by the [1988 drug] Convention. This means that Indonesia as a state party adopting the system of capital punishment against certain Narcotics criminals has the right to determine capital punishment to the Narcotics criminals.[50]

In its judgement, the Court found that Article 24 of the 1988 drug convention actively nullified the effect of Article 6(2) of the International Covenant on Civil and Political Rights. The majority opinion judgement took this logic a step further, commenting that the drug conventions, or at least the Court's own interpretation of them, occupied a higher status in law than did the Covenant as interpreted by the Human Rights Committee.

> The consequences of Indonesia's participation in the Narcotic Drugs and Psychotropic Substances Convention [sic] in order to take more strict national measures in legally eradicating Narcotics crimes shall have a higher degree of binding force in the light of international law sources, as regulated in Article 38 Paragraph (1) of the Statute of International Court of Justice than the opinion of the Human Rights Commission of the United Nations [sic] to the effect that crimes related to the drugs abuse do not belong to the category of the most serious crimes.[51]

The examples cited above illustrate the degree to which both passive and active nullification act as impediments to the evolution of a 'fifth stage' of international drug control law. Were passive nullification the only barrier, then the challenges could be met simply by encouraging the relevant legal bodies to adopt more inter-disciplinary and holistic approaches to their respective mandates. In doing so, the legal contours of a 'fifth stage' approach would organically begin to evolve. However, the risk of active nullification demonstrates that simply promoting inter-disciplinary thinking between the regimes is insufficient to ensure that the outcome is an interpretive approach that safeguards human rights.

[49] 1988 Convention (see chapter 2 n 162) art 24.

[50] *Edith Yunita Sianturi and others* (see chapter 4 n 178) 103, para (i).

[51] Ibid 103, para (j).

Therefore, the question of how actual tensions and conflicts between the regimes should be balanced in a manner that avoids active nullification is critical.

7.4 Towards a 'Fifth Stage' of Drug Control Law

Chapter 5 examined how the norms of international drug control law and international human rights law interact in one of three ways: complementarity, tension or conflict. For the purposes of a dynamic 'fifth stage' of drug control, consideration of complementary or accumulating norms is of little concern, as these norms by definition add to or reinforce the normative content of each other. This is not to suggest that human rights concerns are not still evident. As in the case of access to essential medicines explored earlier, huge gaps in availability exist despite complementary international legal obligations. This section will however focus on the challenges of resolving regime tensions, where the implementation of drug control law, policy or enforcement breach human rights protections without an explicit treaty obligation to undertake such actions; and regime conflicts, where a Party to the drug control and human rights treaties cannot simultaneously comply with its obligations under both regimes.

In the words of South African Supreme Court Justice Albie Sachs, in his spirited dissent to the Court's majority opinion against Prince,

> In my view the majority judgment [against Prince] puts a thumb on the scales in favour of ease of law enforcement, and gives insufficient weight to the impact the measure will have, not only on the fundamental rights of the appellant and his . . . community, but on the basic notion of tolerance and respect for diversity that our Constitution demands for and from all in our society.[52]

Justice Sachs's metaphor of 'a thumb on the scales in favour of ease of law enforcement' neatly describes the process of active nullification of human rights considerations explored above. Therefore, a central challenge in developing a 'fifth stage' of international drug control is, at minimum, to remove the drug enforcement 'thumb on the scales' of justice that causes active nullification, thereby allowing the regimes to rebalance in favour of human rights. Indeed, in some cases a dynamic, human-rights based interpretation will require not simply removing the thumb but moving its

[52] Sachs dissenting opinion, *Prince v President, Cape Law Society and Others* (n 2) para 149.

force squarely onto the human rights side of the scales. Although engaging different interpretive processes and logics, a dynamic interpretive approach demands that both tensions and conflicts between the regimes be resolved in a manner in which the thumb is clearly on the side of the scales that ensures human rights are safeguarded.

7.4.1 Resolving Regime Tensions

Regime tensions are, by definition, not the outcome of a State implementing explicit drug treaty obligations, but rather are the result of how an obligation is interpreted by the State. Because tensions are not a consequence of explicit regime conflicts, and because '[i]n international law, there is a strong presumption against normative conflict',[53] a dynamic interpretive approach must necessarily be one that brings these laws, policies or practices into conformity with international human rights law. The process for resolving tensions through a dynamic approach can be illustrated using the three areas of regime tension explored in Chapter 4: the death penalty for drug offences, compulsory detention in the name of drug treatment and the provision of harm reduction services to active drug users.

7.4.1.1 Death Penalty for Drug Offences

As discussed previously, the death penalty for drugs has been a key area of regime tension between States and international human rights bodies. As seen in the Indonesian case above, it is also an issue that has led to some troubling jurisprudence at the domestic level, where international drug control obligations have been used to actively nullify human rights. However, despite the controversial history of the issue of the death penalty for drug offences, it is actually a question for which a dynamic interpretive approach offers a clear resolution. Given the 'strong presumption against normative conflict' in international law,[54] when balancing competing, or apparently competing, treaty obligations, the preferred interpretation is one that strives for consistency between all concurrent obligations for, as characterised by Jenks, '[i]t seems reasonable to start from a general presumption against conflict'.[55]

A dynamic interpretive approach to international drug control law takes this premise and operationalises it. In this case, none of the three

[53] Fragmentation Report (see chapter 1 n 54) 25, para 37.
[54] Ibid. [55] Jenks (see chapter 4 n 34) 427.

drug treaties makes mention of capital punishment. However, even if one were to accept a suggestion that the silence of the treaties on this question means that the death penalty is an allowable sanction within international drug control law, as was the opinion of the Constitutional Court of Indonesia[56] and the argument of the Government of India,[57] at the same time the drug treaties clearly do not obligate or compel States to enact capital drug laws. Therefore, even if allowed within the terms of the drug conventions, legislating for capital punishment for drug offences is clearly not *required* by the treaties. On the other hand, executions for drug offences are illegal under international human rights law, as described in Chapter 4. As a consequence, the only interpretive conclusion consistent with the international legal environment as a whole, avoiding normative conflict, is that capital punishment for drugs is unacceptable. International drug control law does not obligate capital punishment, therefore *not* executing people for drug offences does not violate any drug treaty obligations. At the same time, executions for drug offences *do* violate international human rights law. Therefore, an abolitionist national drug law is the only option consistent with both legal regimes, violating neither. This approach is again one consistent with the findings of the Fragmentation Report, which concluded that '[i]t is a generally accepted principle that when several norms bear on a single issue they should, to the extent possible, be interpreted so as to give rise to a single set of compatible obligations'.[58]

7.4.1.2 Compulsory Detention in the name of 'Drug Treatment'

A similar exercise undertaken on the question of compulsory detention for drug use again illustrates that adopting a dynamic interpretive approach results in a conclusion that safeguards human rights, and repudiates repressive drug policies. As described in Chapter 4, the compulsory detention *en masse* of persons who use, or are suspected of using, illegal drugs is a widespread issue of concern in a number of countries. It is also a policy that has received criticism from human rights bodies as constituting a form of arbitrary detention, violating the right to liberty

56 *Edith Yunita Sianturi and others* (see chapter 4 n 178).

57 Supreme Court of India (see chapter 4 n 76).

58 International Law Commission, 'Conclusions of the work of the Study Group on the Fragmentation of International Law: Difficulties arising from the Diversification and Expansion of International Law' (adopted at its Fifty-eighth session, 2006), para 4.

and security. The 1961 and 1971 drug treaties create clear obligations for States to provide drug treatment services.[59] However, similar to the question of the death penalty above, this obligation to provide treatment does not create a requirement to force people into treatment, or to detain them against their will for such purpose. In fact, the drafting history of Article 28 of the 1961 Convention reveals just the opposite.

The question of whether involuntary or compulsory drug treatment should be explicitly included within Article 38 was the source of significant debate during the plenipotentiary conference that finalised the draft treaty, driven primarily by the US delegation, which argued that '[t]reatment in liberty had failed wherever it had been tried'.[60] The United States proposed language that States Parties 'shall use their best endeavours to establish facilities for the compulsory treatment of drug addicts in closed institutions'.[61] Although the US proposal received some support,[62] it was eventually amended to remove reference to compulsory treatment in closed facilities, and instead the term 'adequate facilities' was agreed for use in the final treaty text.[63] Given the content of these drafting debates, and the specific and deliberate decision to delete reference to 'compulsory treatment of drug addicts in closed institutions' from the final 1961 treaty, it is difficult to make the case that international drug control law requires the use of involuntary detention or compulsory drug treatment. Moreover, from the perspective of international human rights law, the practice is clearly illegal, constituting breaches of both the right to liberty and security and the right to consent to treatment.[64] As compulsory detention is not required by treaty, the failure to provide it is not a breach of international drug control law. However, the compulsory detention of persons on the basis of providing drug treatment is a violation of international human rights law. Therefore, this tension again is one that is necessarily resolved in favour of human rights, as the prohibition of mass detention for the purposes of drug treatment is the only solution that is consistent with both legal regimes, violating neither.

[59] 1961 Convention amended (see chapter 2 n 171) art 38; 1971 Convention (see chapter 1 n 154) art 20.

[60] 1961 Official Records vol. I (see chapter 2 n 206) 103.

[61] 1961 Official Records vol. II (see chapter 3 n 40) 18. Article 38 of the final treaty was debated as draft Article 47.

[62] The Official Records indicate support from Canada, China, India, Iran and the United Arab Republic. 1961 Official Records vol. I (see chapter 2 n 206) 103, 106.

[63] 1961 Convention amended (see chapter 2 n 171) art 38.

[64] See, for example, UN General Assembly, 'Special Rapporteur Health 2010' (see chapter 1 n 28) para 38, Lines, 'Treatment in Liberty' (see chapter 4 n 108).

7.4.1.3 Harm Reduction

The same result is found when a dynamic process is applied to the question of the provision of harm reduction services such as needle and syringe programmes, access to opioid substitution treatment such as methadone and safe injecting facilities for people who use illicit drugs. Despite the controversy that discussions of harm reduction sometimes generates at both the domestic and international levels,[65] the provision of harm reduction services is not prohibited by the international drug control treaties. Although the approach of the International Narcotics Control Board towards harm reduction has been at best 'lukewarm'[66] and at worst 'generally hostile',[67] the Board does not, in the main, argue that key harm reduction interventions such as needle exchange and methadone are illegal. A significant departure is the Board's opposition to safe injecting facilities, which was discussed in Chapter 4. However the conclusion of the Legal Affairs Section of the UN Drug Control Program in 2002 on the question of harm reduction within the framework of the international drug control treaties was that not only needle exchange and opioid substitution but also safe injecting facilities were legal health interventions under the treaties.[68] Therefore, despite the contentious nature of the harm reduction question within some UN bodies, there is no credible basis upon which to suggest the approach is prohibited under the drug treaties. Within international human rights law, on the other hand, there is growing recognition that access to harm reduction constitutes a component element of the right to health under Article 12 of the International Covenant on Economic, Social and Cultural Rights,[69] essential to the fulfilment of that right among people who use drugs. The UN Special Rapporteur on the Right to Health has specifically highlighted access to harm reduction within the context of Article 12, calling on States to 'ensure that all harm-reduction measures . . . are available to people who use drugs'.[70] Therefore, taking a dynamic approach, the provision of harm reduction services does not breach the drug conventions, while the failure to provide them is increasingly considered to be a violation of the right to health under international human rights law. As a result, provision of

[65] See generally, Bewley-Taylor, *International Drug Control* (see chapter 2 n 2) Chapters 2, 3.

[66] Ibid 232. [67] Ibid 230. [68] See generally, Legal Affairs Section (see chapter 4 n 144).

[69] See, for example, UN Committee on Economic, Social and Cultural Rights, 'Concluding Observations: Tajikistan' (see chapter 4 n 121) para 70; 'Concluding Observations: Ukraine' (see chapter 4 n 122) para 28.

[70] UN General Assembly, 'Special Rapporteur Health 2010' (see chapter 1 n 28) para 76. See also UN Human Rights Council, 'Hunt Sweden Report' (see chapter 4 n 119) para 60.

harm reduction services by States is the only solution that is consistent with both regimes, violating neither.

A dynamic approach therefore offers a clear interpretive pathway for the resolution of the vast majority of human rights violations taking place under the auspices of drug control, namely those resulting from tensions rather than conflicts between the two regimes. Significantly, it offers an approach that has the effect of ensuring human rights are safeguarded, even as drug control treaty obligations are themselves fulfilled. In doing so, the risk of the active nullification of international human rights law is minimised or even eliminated. The second question is how a dynamic approach should be undertaken in instances where the two regimes come into explicit conflict.

7.4.2 *Resolving Regime Conflicts*

Human rights violations resulting from regime tensions are perhaps the most obvious and widespread, and as discussed above are perhaps easiest to resolve in favour of human rights protection using established rules of interpretation. However, the question of conflicts between treaty obligations within the two regimes, ‘where simultaneous compliance with the obligations of different instruments is impossible’,[71] must also be considered. Although these instances are less frequent in the context of human rights and drug control than are the tensions, they nonetheless require attention when considering the development of a ‘fifth stage’ of drug control. This section will explore a dynamic interpretative approach using the two examples of regime conflict described in Chapter 4, the traditional uses of coca and the application of more severe measures.

7.4.2.1 Traditional Uses of Coca

Article 49 of the 1961 Convention is perhaps the clearest example of regime conflict between the drug control and human rights legal systems, creating a positive obligation to eradicate the chewing of the coca leaf,[72] a traditional practice of cultural significance to many indigenous peoples in the Andean region of South America. Article 49 therefore comes into explicit conflict with State obligations to protect the traditional cultural practices of indigenous peoples reflected in multiple human rights

[71] Jenks (see chapter 4 n 34) 451.

[72] 1961 Convention amended (see chapter 2 n 171) art 49(2)(e).

instruments and the work of human rights bodies.[73] The challenge of resolving this conflict is addressed by Pfeiffer and illustrates the inherent limitations of a traditional interpretive approach when balancing obligations in drug control law and human rights law. While not intending to do so, the article affirms the need for a dynamic approach to prevent human rights protection from being actively nullified by drug control law.

Pfeiffer's interpretive approach is built on the assumption that '[g]iven the rigidity of the rules on drug control, it is necessary to consider whether the rules on the rights of indigenous peoples are more flexible in allowing for harmonization and systemic integration'.[74] In other words, he begins the balancing process from the presumption that only human rights obligations offer flexibility or interpretative space in this matter, which has the inevitable consequence of putting 'a thumb on the scales' in favour of international drug control law over international human rights law. The analysis adopts a proportionality test using a human rights framework, yet one in which the drug control norm is deemed sacrosanct and the only relevant interpretive question is to what degree, and under what conditions, it is acceptable to limit indigenous rights. The idea that drug control norms should themselves be open to evolutive interpretation, particularly in the context of the codification and expansion of the international law on indigenous rights in the decades subsequent to the entry into force of the 1961 drug treaty, does not enter into the analysis. Pfeiffer himself recognises the limitations of this approach, which he admits inevitably undermines human rights protection, as 'the rules in question can be harmonized only by restricting the right of indigenous peoples to their customs and traditions'.[75] He continues,

> States who are obliged to implement the prohibition on coca leaf chewing can restrict the right of indigenous peoples to their customs and traditions, but should follow the appropriate procedures to do so in consultation with the peoples concerned, in line with the object and purpose of the relevant instruments. Although this outcome appears legally sound, it is not very favorable to the rights of indigenous peoples, because the balance to be drawn will be tilted in favor of the abolition of coca leaf chewing.[76]

[73] Universal Declaration of Human Rights (see chapter 3 n 86) art 27; International Covenant on Civil and Political Rights (see chapter 4 n 67) art 27; International Covenant on Economic, Social and Cultural Rights (see chapter 4 n 45) art 15; Committee on the Elimination of All Forms of Racial Discrimination (see chapter 1 n 56) paras 4–5; United Nations Declaration on the Rights of Indigenous Peoples (2 October 2007) UN Doc No A/RES/61/295, art 31.

[74] Pfeiffer (see chapter 1 n 60) 313. [75] Ibid 323. [76] Ibid 318.

Pfeiffer's conclusion touches on the critical question in the context of dynamic interpretation, 'whether the rule to abolish coca leaf chewing has lost its legitimacy and whether the principle of harmonization should be applied in this case'.[77] Given the extensive framework of international legal protection for indigenous rights that has emerged since 1961, any interpretive process occurring in a modern legal context cannot be anchored on the notion of Article 49 as a rigid norm. Pauwelyn characterises this type of conflict as a 'conflict in the applicable law', or a case in which '[c]ompliance with, or exercise of the rights under, one of the two norms constitutes breach under the other norm'.[78] In resolving such situations, the question is not 'which of the two norms survives, but which of the two norms applies. In that sense, "conflict of applicable law" is a question of "choice of law"; not one of validity or legality of one norm in the light of another norm'.[79] Says Pauwelyn,

> In terms of state responsibility . . . only the rule that must finally be applied can be breached and result in responsibility. The discarded rule does not apply and can hence *a fortiori* not be breached. However, although this rule is disapplied in the particular circumstances, it is not declared invalid nor is it in any way seen as an 'illegal' rule. It is simply a rule that must give way to another in one of the circumstances. In other circumstances, the discarded rule may continue to apply.[80]

The circumstances described by Pauwelyn neatly characterise the conflict regarding the traditional uses of coca. The application of Article 49 on coca does not universally conflict with international human rights obligations on indigenous rights. For States without a tradition of coca chewing, even those with large indigenous populations, Article 49 poses no inherent human rights conflict. However, for those few countries where traditional indigenous use of coca is evident, a conflict exists for those governments seeking to fulfil their obligations under both regimes. Resolving this conflict demands an evolutive, human rights-based approach. As written by Justice Albie Sachs in his dissent in the Prince case, '[f]or the purposes of balancing, some laws (or parts of laws) will of necessity be more equal than others'.[81]

In this case, and in these States, the laws on indigenous rights are the 'more equal' laws for the purposes of interpretation, and adopting a dynamic approach requires that the international legal protection of the

[77] Ibid 324. [78] Pauwelyn (see chapter 1 n 55) 275. [79] Ibid 327. [80] Ibid.

[81] Sachs dissenting opinion, *Prince v President, Cape Law Society and Others* (n 2) para 154.

cultural rights of indigenous coca-using communities should prevail over Article 49 of the 1961 drug convention. To paraphrase Pauwelyn, the rule in the drug treaty must 'give way' to the rule in human rights law in this particular circumstance, given the current development of international law as a whole. The *Judge v Canada* case before the Human Rights Committee, where the Committee found that 'a broadening international consensus in favour of abolition of the death penalty' was a sufficient basis to 'review . . . the scope of the application of the rights protected' under Article 6 of the International Covenant on Civil and Political Rights[82] offers an instructive parallel example of how a dynamic interpretive approach might look in the case of coca. The Committee found 'that the protection of human rights evolves and that the meaning of Covenant rights should in principle be interpreted by reference to the time of examination and not, as the State party has submitted, by reference to the time the alleged violation took place'.[83] Considering Article 49 of the 1961 drug treaty in this light, it is impossible to conceive of a modern international instrument being adopted in which the eradication of a historically documented indigenous practice is made a core State obligation. Resolving this conflict is therefore not a question of how and where to restrict indigenous rights in order to satisfy the rules of drug control, as suggested by Pfeiffer, but instead an instance where the logic of drug control is not applicable to a modern international legal environment in which indigenous rights have achieved a protected status that did not exist in 1961. The onus should not be on States to restrict their interpretation of human rights law to that as existed at the time the 1961 drug treaty was adopted, but rather to interpret 1961 drug control obligations that engage human rights as evolving in the context of modern international law, or in the words of the Human Rights Committee, it should 'be interpreted by reference to the time of examination'.

Boister writes that although the drug 'conventions are principally concerned with effective crime control, one of their functions should be to protect the human rights of the individuals subject to their processes'.[84] In this context, and in keeping with the *telos* of the drug control regime, protecting and promoting the cultural rights of indigenous communities in the Andean region means that the obligation defined in Article 49 regarding coca must give way. This is not to say the obligation as a whole has 'lost its legitimacy', to use Pfeiffer's term, but rather that in these

[82] Ibid. [83] Ibid, para 10.7.
[84] Boister, 'Suppression Conventions' (n 15) 201.

particular circumstances, in the specific countries where the conflict is extant, international human rights norms must take precedence. Otherwise, what is left is a process that actively nullifies indigenous cultural rights.

The case for dynamic interpretation in this instance is made even more compelling when weighing counter arguments, which are essentially based on the premise that allowing for the indigenous use of coca will weaken the international drug control regime. This was a common theme among the States lodging objections to Bolivia's 2012 reservation to Article 49, which had the effect of allowing traditional uses of coca within the country. The United States, for example, argued that this would mean 'more cocaine will be available for the global cocaine market, further fueling narcotics trafficking and related criminal activities'.[85] Similarly, the United Kingdom objected that allowing traditional uses of coca 'could lead to increases in coca production and . . . weaken international law as it relates to the global effort to tackle drugs'.[86] The International Narcotics Control Board also issued a similar statement.[87] However, given the huge scope of the international illicit market in cocaine, it is difficult to make the case that allowing licit traditional uses among indigenous communities in a handful of countries will truly undermine global drug prohibition. Interestingly, the 2013 UN World Drug Report reports a decline in coca bush cultivation in Bolivia, not the increase predicted in the statements above.[88] It also suggests that 'the growth in global population may be a major driving force in setting the trend for global demand', rather than the available supply driving use.[89]

In testing this opposition to a dynamic approach it is also useful to draw insight from other areas of international law. For example, the United Nations Convention on Biological Diversity provides guidance

[85] Permanent Mission of the United States to the United Nations, 'United States: Objection to the Reservation contained in the in the communication by the Plurinational State of Bolivia' (3 July 2012), UN Doc. No. C.N.101.2012.TREATIES-VI.18 (Depository Notifications) 1.

[86] Permanent Mission of the United Kingdom to the United Nations, 'United Kingdom: Objection to the Reservation contained in the in the communication by the Plurinational State of Bolivia' (14 December 2012), UN Doc No C.N.719.2012.TREATIES-VI.18 (Depository Notifications) 2.

[87] International Narcotics Control Board, 'International Narcotics Control Board Regrets Bolivia's Denunciation of the Single Convention on Narcotic Drugs' (see chapter 4 n 166).

[88] UN Office on Drugs and Crime, 'World Drug Report 2013' (see chapter 1 n 22) 37.

[89] Ibid.

on interpretation under Article 22, 'Relationship with Other International Conventions'.[90] It states that the Convention will only 'affect the rights and obligations . . . deriving from any existing international agreement . . . where the exercise of those rights and obligations would cause a serious damage or threat to biological diversity'.[91] Using this threshold as guidance, it is difficult to credibly argue that allowing the traditional use of coca in a handful of States presents 'serious damage or threat' to the fabric of the international drug control regime. However, it can easily be argued that the obligation to eradicate the use of coca represents a 'serious damage or threat' to the rights of those indigenous communities in which coca forms an important traditional and cultural practice. Using another example from a separate body of international law, the International Whaling Commission recognises 'that indigenous or "aboriginal subsistence" whaling is of a different nature to commercial whaling. It is thus not subject to the [international commercial whaling] moratorium'.[92] This accommodation by the International Whaling Commission to respect the cultural practices of indigenous communities is allowed in only four countries,[93] approximately the same number of States for which there is history of indigenous coca use, and offers a clear example of a regime in which global prohibition (in this case on commercial whaling) is not considered to be weakened or threatened by a specific exception for indigenous cultural practices. Therefore, a dynamic interpretation of this particular conflict must be resolved by placing the 'thumb on the scales' of human rights in those States where the conflict is apparent.

7.4.2.2 Application of More Severe Measures

A second area of conflict explored in Chapter 4 is the permissive obligation common to all three drug treaties allowing States to adopt 'more strict or severe measures' than those required in the treaties themselves.[94] As explored above, the Indonesian Constitutional Court cited Article 24 of the 1988 Convention as a basis to uphold the legality of the death penalty

[90] Convention on Biological Diversity (see chapter 6 n 28) art 22.

[91] Ibid; Pauwelyn (see chapter 1 n 55) 330.

[92] International Whaling Commission, 'Aboriginal Subsistence Whaling' www.iwc.int/aboriginal accessed 14 April 2014.

[93] Denmark, the Russian Federation, St Vincent and The Grenadines and the United States, Ibid.

[94] 1961 Convention amended (see chapter 2 n 171) art 39; 1971 Convention (see chapter 2 n 154) art 23; 1988 Convention (see chapter 2 n 162) art 24.

for drug offences.[95] This case demonstrates how these permissive obligations, enshrined without safeguards or limitations,[96] create a potential justification for the active nullification of human rights obligations and violation of international human rights law. The mere existence of these permissive norms alongside parallel human rights treaties does not in itself create a conflict.[97] The conflict only emerges where the permissive norm is invoked to violate another norm, as occurred in the Indonesian case. In adopting a dynamic approach to considering these permissive norms, it is apparent that appropriate conflict resolution, or even conflict avoidance, must be a process that again places the 'thumb on the scales' of human rights. This conclusion is evident for two reasons.

The first is the consideration of the context of the permissive articles themselves. Although each allows for the application of 'more strict or severe measures', the context of this permission is limited specifically to the terms of the drug conventions. For example, Article 39 of the 1961 Convention states that 'a Party shall not be, or be deemed to be, precluded from adopting measures of control more strict or severe than those provided by this Convention'.[98] Article 24 of the 1988 Convention similarly states that '[a] Party may adopt more strict or severe measures than those provided by this Convention'.[99] Identical wording is used to frame the permissive article in the 1971 Convention.[100] In each case, the provision is situated specifically within the relevant drug treaty, and defines permission to adopt measures only beyond those prescribed in each convention. It does not permit the adoption of more strict or severe measures than those legally allowed elsewhere in international law, or provide permission to exceed safeguards established in other legal regimes.

The context now established, the second consideration is one of appropriate balance. As the nature of the permissive norm is strictly limited to the scope of the drug conventions themselves, the question then is how this obligation interacts with those of other legal regimes, specifically international human rights law. In this case, applying more strict and severe measures of drug control than those outlined in the treaties is allowable only to the degree that the measures in question do not violate other international legal obligations. Given the presumption in

95 *Edith Yunita Sianturi and others* (see chapter 4 n 178) 103, para (i).
96 Boister, *Penal Aspects* (see chapter 1 n 57) 527. 97 Jenks (see chapter 4 n 34) 451.
98 1961 Convention amended (see chapter 2 n 171) art 39.
99 1988 Convention (see chapter 2 n 162) art 24.
100 1971 Convention (see chapter 2 n 154) art 23.

international law against normative conflict, the correct application of these permissive obligations must be one that maintains coherence with parallel international human rights obligations, and places a 'thumb on the scales' of human rights. Herein lies the essential error at the heart of the Indonesian Constitutional Court's application of this provision. As the permissive obligations within the drug conventions are limited narrowly to the measures within the drug treaties, the Court's invoking Article 24 as justification to override Article 6(2) of the International Covenant on Civil and Political Rights is a misapplication of the provision, creating a breach of international human rights law. As described by Jenks, '[t]here is no conflict if... it is possible to comply with the obligations of one instrument by refraining from exercising a privilege or discretion accorded by another'.[101] Therefore, international human rights law must always act as a limiting control on the interpretation of these permissive obligations in order to avoid or mediate regime conflict.

7.5 Conclusion

International drug control law and international human rights law engage each other in multiple ways, and in multiple fora, both international and domestic. In many cases, this engagement results in tensions or even conflicts between the regimes, resulting in undermining human rights protections. Resolving these engagements in a manner that protects fundamental human rights norms is the key challenge in the evolution of a 'fifth stage' of drug control. Chapter 7 has explored how this evolution might look in practice, outlining the legal bodies and fora through which a dynamic, human rights-based approach to drug control must evolve, and outlining the basic principles that should guide the necessary balancing tests. Moving beyond the approaches of passive and active nullification that have historically impeded progressive legal evolution in this area, a dynamic approach offers clear guidance to ensure that the balancing exercise between human rights and drug control, upholding that human rights standards in a manner consistent with the *telos* of the drug control regime, and in most cases the obligations it enshrines.

[101] Jenks (see chapter 4 n 34) 451.

8

The Future for a 'Fifth Stage' of Drug Control

This book has explored the question of treaty interpretation within international drug control law. Specifically, it has addressed the problem of human rights violations occurring in the name of drug control and enforcement, and proposed an interpretive approach to resolving tensions and conflicts between drug control law and human rights law to prevent such abuses. Through this process, it has proposed a framework and possible interpretive fora for the development of a 'fifth stage' of drug control, one that ensures obligations enshrined within international drug control law are carried out in a manner that is human rights compliant.

At the time of this writing, such a 'fifth stage' of drug control remains far from being achieved. Although United Nations human rights mechanisms and Special Procedures have in recent years become more active in addressing drug control issues within their mandates, examples are still so rare as to be notable when they occur. The Office of the High Commissioner for Human Rights, for example, made its first public statement on drug control in only 2009.[1] While the Special Rapporteurs on torture and on the right to health have done important thematic work on drug control within their mandates, in 2009[2] and 2010[3] respectively, as has the UN Working Group on Arbitrary Detention in 2015,[4] such cross-cutting work by the Special Procedures remains the exception.

The UN drug control system has also taken some steps towards recognising human rights concerns, although the examples are again rare and unconvincing. The first and only human rights resolution by the

1 Office of the UN High Commissioner for Human Rights, 'High Commissioner calls for focus on human rights and harm reduction in international drug policy' (see chapter 4 n 129).

2 UN Human Rights Council, 'Nowak Report' (see chapter 1 n 41).

3 UN General Assembly, 'Special Rapporteur Health 2010' (see chapter 1 n 28).

4 WGAD 2015 (see chapter 4 n 86).

Commission on Narcotic Drugs was adopted in 2008.[5] Although highly contentious at the time, use of basic language acknowledging human rights has subsequently become relatively routine in Commission resolutions.[6] In 2010, the outgoing Executive Director of the UN Office on Drugs and Crime released an important conference room paper during the Commission on Narcotic Drugs session, addressing the question of a human rights perspective on drug control and crime prevention.[7] This was followed two years later by a guidance paper on human rights and drug enforcement by the Office on Drugs and Crime.[8]

However, despite these positive steps, the UN drug control bodies still struggle to fully embrace a human rights perspective in their deliberations. The more common appearance of the term 'human rights' in resolutions of the Commission on Narcotic Drugs has not resulted in concrete operational commitments to ensure rights are considered within, let alone at the centre of, drug control efforts. Despite the positive recommendations contained in its 2012 human rights guidance paper, the UN Office on Drugs and Crime has yet to operationalise its key recommendations, and the report has largely disappeared within the agency. In 2014, a paper on international drug control law prepared for the Commission on Narcotic Drugs returned to using the 'evil', threat-based language explored in Chapter 3. According to that document, 'people become dependent on drugs, slaves of drug dealers, isolated from the community, deprived of mental health and cognitive/affective abilities. This is inconsistent with basic human rights'.[9] Within this conception of drug control, fighting drug dealers and traffickers who inflict 'chemical slavery' becomes synonymous with advancing rights, a road that quickly becomes a tool for justifying

[5] UN Commission on Narcotic Drugs, 'Strengthening cooperation between the United Nations Office on Drugs and Crime and other United Nations entities for the promotion of human rights in the implementation of the international drug control treaties' (March 2008) Res 51/12.

[6] See, for example, UN Commission on Narcotic Drugs, 'Preventing the use of illicit drugs within Member States and strengthening international cooperation on policies of drug abuse prevention' (March 2010) Res 53/2, preamble.; 'Achieving universal access to prevention, treatment, care and support for drug users and people living with or affected by HIV' (March 2010) Res 53/9, preamble.

[7] UN Commission on Narcotic Drugs, 'Drug control, crime prevention and criminal justice: A Human Rights perspective. Note by the Executive Director' (March 2010) UN Doc No E/CN.7/2010/CRP.6-E/CN.15/2010/CRP.1.

[8] UN Office on Drugs and Crime, 'UNODC and the Promotion and Protection of Human Rights: A Position Paper' (2012) United Nations Office on Drugs and Crime.

[9] UN Commission on Narcotic Drugs, 'Drug policy provisions from the international drug control Conventions' (10 February 2014) UN Doc No E/CN.7/2014/CRP.5, 14.

abusive State policies and practices, including the death penalty. Given this context, what is the future outlook for a 'fifth stage' of drug control?

An indication of the continuing challenge within the drug control regime was apparent during the preparations for the April 2016 United Nations General Assembly Special Session (UNGASS) on drugs. The text of the resolution adopted by consensus at the General Assembly was agreed among Member States at the 2016 Commission on Narcotic Drugs session in March, and reflects the continuing tensions between human rights and drug control. While the document importantly eschews the threat- and fear-based framing so common in previous similar resolutions,[10] by the time the final text was negotiated, specific references to the right to health and the right to informed consent to treatment found in the first draft in January has been stripped out, as had a call for annual reporting on human rights and drug control to the Commission on Narcotic Drugs.[11] A caveat that the content of certain provisions must conform to applicable national laws, thereby allowing States significant discretion in observing (or not) international human rights norms, was inserted throughout.

Interestingly, despite the often fraught drafting debates, the final resolution included the strongest ever operational paragraph on human rights ever adopted in a UN drug control resolution. It states that governments will

> Promote and implement effective criminal justice responses to drug-related crimes to bring perpetrators to justice that ensure legal guarantees and due process safeguards pertaining to criminal justice proceedings, including practical measures to uphold the prohibition of arbitrary arrest and detention and of torture and other cruel, inhuman or degrading treatment or punishment and to eliminate impunity, in accordance with relevant and applicable international law and taking into account United Nations standards and norms on crime prevention and criminal justice, and ensure timely access to legal aid and the right to a fair trial.[12]

Rather than the usual and vague aspirational human rights language found in this and previous drug control resolutions, this paragraph creates operational commitments for governments to 'implement effective . . . responses' to prohibit abuses such as arbitrary detention and

[10] UN Commission on Narcotic Drugs (see chapter 4 n 54).

[11] 'UNGASS 2016: Our joint commitment in addressing the world drug problem' Draft Outcome Document (14 January 2016) Prepared by the UNGASS Board for consideration by the Commission on Narcotic Drugs, paras 4(e), 1(h), 4(f).

[12] UN Commission on Narcotic Drugs (chapter 4 n 54) p 16, para O.

torture and other cruel, inhuman or degrading treatment or punishment. This clearly creates a mandate for UN Charter-based human rights bodies, such as the Office of the High Commissioner, the Human Rights Council and the Special Procedures, to engage in drug control issues in a sustained manner within their own working practices.[13] For example, there is a growing consensus within international human rights law that the use of death penalty in any context constitutes a form of torture, or cruel, inhuman or degrading treatment, a perspective that the UN Special Rapporteur on Torture describes as one that 'is developing into a norm of customary law, if it has not already done so'.[14] Significantly, the paragraph does not contain the usual caveat making it subject to applicable domestic law, instead clearly stating it will be implemented 'in accordance with relevant and applicable international law'. Therefore, this provision potentially offers a tool to press for abolition of the death penalty for drug offences within UN drug control fora, and an invitation for UN human rights bodies to engage directly with drug control mechanisms on this and other key issues.

Despite small progress, the challenges and barriers inherent to overcoming fifty years of institutional inertia on these issues within both systems, and of bridging the 'parallel universes' identified by Paul Hunt, should not be underestimated. Every year since 1990, the UN General Assembly has adopted a major resolution on drug control, in part '[r]ecognizing that the fight against drug abuse and illicit trafficking should be pursued in full conformity with the principles enshrined in the Charter of the United Nations, and the principles of international law'.[15] In 1993, the resolution '[re]affirm[ed] that the international fight against drug trafficking should not in any way justify violation of the principles enshrined in the Charter of the United Nations and international law'.[16]

[13] For a more detailed analysis of this provision, see Rick Lines and Damon Barrett, 'The human rights "win" at the UNGASS on drugs that no one is talking about, and how we can use it' (Human Rights Centre Blog, University of Essex, 9 May 2016) https://hrcessex.wordpress.com/2016/05/09/the-human-rights-win-at-the-ungass-on-drugs-that-no-one-is-talking-about-and-how-we-can-use-it accessed 23 May 2016.

[14] UN General Assembly, 'Interim report of the Special Rapporteur on torture and other cruel, inhuman or degrading treatment or punishment' (9 August 2012) UN Doc No A/67/279, para 74.

[15] UN General Assembly, 'Respect for the principles enshrined in the Charter of the United Nations and international law in the fight against drug abuse and illicit trafficking' (18 December 1990) UN Doc No A/RES/45/147, paras 2, 8.

[16] UN General Assembly, 'International action to combat drug abuse and illicit production and trafficking' (20 December 1993) UN Doc No A/Res/48/112, para I(3).

Beginning in 1997, this annual resolution began to make specific reference to human rights, that year '[s]tressing that respect for human rights is and must be an essential component of measures taken to address the drug problem'.[17] In more recent years, the agreed language in this regard has been strengthened, and the 2011 resolution read that the General Assembly,

> *Reaffirms* that countering the world drug problem . . . must be carried out in full conformity with the purposes and principles of the Charter of the United Nations and other provisions of international law, the Universal Declaration of Human Rights and the Vienna Declaration and Programme of Action on human rights, and, in particular, with full respect for the sovereignty and territorial integrity of States, for the principle of non-intervention in the internal affairs of States and for all human rights and fundamental freedoms, and on the basis of the principles of equal rights and mutual respect.[18]

In one sense then, the need to reconcile international drug control law obligations with those of other international legal regimes has been repeatedly articulated. However, despite more than twenty years of General Assembly acknowledgement of this gap, examples of these principles being put into practice remain few and far between.

However, there have been some instances of promise, where the potential impacts of a 'fifth stage' interpretive process have been demonstrated. For example, in March 2014, the International Narcotics Control Board issued a public statement 'encourag[ing] States to consider the abolition of the death penalty for drug related offences'.[19] This statement was important for at least two reasons. The first is that it was a reversal of the Board's long standing position that the drug treaties gave States the latitude to determine criminal penalties and sanctions themselves, placing it beyond the mandate of the Board to comment upon issues such as capital punishment.[20] More significant, however, was the Board's assertion that in reaching this new position, it was accepting the relevance of international human rights law. While re-affirming its previous position that 'specific sanctions applicable to drug-related offences remains the

[17] UN General Assembly, 'International action to combat drug abuse and illicit production and trafficking' (28 January 1997) UN Doc No A/RES/51/64, 3.

[18] UN General Assembly, 'International cooperation against the world drug problem' (see chapter 3 n 109) p 4, para 2.

[19] United Nations Information Service, 'INCB encourages States to consider the abolition of the death penalty for drug-related offences' (5 March 2014) UN Doc No UNIS/NAR/1199.

[20] See Chapter 4.

prerogative of States Parties', it explained that its new position 'takes into account the relevant international conventions and protocols, and resolutions of the General Assembly, the Economic and Social Council and UN bodies pertaining to the death penalty'.[21] While conspicuously avoiding any explicit acknowledgement of such, the Board's statement accepts the relevance of human rights norms and standards within its own deliberations, and in doing so exhibits a human rights-based evolution of its interpretation of the question of capital punishment. Although when questioned by the author during the 2014 session of the Commission on Narcotic Drugs, Board President Raymond Yans refused to acknowledge that this approach was relevant to other areas of the Board's mandate such as harm reduction,[22] the statement clearly opens the potential for future engagement with human rights norms. The Board's statements on human rights continued the following year. In his address to the 2015 special session of the Commission on Narcotic Drugs, Board President Lochlan Naidoo stated that

> Drug-related policies and strategies must reflect due regard to human rights... Once again and in line with developments within the United Nations, the Board urges all countries that continue to retain the death penalty for drug-related offences to consider abolishing capital punishment for this category of offences.[23]

Dr Naidoo also emphasised that 'Nothing in the [Drug] Conventions requires States to incarcerate drug users'.[24] In his March 2016 speech to the Commission on Narcotic Drugs, Board President Werner Sipp went further, stating that 'respect for human rights' is one of three 'fundamental principles the drug control system is based on'.[25] These statements offer clear examples of the potential for the Board to be a forum where evolutive human rights-based interpretation can occur, and also hint at its as yet unrealised potential to promote the operationalisation of human

21 United Nations Information Service (n 19).

22 Author's notes from the meeting, 18 March 2014, United Nations Headquarters, Vienna.

23 International Narcotics Control Board, 'Statement by Dr. Lochlan Naidoo, President, International Narcotics Control Board', Fifty-eighth session of the Commission on Narcotic Drugs Special segment on preparations for the special session of the General Assembly on the world drug problem (UNGASS) to be held in 2016 Vienna, 9–17 March 2015.

24 Ibid.

25 International Narcotics Control Board, 'Statement by Mr. Werner Sipp, President, International Narcotics Control Board (INCB), Fifty-ninth session of the Commission on Narcotic Drugs, Preparations for the special session of the General Assembly on the world drug problem to be held in 2016' (14 March 2016) 2.

rights-based approaches to drug policy within its mandate to engage with States.

Some positive steps were also seen within the UN human rights system in 2015, when the Human Rights Council passed a specific resolution on drug control at its twenty-eighth session. The resolution, a first for the Council, was intended to promote the engagement of the Council and the Office of the High Commissioner for Human Rights with the UN General Assembly Special Session on Drugs in April 2016. It specifically requested the High Commissioner's office

> [T]o prepare a study [for the Council] . . . on the impact of the world drug problem on the enjoyment of human rights, and recommendations on respect for and the protection and promotion of human rights in the context of the world drug problem, with particular consideration for the needs of persons affected and persons in vulnerable situations.[26]

In addition, the resolution called for a thematic panel on drug policy and human rights, as well as promoting enhanced engagement between the High Commissioner's office and the Commission on Narcotic Drugs.[27] That panel on 'the impact of the world drug problem on the enjoyment of human rights' was held during the Council's 30th session in September 2015.[28]

The preparation of the High Commissioner's report for the Council was notable for the significant number of submissions contributed to the process. In total, twenty-four Member States, three UN agencies, the Council of Europe, four national human rights institutions and over thirty civil society organisations from all regions of the world made submissions to the High Commissioner's office.[29] This unprecedented level of participation, unimaginable even five years earlier, is an indication of the growing awareness of the human rights impacts of drug control efforts. The High Commissioner's report was published in early September 2015 in advance of the Human Rights Council session.[30] In December 2015, the Special

[26] UN Human Rights Council, 'Contribution of the Human Rights Council to the special session of the General Assembly on the world drug problem of 2016' (2 April 2015) UN Doc No A/HRC/RES/28/28, para 1.

[27] Ibid paras 2–4.

[28] UN Human Rights Council, 'Annotations to the agenda for the thirtieth session of the Human Rights Council' (5 August 2015) UN Doc No A/HRC/30/1, 20.

[29] For details of these submissions, see UN High Commission for Human Rights, 'The impact of the world drug problem on the enjoyment of human rights' www.ohchr.org/EN/HRBodies/HRC/Pages/WorldDrugProblem.aspx accessed 18 September 2015.

[30] Office of the UN High Commissioner for Human Right (see chapter 4 n 73).

Rapporteur on the Right to Health made a written submission to the General Assembly Special Session on drugs 'to reflect upon the achievements and challenges of international drug control, and its impact upon the enjoyment of human rights and fundamental freedoms'.[31]

Evidence of a dynamic, as opposed to a nullifying, interpretive approach can also be found at domestic level, where important examples exist of national courts playing a positive role in mitigating the negative human rights impacts of drug laws. A significant example is found in the jurisprudence of the Supreme Court of Canada. As described in Chapter 4, a series of domestic court cases were taken by the Canadian federal government in an attempt to force the closure of 'Insite', a safe injecting facility in Vancouver, British Columbia, which operated with the support of both the city and the province. Specifically, the federal government argued that in knowingly allowing people to possess and consume illegal drugs within the facility, Insite was in violation of the federal Controlled Drugs and Substances Act (CDSA).[32] When the facility was first established some years earlier, the previous Liberal federal government had issued a waiver to the relevant provisions of the Act to enable the facility to operate its health services within the law. However, the subsequent Conservative federal government refused to renew the waiver, thereby placing Insite in violation of the Act. The case eventually went to the Supreme Court in 2011.

An element of the Court's deliberations in this case, and one of direct relevance to a 'fifth stage' approach to interpretation, was its testing of the relevant drug control provisions in light of Article 7 of the Canadian Charter of Rights and Freedoms,[33] assessing whether subsections '4(1) and 5(1) of the CDSA, which prohibit possession and trafficking respectively, are invalid because they limit the claimants' s[ection] 7 rights to life, liberty and security of the person'.[34] The Court found that subsection 4(1) of the Controlled Drugs and Substances Act prohibiting possession constituted a violation of the rights to life, liberty and security of the

31 Office of the High Commissioner for Human Rights, 'Open Letter by the Special Rapporteur on the right of everyone to the highest attainable standard of mental and physical health, Dainius Pūras, in the context of the preparations for the UN General Assembly Special Session on the Drug Problem (UNGASS), which will take place in New York in April 2016' (7 December 2015).

32 Controlled Drugs and Substances Act (S.C. 1996, c. 19).

33 Canadian Charter of Rights and Freedoms, s 2, Part I of the Constitution Act, 1982, being Schedule B to the Canada Act 1982 (UK), 1982, c 11.

34 *Attorney General v PHS Community Services Society*, 2011 SCC 44 (SSC), para 75.

person of Insite staff because 'by operating the premises – opening the doors and welcoming prohibited drugs inside – the staff responsible for the centre may be "in possession" of drugs brought in by clients' and 'their minimal involvement with clients' drugs may bring them within the legal concept of illegal possession of drugs, contrary to s. 4(1)'.[35] The Court concluded that the violations of the rights of staff in this regard would inevitably result in further violations of the rights of the people using the health clinic. According to the judgement,

> [W]ithout an exemption from the application of the CDSA, the health professionals who provide the supervised services at Insite will be unable to offer medical supervision and counselling to Insite's clients. This deprives the clients of Insite of potentially lifesaving medical care, thus engaging their rights to life and security of the person. The result is that the limits on the s. 7 rights of staff will in turn result in limits on the s. 7 rights of clients.[36]

The justices took this argument a step further, finding not only an indirect violation of the rights of people who use Insite but also a direct violation of their rights, as '[i]n order to make use of the lifesaving and health-protecting services offered at Insite, clients must be allowed to be in possession of drugs on the premises. To prohibit possession by drug users *anywhere* engages their liberty interests; to prohibit possession at Insite engages their rights to life and to security of the person'.[37]

In an approach relevant to that proposed here, the Supreme Court's consideration of the case was informed by its assessment of what it called 'the dual purpose of the *CDSA*: the protection of both public safety and public health'.[38] In effect, the objective of the control measures defined within the national drug legislation was not control for the sake of control, but rather control to promote other public interests, in this case public health. If elements of that law were found to undermine public health, then clearly those measures were neither consistent with human rights protections, nor with the objectives of the drug legislation itself. The Insite decision offers a clear window into the potential benefits of a 'fifth stage' interpretive approach at domestic level, where a nullification approach is pushed aside in favour of a human rights-based balancing of the relevant legal tensions.

There is also a growing body of 'fifth stage' jurisprudence within the Latin American courts, examining the criminalisation of drug possession

[35] Ibid paras 89–90. [36] Ibid para 91. [37] Ibid para 92. [38] Ibid para 41.

for personal use within the context of the right to privacy, and whether the private activities of adults are improperly infringed by drug laws. Two significant cases in this regard are found in the Argentinian courts, where the right to privacy enshrined in Article 19 of the Constitution has been successfully used to challenge the criminalisation of possession for personal use under the States drug legislation.

The leading case in this regard is that of *Gustavo Bazterrica*, which was heard by the Supreme Court in 1986.[39] In the case, the plaintiff appealed a conviction for drug possession, arguing that personal drug consumption constituted private behaviour, and therefore protected within the context of Article 19, which states

> The private actions of men which in no way offend public order or morality, nor injure a third party, are only reserved to God and are exempted from the authority of judges. No inhabitant of the Nation shall be obliged to perform what the law does not demand nor deprived of what it does not prohibit.[40]

As described by Fusero, this provision is understood to protect 'not only the actions that are performed in private, but as those who do not harm others'.[41] The judgement agreed that there were legitimate limitations on the scope right to private behaviour, in particular where those private actions harm others. However, the Court also noted that although harms to third parties were 'repeatedly affirmed' in the context of drug use, there was no actual proven causal link between personal drug consumption and harm to others.[42] The majority decision found that 'to punish the mere creation of a risk allows the interpreter to refer simply to abstract potential damage and dangers and not to specific harm to others and the community'. According to the Court, '[t]he failure to establish a reasonable link between conduct and the damage it causes' means that no distinction was made between 'actions that offend public morality or prejudice others' and those that are strictly 'individual', and that Article 19 demands that

[39] 'Bazterrica, Gustavo Mario' (29 August 1986) LL 1986-D-582.

[40] The original Spanish text reads 'Las acciones privadas de los hombres que de ningún modo ofendan al orden y a la moral pública, ni perjudiquen a un tercero, están sólo reservadas a Dios, y exentas de la autoridad de los magistrados. Ningún habitante de la Nación será obligado a hacer lo que no manda la ley, ni privado de lo que ella no prohíbe.' Constitucion de la Nacion Argentina (Sancionada: Diciembre 15 de 1994. Promulgada: Enero 3 de 1995) art 19.

[41] Mariano Fusero, 'Conceptos Basicos para un Cambio de Paradigma Posible', La Asociación de Pensamiento Penal, 2015, 38.

[42] Bazterrica (n 39) para 9.

just such a distinction be made.[43] In deciding to strike down the conviction of the plaintiff, the judgement concluded that 'the constitutional prohibition to interfere with private conduct . . . responds to a conception that the state should not impose ideals of life to individuals, but to offer them the freedom to choose, and that is sufficient in itself to invalidate the art. 6 [of the national drug law]'.[44] Although the *Bazterrica* judgement was overturned by the Supreme Court in the 1990,[45] it was later reaffirmed in the 2009 case of *Arriola*, in which the Court again concluded that the relevant provision of the national drug legislation 'violates Article 19 of the Constitution, to the extent that invades the sphere of personal freedom excluded from authority of state bodies'.[46] Similar jurisprudence is found in the case law of Colombia,[47] where the Constitutional Court found as early as 1994 that legislation outlawing possession for personal use violated Article 49 of the Constitution, which enshrines a Constitutional right to health.[48]

While the mandate of national courts in providing human rights checks and balances on abusive domestic laws and practices is clear, as is the potential role of the International Narcotics Control Board on influencing treaty interpretation, the role of international human rights bodies is somewhat more ambiguous. The primary challenge is to determine whether international human rights bodies have a mandate to influence the interpretation of international drug control law, above and beyond the scope to adjudicate individual complaints.[49] Is there any possibility of a systemic influence of human rights bodies on the development of the international drug control regime as a whole? A useful approach to this question, one that provides a model for dynamic human rights-based interpretation of the drug conventions, is found in the jurisprudence of the Inter-American Court of Human Rights.

As was discussed in Chapter 6, the Inter-American Court embraces an evolutive approach, finding that 'to determine the legal status of the American Declaration [of the Rights and Duties of Man] it is appropriate to look at the inter-American system of today in light of the evolution

[43] Ibid. [44] Ibid para 12.

[45] Fallo 'Colavini, Ariel Omar' (28 March 1978) fallos 300, t I-254.

[46] Fallo 'Arriola, Sebastián y otros s/ causa n° 9080' (25 August 2009) A. 891. XLIV. para 36.

[47] Columbian Constitutional Court, 'Drug Use as Personal Use', decision C-221/1994.

[48] Colombia's Constitution of 1991 (with Amendments through 2005), art 49.

[49] The lone exception to this is the Committee on the Rights of the Child, as Article 33 of the Convention on the Rights of the Child makes specific mention of drug control, bringing consideration of these issues clearly within the Committee's mandate.

it has undergone since the adoption of the Declaration'.[50] Significant to the question of a dynamic human rights-based interpretation of the drug control conventions is the fact that, over the course of a series of opinions, the Court has established its 'jurisdiction to interpret, in addition to the American Convention [on Human Rights], "other treaties concerning the protection of human rights in the American States"'.[51] The Court has furthermore adopted a broad perspective on the question of which 'other treaties' concern human rights, one not limited by either the subject matter of the treaty itself or the scope of the States Parties. According to its Advisory Opinion on *'Other Treaties' Subject to the Consultative Jurisdiction of the Court*,

> By unanimous vote . . . the advisory jurisdiction of the Court can be exercised, in general, with regard to any provision dealing with the protection of human rights set forth in any international treaty applicable in the American States, regardless of whether it be bilateral or multilateral, whatever be the principal purpose of such a treaty, and whether or not non-Member States of the inter-American system are or have the right to become parties thereto.[52]

In the Court's Advisory Opinion on *The Right to Information on Consular Assistance*, it utilised this approach to conclude that individual due process rights of detainees are contained in the Vienna Convention on Consular Relations, an instrument of general international law outlining relations between States. In effect, the Court adopted a dynamic human-rights based approach to the Vienna Convention, in which it engaged parallel obligations within the International Covenant on Civil and Political Rights, concluding that 'the individual's right to information established in Article 36(1)(b) of the Vienna Convention on Consular Relations allows the right to the due process of law recognized in Article 14 of the International Covenant on Civil and Political Rights to have practical effects in concrete cases'.[53] According to Lixinski, 'the Court said through that

[50] *Interpretation of the American Declaration of the Rights and Duties of Man Within the Framework of Article 64 of the American Convention on Human Rights*, Advisory Opinion OC-10/89, Inter-American Court of Human Rights Series A No 10 (14 July 1989), para 37.

[51] *The Right to Information on Consular Assistance in the Framework of Guarantees of the Due Process of Law* (see chapter 6 n 15) para 69.

[52] *'Other Treaties' Subject to the Consultative Jurisdiction of the Court (Art. 64 of the American Convention on Human Rights)*, Advisory Opinion OC-1/82, Inter-American Court of Human Rights Series A No 1 (24 September 1982), opinion para 1.

[53] *The Right to Information on Consular Assistance in the Framework of Guarantees of the Due Process of Law* (see chapter 6 n 15) opinion para 6.

Opinion that human rights considerations permeate other areas of international law, and that when human rights interests are concerned legal obligations should be interpreted in a dynamic manner, so as to cover new situations on the basis of pre-existing rights'.[54] As described in the Concurring Opinion of Court President Judge Cançado Trinade,

> The progressive development of international law is likewise accomplished by means of application of human rights treaties . . . We are, thus, before a phenomenon much deeper than the sole recourse *per se* to rules and methods of interpretation of treaties. The intermingling between Public International Law and the International Law of Human Rights gives testimony of the recognition of the centrality, in this new *corpus juris*, of the universal human rights, what corresponds to a new *ethos* of our times.[55]

This approach has significance for the development of a human rights-based interpretation of international drug control. As has been explored in earlier chapters, there is a compelling case that the three drug conventions fall into that category of 'other treaties concerning the protection of human rights'. First, as explored in Chapter 5, the *telos* of the drug control regime, to promote 'the health and welfare of mankind', itself engages human rights concepts, concerns and parallel treaty obligations. The second is because the nature of many obligations within the drug treaties potentially create an environment of heightened human rights risk. As described by Boister, '[t]he suppression conventions threaten the human rights of the individuals caught up in the panoply of national laws derived from the conventions in many different ways. Consider, for example, the drug suppression conventions. . . . They have enormous potential for human rights violation'.[56] If the approach of the Inter-American Court were to be embraced by other regional and international human rights bodies, it would provide an important mechanism to review and assess the human rights implications of the drug treaty obligations themselves, not simply their domestic implementation by various States. In this manner, the Inter-American Court's approach to considering 'other treaties' opens a door to the international human rights system to engage directly with

54 Lucas Lixinski, 'Treaty interpretation by the Inter-American Court of Human Rights: expansionism at the service of the unity of international law' (2010) 21/3 European Journal of International Law 585, 590.

55 *The Right to Information on Consular Assistance in the Framework of Guarantees of the Due Process of Law* (see chapter 6 n 15) Concurring Opinion of Judge A.A. Cançado Trindade, paras 33–34.

56 Boister, 'Suppression Conventions' (see chapter 7 n 15) 200–201.

the terms of the international drug treaties, with a potential to influence the development of a 'fifth stage' drug control paradigm.

The need to bridge the 'parallel universes' of drug control and human rights is a clear one and is a need increasingly acknowledged by both international regimes. However, despite the interpretative challenges to resolving or preventing conflicts and tensions between the two bodies of law, the potential for the development of drug control's 'fifth stage' exist in law and practice, and examples of this approach in action can be identified and built upon. In this process, the leadership of the international bodies established within both regimes is critical, and the institutional inertia that has historically characterised the relationship between drug control and human rights law must be broken down and transformed into active leadership on human rights issues and the progressive development of international law. To paraphrase the words of Justice Albie Sachs, the 'fifth stage' of drug control must put a thumb on the scales in favour of human rights[57] and ensure when balancing obligations between the two regimes that human rights, and the health and welfare of humankind, are promoted, protected and fulfilled.

57 Sachs dissenting opinion, *Prince v President, Cape Law Society and Others* (see chapter 7 n 2) para 149.

BIBLIOGRAPHY

All Party Parliamentary Group on Drug Policy Reform, 'Guidance on Drug Policy: Interpreting the UN Drug Conventions', August 2015.

Ansley N., 'International Efforts to Control Narcotics' (1959–1960) 50 *Journal of Criminal Law and Criminology* 105.

Anslinger H. J., 'Report of Progress in Drafting the "Single Convention", a Proposed Codification of the Multilateral Treaty Law on Narcotic Drugs' (1958) 13 *Food, Drug, and Cosmetic Law Journal* 692.

Aoyagi M. T., 'Beyond Punitive Prohibition: Liberalizing the Dialogue on International Drug Policy' (2005) 37 *NYU Journal of International Law and Policy* 555.

Barrett D., '*Unique in International Relations?: A Comparison of the International Narcotics Control Board and the UN Human Rights Treaty Bodies*' (International Harm Reduction Association 2008).

'*Backgrounder: Bolivia's Concurrent Drug Control and other International Legal Commitments*' (International Centre on Human Rights and Drug Policy 2011).

'*Intersections between the International Legal Regimes for Drug Control and Human Rights*' (Human Rights and Drugs Conference, Human Rights Centre, University of Essex, 8 February 2014).

Barrett D. and Nowak M., 'The United Nations and Drug Policy: Towards a Human Rights-Based Approach' in A. Constantinides and N. Zaikos (eds), *The Diversity of International Law: Essays in Honour of Professor Kallopi K. Kpufa* (Martinus Nijhoff 2009).

Barrett D. and Tobin J., 'Article 33: Protection from Narcotic Drugs and Psychotropic Substances' in J. Tobin and P. Alston (eds) *A Commentary to the United Nations Convention on the Rights of the Child* (Oxford University Press, in press).

Barrett D. and Veerman P. E., 'Article 33: Protection from Narcotic, Drugs and Psychotropic Substances' in A. Alen, J. Vande Lanotte, E. Verhellen, F. Ang, E. Berghmans, M. Verheyde and B. Abramson (eds) *A Commentary on the United Nations Convention on the Rights of the Child* (Martinus Nijoff 2012).

Barrett D., Lines R., Schleifer R., Elliott R. and Bewley-Taylor D., '*Recalibrating the Regime: The Need for a Human Rights-Based Approach to International Drug Policy*' (Beckley Foundation Drug Policy Programme 2008).

Bassiouni M. C., 'International Aspects of Drug Abuse: Problems and a Proposal' (1975–1976) 9 *The John Marshall Journal of Practice and Procedure* 3.

'Critical Reflections on International and National Control of Drugs' (1989–1990) 18 *Denver Journal of International Law and Policy* 311.

'A Comprehensive Strategic Approach on International Cooperation for the Prevention, Control and Suppression on International and Transnational Criminality, including the Establishment of an International Criminal Court' (1991) 15 *Nova Law Review* 353.

Bevans C. I., 'International Conventions in the Field of Narcotic Drugs' (1963–1964) 37 *Temple Law Quarterly* 41.

Bewley-Taylor D. R., *The United States and International Drug Control, 1909–1997* (Continuum 1999).

'Challenging the UN Drug Control Conventions: Problems and Possibilities' (2003) 14 *International Journal of Drug Policy* 171.

International Drug Control: Consensus Fractured (Cambridge University Press 2012).

Bewley-Taylor D. R. and Jelsma M., '*Fifty Years of the 1961 Single Convention on Narcotic Drugs: A Reinterpretation*' (Transnational Institute Series on Legislative Reform of Drug Policies Nr 12 2011).

Bewley-Taylor D. R. and Trace M., Stevens A., '*Incarceration of drug offenders: costs and impacts*' (Beckley Foundation Drug Policy Programme, 2005).

Bland J. O. P., 'The Opium Abolition Question' (1912–1913) 3 *Journal of Race Development* 302.

Blickman T., '*A Beginner's Guide to Coca*' (Transnational Institute 2011).

Blum Y. Z., 'Extradition: A Common Approach to the Control of International Terrorism and Traffic in Narcotic Drugs' (1978) 13 *Israeli Law Review* 194.

Bogaard W., 'Limits to National Penal Policies Concerning Narcotic Drugs as Set by the International Treaties: The Dutch Example' (1975) 10 *Journal of International Law and Economics* 747.

Boister N., '*The Suppression of Narcotic Drugs through International Law*' (PhD thesis, University of Nottingham 1998).

'The Interrelationship between the Development of Domestic and International Drug Control Law' (1995) 7 *African Journal of International and Comparative Law* 906.

Penal Aspects of the UN Drug Conventions (Kluwer 2001).

'Human Rights Protections in the Suppression Conventions' (2002) 2 *Human Rights Law Review* 199.

Bonnie R. J., 'The Virtues of Pragmatism in Drug Policy' (2010) 13 *Journal of Health Care Law and Policy* 7.

Bonino E., 'Crimes without Victims: Appropriate Policy Responses to Drug Use' in Protecting the Human Rights of Injection Drug Users: The Impact of HIV and AIDS (Open Society Institute 2005).

Borgen C. J., 'Resolving Treaty Conflicts' (2005) 37 *George Washington International Law Review* 573.

Buffard I. and Zemanek K., 'The "Object and Purpose" of a Treaty: An Enigma?' (1998) 3 *Austrian Review of International & European Law* 311.

Campos I., *Home Grown: Marijuana and the Origins of Mexico's War on Drugs* (University of North Carolina Press 2012).

Cannizzaro E. (ed), *The Law of Treaties: Beyond the Vienna Convention* (Oxford University Press 2011).

Chatterjee S. K., *Legal Aspects of International Drug Control* (Martinus Nijhoff 1981).

Cohrerrsen J. J. and Hoover L. H., 'The International Control of Dangerous Drugs' (1974) 9 *The Journal of International Law and Economics* 63.

Collins J. (ed), *Ending the Drug Wars: Report of the LSE Expert Group on the Economics of Drug Policy* (LSE Ideas 2014).

Regulations and Prohibitions: Anglo-American Relations and International Drug Control, 1939–1964, PhD thesis, Department of International History, London School of Economics London, January 2015.

'Control of Dangerous Drugs' (1930) 2/3639 *British Medical Journal* 572.

Corten O. and Klein P. (eds), *The Vienna Convention on the Law of Treaties: A Commentary*, Vol. I (Oxford University Press 2011).

Csete J., 'Overhauling Oversight: Human Rights at the INCB' in J. Collins (ed) *Governing The Global Drug Wars LSE Ideas: Special Report* (LSE Ideas 2012).

'Costs and Benefits of Drug-Related Health Services' in J. Collins (ed) *Ending the Drug Wars: Report of the LSE Expert Group on the Economics of Drug Policy* (LSE Ideas 2014).

Csete J. and Wolfe D., 'The International Narcotics Control Board and HIV/AIDS' (Canadian HIV/AIDS Legal Network/Open Society Institute 2007).

de Londras F., 'The Right to Challenge the Lawfulness of Detention: An International Perspective on US Detention of Suspected Terrorists' (2007) 12/2 *Journal of Conflict and Security Law* 223.

Dikotter F., Laamann L. and Zhou X., *Narcotic Culture: A History of Drugs in China* (University of Chicago Press 2004).

Dorr O. and Schmalenbach (eds), *Vienna Convention on the Law of Treaties: A Commentary* (Springer 2012).

Dorn W. A., '*The League Covenant and the UN Charter: A side-by side (full text) comparison*' (12 May 2008) Royal Military College of Canada.

Drug Policy Alliance, '*Drug Courts are Not the Answer: Towards a Health Centered Approach to Drug Use*' (Drug Policy Alliance 2011).

Dupuy P-M, 'Evolutionary Interpretation of Treaties: Between Memory and Prophecy' in E. Cannizzaro (ed) *The Law of Treaties: Beyond the Vienna Convention* (Oxford University Press, 2011).

Elliott R., Csete J., Wood E. and Kerr T., 'Harm Reduction, HIV/AIDS, and the Human Rights Challenge to Global Drug Control Policy' (2005) 8/2 *Health and Human Rights* 104.

Elliott R., Lines R. and Schleifer R., '*Treatment or Torture? Applying International Human Rights Standards to Drug Detention Centers*' (Open Society Foundations 2011).

Evans, M. D. (ed) *International Law* (3rd ed, Oxford University Press 2010).

Fairbank J. K., 'The Legalization of the Opium Trade before the Treaties of 1858' (1933–1934) 17 *Chinese Social and Political Science Review* 215.

Fisher K., 'Trends in Extraterritorial Narcotics Control: Slamming the Stable Door after the Horse Has Bolted' (1983–1984) 16 *New York University Journal of International Law and Politics* 353.

Fitzmaurice M., 'The Practical Working of the Law of Treaties' in M. Evans (ed) *International Law* (3rd ed, Oxford University Press 2010).

Fitzmaurice M., Elias O. and Merkouris P. (eds), *Treaty Interpretation and the Vienna Convention on the Law of Treaties: 30 Years on* (Martinus Nijhoff 2010).

Flacks S., 'Drug Control, Human Rights, and the Right to the Highest Attainable Standard of Health: A Reply to Saul Takahashi' (2011) 33 *Human Rights Quarterly* 856.

Fusero M., '*Conceptos Basicos para un Cambio de Paradigma Posible*' (2015) La Asociación de Pensamiento Penal.

Gallahue P., '*The Death Penalty for Drug Offences: Global Overview 2011*' (International Harm Reduction Association 2011).

Gallahue P. and Lines R., '*The Death Penalty for Drug Offences: Global Overview*' (International Harm Reduction Association 2010).

Gallahue P. and Lines R., 'The Death Penalty for Drug Offences: Shared responsibility and shared consequences' in P. Hodgkinson (ed) *The International Library if Essays on Capital Punishment*, Volume III: Policy and Governance (Ashgate 2013).

Gallahue P. and Saucier R., Barrett D., '*Partners in Crime: International Funding for Drug Control and Gross Violations of Human Rights*' (International Harm Reduction Association, 2012).

Gardiner R. K., *Treaty Interpretation* (Oxford University Press 2008).

'The Vienna Convention Rules on Treaty Interpretation' in D. B. Hollis (ed) *The Oxford Guide to Treaties* (Oxford University Press 2012).

Gearty C. A., 'Terrorism and Human Rights' [2005] European Human Rights Law Review 1.

Geraghty A. H., 'Universal Jurisdiction and Drug Trafficking: A Tool for Fighting one of the World's Most Pervasive Problems' (2004) 16 *Florida Journal of International Law* 371.

Gilmore N., 'Drug Use and Human Rights: Privacy, Vulnerability, Disability, and Human Rights Infringements' (1996) 12 *Journal of Contemporary Health Law and Policy* 355.

Global Commission on Drug Policy, 'The Global Crisis of Avoidable Pain: Drug Control's Negative Impact on Public Health', September 2015.

Gregg R. W., 'The Single Convention for Narcotic Drugs' (1961) 16/4 *Food, Drugs and Cosmetic Law Journal* 187.

Gupta J., 'Interpretation of Reverse Onus Clauses' (2012) 5/1 *NUJS Law Review* 49.

Harding J. L., 'International Narcotics Control: A Proposal to Eradicate an International Menace' (1984) 14 *California Western International Law Journal* 530.

Harm Reduction International, 'Commanding General Confidence? Human Rights, International Law and the INCB Annual Report for 2011' (2012).

Harrington S. L., 'Death, Drugs and Development: Malaysia's Mandatory Death Penalty for Traffickers and the International War on Drugs' (1991) 29 *Columbia Journal of Transnational Law* 365.

Harris D. J., O'Boyle M., Bates E. and Buckley C., *Law of the European Convention on Human Rights* (2nd ed, Oxford University Press 2009).

Hedrich D., Kerr T. and Dubois-Arber F., 'Drug Consumption Facilities in Europe and Beyond' in T. Rhodes and D. Hedrich (eds) *Harm Reduction: Evidence, Impacts and Challenges* (Publications Office of the European Union 2010).

Heilmann D., 'The International Control of Illegal Drugs and the U.N. Treaty Regime: Preventing or Causing Human Rights Violations' (2011) 19/2 *Cardozo Journal of International and Comparative Law* 237.

Helmersen S. T., 'Evolutive Treaty Interpretation: Legality, Semantics and Distinctions' (2013) 6/1 *European Journal of Legal Studies* 127.

Hepburn W. M., 'International Legislation on Social Questions' (1931–1932) 9 *New York University Law Review* 310.

Hood R. and Hoyle C., *The Death Penalty: A Worldwide Perspective* (4th ed, Oxford University Press 2008).

Hor M., 'Singapore's Innovations to Due Process' (International Society for the Reform of Criminal Law Conference on Human Rights and the Administration of Justice, Johannesburg, December 2000) www.isrcl.org/Papers/Hor.pdf accessed 13 May 2014.

Human Rights Watch, '*Not Enough Graves: The War on Drugs, HIV/AIDS, and Violations of Human Rights*' (Human Rights Watch 2004), Vol 16, No 8 (C).

'"Skin on the Cable" The Illegal Arrest, Arbitrary Detention and Torture of People Who Use Drugs in Cambodia' (2010).

'The Rehab Archipelago Forced Labor and Other Abuses in Drug Detention Centers in Southern Vietnam' (2011).

Hunt P., '*Human Rights, Health and Harm Reduction: States' Amnesia and Parallel Universes*' (International Harm Reduction Association 2008).

Hussein M., '*Abdullah Defends Death Penalty for Drug Traffickers*' Bernama Malaysian National News Agency (22 February 2006).

Hyde C. C., 'Concerning the Interpretation of Treaties' (1909) 3 *American Journal of International Law* 46.

International Drug Policy Consortium, '*The International Narcotics Control Board: Current Tensions and Options for Reform*', International Drug Policy Consortium Briefing Paper (February 2008).

International Harm Reduction Association, '*What is Harm Reduction*?' (International Harm Reduction Association 2009).

International Harm Reduction Development Program, '*Human Rights Abuses in the Name of Drug Treatment: Reports from the Field*", Public Health Fact Sheet (March 2009).

Jelsma M., '*The Development of International Drug Control: Lessons Learned and Strategic Challenges for the Future*': Working Paper Prepared for the First Meeting of the Global Commission on Drug Policy (24–25 January 2011).

Jenks C. W., 'The Conflict of Law-Making Treaties' (1953) 30 *British Yearbook of International Law* 401.

Jurgens R. and Csete J., 'In the Name of Treatment: Ending Abuses in Compulsory Drug Detention Centers' (2012) 107/4 *Addiction* 689.

Kelsen H., *General Theory of Law and State* (Anders Wedberg tr, Harvard University Press, 1949).

The Law of the United Nations (Stevens & Sons Ltd, 1950).

General Theory of Norms (Michael Hartney tr., Clarendon Press, 1991).

Kiefer H. L., 'Just Say No: The Case against Expanding the International Criminal Court's Jurisdiction to Include Drug Trafficking' (2009) 31 *Loyola of Los Angeles International and Comparative Law Review* 157.

Klabbers J., 'Some Problems Regarding the Object and Purpose of Treaties' (1997) 8 *Finnish Yearbook of International Law* 160.

Lande A., 'The Adjustment of the International Opium Administration to an Eventual Dissolution of the League of Nations' (1945) 45 *Columbia Law Review* 392.

Legac S., 'The Negative Impacts of the Global War on Drugs: Can International Drug Enforcement be Successful Without Infringing on Human Rights?' (2010) 3 *Albany Government Law Review* 823.

Linderfalk U., On the Meaning of the 'Object and Purpose' Criterion, in the Context of the Vienna Convention on the Law of Treaties, Article 19' (2003) 72 *Nordic Journal of International Law* 429.

On the Interpretation of Treaties: The Modern International Law as Expressed in the 1969 Vienna Convention on the Law of Treaties (Springer 2007).

'Doing the Right Thing for the Right Reason: Why Dynamic or Static Approaches Should be Taken in the Interpretation of Treaties' (2008) 10 *International Community Law Review* 109.

Lindesmith A. R., 'The Drug Addict: Patient or Criminal?' (1941) 31/5 *Journal of the American Institute of Criminal Law and Criminology* 531.

Lines R., '*The Death Penalty for Drug Offences: A Violation of International Human Rights Law*' (International Harm Reduction Association 2007).

'*A "most serious crime"? International Human Rights Law and the Death Penalty for Drug Offences*' (18th International Conference on the Reduction of Drug-Related Harm, Warsaw, 15 May 2007).

'A "Most Serious Crime"? The Death Penalty for Drug Offences and International Human Rights Law' (2010) 21 *Amicus Journal* 21.

'"Treatment in Liberty" – Compulsory Detention for Drug Use and Human Rights' (2016) 3 *Journal of International Law and Drug Policy* (in press).

Lines R. and Barrett, D., '*The Human Rights "Win" at the UNGASS on Drugs that No One is Talking about, and How We Can Use It*' (Human Rights Centre Blog, University of Essex, 9 May 2016) hrcessex.wordpress.com/2016/05/09/the-human-rights-win-at-the-ungass-on-drugs-that-no-one-is-talking-about-and-how-we-can-use-it/ accessed 23 May 2016.

Lines R. and Elliott R., 'Injecting Drugs into Human Rights Advocacy' (2007) 18 *International Journal of Drug Policy* 453.

Lixinski L., 'Treaty Interpretation by the Inter-American Court of Human Rights: Expansionism at the Service of the Unity of International Law' (2010) 21/3 *European Journal of International Law* 585.

Madrazo Lajous, A 'The Constitutional Costs of the "War on Drugs" in J. Collins (ed) *Governing The Global Drug Wars LSE Ideas: Special Report* (LSE Ideas 2012).

Mass F., 'Alternatives to Indirect Control of International Narcotics Traffic' (1975–1976) 8 *New York University Journal of International Law and Politics* 241.

Makowski K. W., 'Narcotics Regulation: A Study in Irresolution' (1960–1961) 34 *Temple Law Quarterly* 310.

Mackenzie J., 'Pope Francis warns on "evil" of drugs, opposes legalization' Reuters (20 June 2014).

May H. L, 'Narcotic Drug Control' (1951–1952) 29 *International Conciliation* 491.

Mayss A., *Principles of Conflict of Laws* (3rd ed, Cavendish 1999).

McAllister W. B., *Drug Diplomacy in the Twentieth Century: An International History* (Routledge 2000).

McCoy A., *The Politics of Heroin: CIA Complicity in the Global Drug Trade, Afghanistan, Southeast Asia, Central America*, Colombia (3rd ed, Lawrence Hill Books 2003).

McLachlan C., 'The Principle of Systemic Integration and Article 31(3)(c) of the Vienna Convention' (2005) 54 *International and Comparative Law Quarterly* 279.

Miller D. H., *The Drafting of the Covenant*, vol. I (GP Putnam's Sons 1928).

The Drafting of the Covenant, vol. 2 (GP Putnam's Sons 1928).

Morgan E. M., 'Traffic Circles: The Legal Logic of Drug Extraditions' (2009–2010) 31 *University of Pennsylvania Journal of International Law* 373.

Nadelmann E., 'Global Prohibition Regimes: The Evolution of Norms in International Society' (1990) 44 *International Organization* 479.

Noll A., 'International Treaties and the Control of Drug Use and Abuse' (1977) 6 *Contemporary Drug Problems* 17.

Pauwelyn J., *Conflict of Norms in Public International Law: How WTO Law Relates to Other Rules of International Law* (Cambridge University Press 2003).

Pauwelyn J. and Elsig M., 'The Politics of Treaty Interpretation: Variations and Explanations Across International Tribunals' in J. L. Dunoff and M. A. Pollack (eds) *Interdisciplinary Perspectives on International Law and International Relations: The State of the Art* (Cambridge University Press 2013).

Pearshouse R., '*Compulsory Drug Treatment in Thailand*' (Canadian HIV/AIDS Legal Network 2009).

Pfeiffer S., 'Rights of Indigenous Peoples and the International Drug Control Regime: The Case of Traditional Coca Leaf Chewing' (2013) 5/1 *Getting Journal of International Law* 287.

Pressly L., 'The Rehab Centres that Lock up Addicts against Their Will' *BBC Radio* 4 (27 August 2014).

Renborg B. A., 'Principles of International Control of Narcotics' (1943) 37 *American Journal of International Law* 436.

International Drug Control: A Study of International Administration by and Through the League of Nations (Carnegie Endowment for Peace 1947).

'International Control of Narcotics' (1957) 22 *Law and Contemporary Problems* 86.

Room R., 'Addiction Concepts and International Control' (2006) 20 *The Social History of Alcohol and Drugs* 2006.

Room R. and MacKay S., *Roadmaps to Reforming the UN Drug Conventions* (Beckley Foundation Press 2012).

Sabharwal Y. K., '*Keynote Address*' (National Seminar and Training Programme on Narcotic Drugs and Psychotropic Substances', 25 March 2006, New Delhi) www.supremecourtofindia.nic.in/speeches/speeches_2006/ndps.pdf accessed 14 June 2014.

Sadat-Akhavi S-A, *Methods of Resolving Conflicts between Treaties* (Brill Academic Publishers 2003).

Samuels J. W., 'International Control of Narcotic Drugs and International Economic Law' (1969) 7 *Canadian Yearbook of International Law* 192.

Saucier R., Wolfe D., Kingsbury K. and Silva P. (eds) '*Treated with Cruelty: Abuses in the name of Drug Rehabilitation*' (Open Society Foundations 2011).

Schabas W. A., *The Abolition of the Death Penalty in International Law* (3rd ed, Cambridge University Press 2002).

Shaw M. N., *International Law* (6th ed, Cambridge University Press 2008).

Simma B. (ed), *The Charter of the United Nations: A Commentary* (Oxford University Press 1994).

Sorel J-M and Eveno V. B., 'Article 31: General rule of interpretation' in O. Corten and P. Klein (eds) *The Vienna Convention on the Law of Treaties: A Commentary*, Vol. I (Oxford University Press 2011).

Speaker S. L., '"The Struggle of Mankind against its Deadliest Foe": Themes of Counter-Subversion in Anti-Narcotics Campaigns, 1920—1940' (2001) 34/3 *Journal of Social History* 591.

Stanley L. L., 'Narcotic Drugs and Crime' (1921) 12/1 *Journal of the American Institute of Criminal Law and Criminology* 110.

Steiner H. J., Alston P. and Goodman R., *International Human Rights in Context: Law, Politics, Morals* (3rd ed, Oxford University Press 2008).

Stewart D. P., 'Internationalizing The War on Drugs: The UN Convention Against Illicit Traffic in Narcotic Drugs and Psychotropic Substances' (1989–1990) 18 *Denver Journal of International Law and Policy* 387.

Sunter A. F., 'The Harm of Drug Trafficking: Is There Room for Serious Debate?' (2006–2008) 32 *Manitoba Law Journal* 174.

Takahashi S., 'Drug Control, Human Rights, and the Right to the Highest Attainable Standard of Health: By No Means Straightforward Issues' (2009) 31 *Human Rights Quarterly* 748.

'*Drug Control and Human Rights: Frequently Asked Questions*' (World Federation Against Drugs 2013).

(ed) *Human Rights, Human Security, and State Security: The Intersection*, vol. 1 (Praeger, 2014).

Tams C. J., *Enforcing Obligations Erga Omnes in International Law* (Cambridge University Press 2005).

Taylor A. H., *American Diplomacy and the Narcotics Traffic, 1900–1939: A Study in International Humanitarian Reform* (Duke University Press 1969).

'The International Opium Conference' (1911) 5/2 *American Journal of International Law* 466.

'The Traffic in Narcotic Drugs' (1923) 2/3283 *British Medical Journal* 1053.

'The Traffic in Narcotic Drugs' (1933) 2/3795 *British Medical Journal* 618.

'The Opium Evil' (1924) 2/3328 *British Medical Journal* 678.

Thirlway H., 'The Law and Procedure of the International Court of Justice 1960–1989, Supplement 2006: Part Three' (2006) 77 *British Yearbook of International Law* 1.

Thompson N., '*Detention as Treatment: Detention of Methamphetamine Users in Cambodia, Laos, and Thailand*' (International Harm Reduction Development Program 2010).

Transnational Institute, 'The Erratic Crusade of the INCB', *TNI Drug Policy Briefing, Nr* (Transnational Institute 2003).

'Treaties and Documents Concerning Opium' (1909) 3/3 *American Journal of International Law* 253.

Tzevelekos V. P., 'The Use of Article 31(3)(C) of the VCLT in the Case Law of the ECtHR: An Effective Anti-Fragmentation Tool or a Selective Loophole for the Reinforcement of Human Rights Teleology? Between Evolution and Systemic Integration' (2009–2010) 31 *Michigan Journal of International Law* 621.

van Aaken A., 'Defragmentation of Public International Law Through Interpretation: A Methodological Proposal' (2009) 16 *Indiana Journal of Global Legal Studies* 483.

van der Kruit P. J. J., '*Maritime Drug Interdiction in International Law*' (PhD thesis, Utrecht University 2007).

Villager M. E., *Commentary on the 1969 Vienna Convention on the Law of Treaties* (Martinus Nijhoff 2009).

'The Rules on Interpretation: Misgivings, Misunderstandings, Miscarriage? The "Crucible" Intended by the International Law Commission" in E. Cannizzaro (ed) *The Law of Treaties: Beyond the Vienna Convention* (Oxford University Press 2011).

Volkow N., 'Addiction is a Disease of Free Will' The Huffington Post (12 June 2015).

Vranes E., 'The Definition of "Norm Conflict" in International Law and Legal Theory' (2006) 17/2 *The European Yearbook of International Law* 395.

Waddell I. G., 'International Narcotics Control' (1970) 64 *American Journal of International Law* 310.

Weber A. J., 'China's Future Opium Evil Problem' (1919) 9/4 *Journal of the American Institute of Criminal Law and Criminology* 530.

Windle J., 'How the East Influenced Drug Prohibition' (2013) 35/5 *The International History Review* 1185.

Wolfe D. and Tomasini-Joshi D., '*Drug Users Burned by the System in Peru*', Open Society Foundation Voices (13 May 2012).

Wolfram K., 'Conflicts between Treaties' in R. Bernhardt (ed) *Encyclopedia of Public International Law* (1984) vol VII, 467.

Wolfrum R. and Matz N., *Conflicts in International Environmental Law* (Springer Verlag 2003).

Wright H., 'The International Opium Commission' (1909) 2/4 *American Journal of International Law* 828.

'The International Opium Commission, Part 1' (1909) 3/3 *American Journal of International Law* 648.

Wright Q., 'The Opium Question' (1924) 18/2 *American Journal of International Law* 281.

'The Opium Conferences' (1925) 19/3 *American Journal of International Law* 559.

'The Narcotics Convention of 1931' (1934) 28 *American Journal of International Law* 475.

Wu Z., 'Arguments in Favour of Compulsory Treatment of Opioid Dependence' (2013) 91/2 *Bulletin of the World Health Organization* 142.

Young R., 'The Development of International Law: The International Control of Narcotic Drugs' (1952) 38 *American Bar Association Journal* 778.

INDEX

Lightning Source UK Ltd.
Milton Keynes UK
UKHW021937180220
358952UK00008B/20

9 781107 171176